Modern Corporate Finance

Modern Corporate Finance

ALAN C. SHAPIRO

University of Southern California

MACMILLAN PUBLISHING COMPANY
New York

COLLIER MACMILLAN PUBLISHERS
London

Editors: Caroline Carney, Ken MacLeod, Chip Price
Production Supervisor: Ron Harris
Production Manager: Rick Fischer
Text Designer: Natasha Sylvester
Cover Designer: Natasha Sylvester
Cover illustration: Leslie Bakshi
Illustrations: Wellington Studios
This book was set in Zapf Book by Waldman Graphics, printed and bound by
Von Hoffmann Press, Inc. The cover was printed by Von Hoffmann Press, Inc.

Macmillan Publishing Company
866 Third Avenue, New York, New York 10022

Collier Macmillan Canada, Inc.

Library of Congress Cataloging in Publication Data
Shapiro, Alan C.
    Modern corporate finance / Alan C. Shapiro.
        p. cm.
    Includes index.
    ISBN 0-02-409530-3
    1. Corporations—Finance.   I. Title.
HG4026.S44   1990
658.1′5—dc 19   89-2503
                        CIP

We gratefully acknowledge permission to reprint from the following: Edward I.
Altman, *Investing in Junk Bonds* (New York: John Wiley & Sons, 1987), pp. 209,
212 • AMAX Inc., Greenwich, CT • AT&T, New York, NY • Beneficial
Corporation, Wilmington, DE • Bethlehem Steel Corporation, Bethlehem,
PA • The Boeing Company, Seattle, WA • © 1986 *The Economist* Newspaper,
Limited, London • Financial Management Association, College of Business
Administration, University of South Florida, Tampa, FL • Florida Power & Light
Company, Miami, FL. • Reprinted by permission of *Forbes* magazine, October
8, 1984. © Forbes Inc., 1984 • *Fortune* magazine, © 1979, 1984, 1986, 1987, 1988,
Time Inc. All rights reserved • Helen of Troy Corporation, El Paso,
TX • Ingersoll-Rand, Woodcliff Lake, NJ • Richard D. Irwin Inc., *Financial
Strategy: Studies in the Creation, Transfer, and Destruction of Shareholder
Value* by William E. Fruhan, Jr. © 1979, *Journal of Financial Economics* and
Clifford W. Smith, Jr., University of Rochester, Rochester, NY • *Journal of
General Management* and Professor Allen Michel, Boston University •
Macmillan, Inc., New York, NY • Manufacturers Hanover Leasing Corporation,
New York, NY • M Corp, Dallas, TX • *Midland Journal of Corporate Finance*,
Donald H. Chew, editor, New York, NY, © 1985, p. 13 • New United Motor
Manufacturing, Fremont, CA • NWA Inc. and Northwest Airlines, St. Paul,
MN • Polycast Technology Corporation, Stamford, CN • G.D. Searle & Co.,
Chicago, IL • StorageTek, Louisville, CO • Robert A. Taggart, Jr., Boston
University • Tenneco Inc., Houston, TX • Union Pacific Corporation,
Bethlehem, PA • Reprinted by permission of *The Wall Street Journal*, © Dow
Jones & Company, Inc., 1985, 1986, 1987, 1988. All Rights Reserved
Worldwide • John Wiley & Sons, Inc., *Handbook of Corporate Finance*, Edward
I. Altman, editor, © 1986

Printing: 1 2 3 4 5 6 7 8   Year: 0 1 2 3 4 5 6 7 8

To Diane, for giving new meaning to my life.

ABOUT THE AUTHOR

Alan C. Shapiro is Professor of Finance and Business Economics at the School of Business Administration, University of Southern California. Prior to joining USC in 1978, he was an Assistant Professor at the Wharton School of the University of Pennsylvania. He has been a Visiting Professor at UCLA, the Stockholm School of Economics, and the University of British Columbia. During 1990 he will be a Visiting Professor at Yale University.

His specialty is international financial management. His best-selling textbook, *Multinational Financial Management*, Third Edition (1989), is in use in most of the leading MBA programs around the world. He has also written *International Corporate Finance* (1989).

Dr. Shapiro is currently researching the links between corporate finance and corporate strategy. He has engaged in consulting assignments with numerous firms and banks, including Texas Instruments, GTE, Caltex Petroleum, Computer Sciences Corporation, Citicorp, and Bank of America.

He has taught in numerous executive education programs and has conducted in-house training programs for banks, corporations, consulting firms, and law firms in the areas of corporate finance and international finance and economics. Dr. Shapiro has published over 40 articles in leading academic and professional journals.

Preface

Money has a universal fascination but few people seem to understand it very well. It is the subject of countless myths, false theories, and illogical beliefs. One of the few organized attempts to study the relationship between money—past, present, and future—and financial markets and financial decision making is provided by the discipline of financial economics. In the course of their work, financial economists have dispelled many of the myths and ad hoc reasoning surrounding traditional financial advice and substituted an insightful and subtle logic firmly grounded in economic analysis.

My basic objective in writing *Modern Corporate Finance* is to make accessible to students and practitioners alike the practical implications for corporate financial management of the exciting new theoretical and empirical breakthroughs in financial economics. The book is written so as to help the reader understand how and why finance matters, regardless of whether the reader intends to pursue a career in finance. I have tried to motivate the nonfinance major by illustrating the application of financial analysis and reasoning to problems faced by executives in marketing, operations, and personnel. It is suitable for use by first-year MBA students taking their introductory corporate finance course, advanced undergraduates, and managers enrolled in executive education programs.

Although the book relies on material that is covered in economics, accounting, and statistics courses, it is self-contained in that prior knowledge of those areas is useful but not essential. The only real prerequisites are algebra and an interest in understanding how the world works.

Distinctive Features

Modern Corporate Finance identifies the discipline that the external financial market imposes on the financial affairs of the firm. It also attempts to decipher the messages the market sends about the proper objectives of corporate financial decision making and the appropriate tactics and strategies for achieving them. Throughout, the text emphasizes value creation and the role of corporate finance in facilitating this process.

To achieve these aims this book tells finance as a single coherent story, rather than as a collection of short stories. It also includes features that distinguish it from its competitors.

Practical Approach.   There is nothing quite so practical as a theory that works. I have tried to reinforce this belief by taking a commonsense approach to finance. This involves showing students *why* the various theories discussed make sense and *how* to use these theories to solve problems. The book relates the subject matter to material students are already familiar with or have learned in previous chapters, making it less intimidating and more interesting. Basic intuition is emphasized throughout.

Numerous Applications of Finance Principles.   In keeping with its down-to-earth approach, the book contains numerous real-world examples and vignettes that help illustrate the application of financial theories and demonstrate the use of financial analysis and reasoning to solve financial problems. No other text has as many or as interesting examples of finance in practice. These examples promote understanding of basic theory and add interest to finance.

Appeal to Nonfinance Majors.   Since so many of the issues dealt with by nonfinancial executives have financial implications, from determining advertising budgets and credit policies to investing in management training programs, it is clear that financial theory has broad application to general management as well. Persuading readers who are not interested in pursuing a career in finance of this fact is a different matter. I have attempted to motivate these doubting Thomases by using numerous illustrations, scattered throughout the text, of the application of financial analysis to nonfinancial problems. Moreover, I have attempted to concentrate on those aspects of corporate finance that are most important to financial and nonfinancial executives. In this way I have tried to highlight why the reader should care about the topics covered.

Emphasis on Value Creation.   The text emphasizes two related issues: how companies create value and how corporate finance can facilitate the process of value creation. Since this is a book on corporate finance, the focus is on how the financial manager can add value to the firm. The viewpoint taken in this text is that the comparative advantage of the financial manager lies in understanding the intricacies of the modern financial marketplace and using this knowledge to full advantage to manage the firm's financial affairs.

Its guiding principle is that financial management is subordinate to the "real" business of the firm, which is to produce and sell goods and services. This does not, of course, preclude the financial manager from finding and exploiting profitable opportunities that may occasionally arise in financial markets. It does, however, require that the financial executive be able to recognize when these circumstances exist or are likely to exist. This necessitates a firm grounding in modern finance theory.

Initial Overview of Basic Financial Principles.   To bring the full power of modern finance theory to bear on the subject matter of corporate financial management, we require a unified theory of how and why individuals behave in the presence of choice situations involving limited resources, current versus future consumption, and uncertainty. This is supplied by the general equilibrium framework of financial economics, which attempts to study how all the financial factors mentioned earlier interact simultaneously. I introduce this material in Chapter 1 by discussing a series of deceptively simple principles and then applying those principles to specific problems faced by the modern financial manager. By providing an overview of the basic concepts and principles applicable to the practice of corporate finance in the first chapter, readers have a clear road map of where we are headed and why. This discussion also helps set these ideas in perspective.

Incorporation of the Human Factor in Finance.   Although this text takes its basic driving principle to be the maximization of shareholder wealth, it recognizes that the separation between ownership and control can help explain the frequent discrepancy between observed corporate financial policy and neoclassical economic predictions. This is the topic known as agency theory and it is utilized to analyze manager–owner and stockholder–bondholder conflicts in professionally managed firms. The material is also useful in helping to understand the wave of corporate restructuring that is now occurring.

By integrating agency theory—and its companion, information asymmetry—and their applications throughout, I have tried to illustrate the human factor in financial decision making. The basic perspective taken is that seemingly irrational managerial actions (from the standpoint of the shareholder) can best be understood as the rational response of managers to uncertainty and specific evaluation criteria and mechanisms.

Coverage of International Topics.   On a more personal note, I believe that managers must view business from a global perspective; **international** is not just another section of the domestic economy, like office machines or autos, that can be ignored at no cost. Instead, an international orientation has become a business necessity, not a luxury. Those American television manufacturers determined to remain purely domestic operations learned this lesson the hard way; their greatest competitive threat came from companies located 8,000 miles away, across the Pacific, not from other American producers. To facilitate the development of a global perspective, I have tried to integrate domestic and international financial management throughout the book. To the extent I have succeeded, this is one of the distinctive features of the text.

At the same time, the book contains a separate chapter (31) that supplies the basic equilibrium framework for international financial management, while also dealing with the identification and management of foreign exchange risk.

Comprehensive Coverage.   The extensive coverage of corporate finance allows instructors to delete or assign as outside reading topics that they may not want to devote class time to. Comprehensive coverage is a plus for MBA programs that have just one finance course. Students also benefit because they can keep the text as a comprehensive reference after completing the course.

Numerous Questions and Problems.   Another distinctive feature of *Modern Corporate Finance* is the large number of end-of-chapter questions and problems and their close relationship to the material in the chapters. Good conceptual questions are as important as computational problems in promoting understanding and the ones in the book are consistently challenging, interesting, and extremely useful. They provide practical insights into the types of decisions faced by financial executives and offer practice in applying financial concepts and theories.

Additional Features.   The book also includes a number of other distinguishing features that relate to the subject matter covered; it

- Stresses the value of international, as opposed to domestic, diversification (Chapter 4).
- Contains an early introduction to option pricing and contingent claims, which allows these concepts to be used for valuing growth options and explaining stockholder–bondholder conflicts in later discussions of capital structure and financial strategy (Chapter 5).
- Features a detailed discussion of estimating project cash flows, including incremental versus total cash flows, the effects of inflation on cash flows, and the valuation of growth options. It gives students hands-on experience in estimating project cash flows and helps them gain an appreciation for the real-world difficulties in valuing projects (Chapter 7).
- Provides a discussion of risk that points out the many ways in which total risk can affect expected future cash flows, even if it does not affect the discount rate (Chapter 8).
- Features a separate chapter on corporate strategy that helps readers understand the origins and characteristics of positive net present value projects (Chapter 10).
- Contains a unique chapter on how companies create value—including value-based analysis and corporate restructuring—as well as the links between return on investment, required return on capital invested, and the pricing of stocks. It also deals with issues of executive compensation from a financial standpoint (Chapter 11).
- Features a detailed presentation of financing patterns of companies around the world and discusses the evolution of these financing patterns, particularly the rise of securitization, that helps to put financing options and patterns into perspective (Chapter 12).
- Addresses the qualitative factors that determine financial strategy, concentrating on the costs of financial distress and the value of financial flexibility, thereby putting the design of financial packages in perspective (Chapters 15 and 16).
- Includes a detailed discussion of junk bonds and their role in corporate financing, thereby helping students understand the role and limitations of this important new financial instrument (Chapter 19).
- Emphasizes the distinction between accounting and economic performance (Chapter 22).
- Includes the most comprehensive discussion and illustration of financial statement analysis available; shows students how to conduct a detailed financial analysis and points out the numerous pitfalls involved in such an analysis; and provides a unique discussion of the qualitative aspects of corporate control (Chapter 23).
- Includes chapters on working capital that emphasize its links with overall corporate strategy, thereby helping to place the role of working capital policy in perspective (Chapters 24–29).
- Contains a discussion of just-in-time inventory systems that helps students understand this important new competitive weapon (Chapter 28).
- Contains the most comprehensive discussion of mergers and acquisitions available in a corporate finance text (Chapter 30).

• Has a unique chapter on financial hedging strategy that acquaints readers with financial risk management techniques and instruments, including futures, forwards, swaps, and options (Chapter 33).

Organization

Although the ideas underlying financial economics are interrelated, by necessity they must be elaborated individually. Eventually, they must also be integrated because they are all part of a grand framework. To accomplish this objective, the book is divided into seven parts, each of which builds on the previous material.

Part I, consisting of Chapters 2–5, provides students with a firm grounding in the essentials of modern corporate finance: the time value of money, the pricing of stocks and bonds, portfolio theory and the capital asset pricing model, market efficiency, the nature and pricing of options, and the crucial distinction between accounting profits and cash flow. This material supplies the foundation that enables students to see financial problems from a different frame of reference. Above all else, my aim is to get students to begin thinking in the distinctive way that characterizes the mindset of a financial economist.

Part II applies these basic financial principles to the capital-budgeting decision. This part, which consists of Chapters 6–11, is concerned with the most important problem facing management—finding or creating investment projects worth more than they cost. Topics covered include the basics of capital budgeting, the estimation of project cash flows and the project cost of capital, risk analysis in capital budgeting, and corporate strategy and its relationship to the capital-budgeting decision. Throughout, this part emphasizes how management creates value for its shareholders.

Part III is concerned with developing a long-term financing strategy. It discusses the long-term financing options that firms have, how firms go about raising long-term capital, the theory and practice surrounding capital structure, and dividend policy. Throughout this part, which consists of Chapters 12–17, the emphasis is on how financing can add value.

Part IV takes a closer look at the long-term financing options available to the firm. It examines the fundamental nature of debt, the institutional features and costs associated with bonds and term loans, the valuation of convertibles and warrants, and lease financing. The focus of this part, which consists of Chapters 18–21, is on the rationale for the wide variety of debt securities that we see in the marketplace and, by extension, the circumstances in which it makes sense to use each type of debt instrument.

Part V discusses financial planning and the evaluation and control of operations. It presents the basic financial statements and shows how management, investors, lenders, and other interested parties can analyze these statements to check on a firm's financial well-being. It also shows how financial managers can forecast future financial statements and use these projections to develop an overall financial plan for the firm. This part consists of Chapters 22–24.

Part VI deals with the efficient use of the firm's current assets and how these assets should be financed. It begins with an overview of working capital policy, and then analyzes the specific components of working capital—cash and marketable securities, accounts receivable, inventory, and current liabilities. This part, which consists of Chapters 25–29, emphasizes the relationship between working capital policy and overall corporate strategy.

Part VII, comprising Chapters 30–33, covers special topics in financial management, including mergers and acquisitions, international finance, bankruptcy and reorganization, and financial hedging techniques. These important subjects are treated as applications of concepts and principles developed previously.

Teaching Aids and Supplements

Modern Corporate Finance has a complete set of auxillary materials containing the following elements:

1. An *Instructor's Manual* includes chapter outlines, key terms and concepts with brief definitions, chapter summaries that highlight the key information in the chapter, answers to all end-of-chapter questions, worked-out solutions to all end-of-chapter problems, and transparency masters reproduced from the illustrations in the text.
2. A *Study Guide* will provide students with outstanding self-instructional content. It contains chapter learning objectives, key terms and concepts, chapter summaries, true–false, multiple choice, and written answer questions, as well as worked-out numerical examples. This guide will be particularly helpful for those students requiring assistance working numerical problems in finance.
3. The *Test Bank* by Professor John Stowe of the University of Missouri contains an average of 25 multiple choice questions and 10 problems for each of the 33 chapters in the text. All questions and problems will be keyed to the section of the text that they are drawn from for ease of designing examinations.
4. *Software* developed by Professor David Shimko of the University of Southern California contains teaching software designed to cover specific types of finance techniques, such as the Black–Scholes Option Pricing model; Lotus® problems that offer practical applications of users' Lotus skills; and teaching materials, such as tables and graphs. This software is designed to focus the student's attention on learning the underlying concepts and techniques of finance by lessening the time and effort spent on computations.

Acknowledgments

This book has benefited greatly from the comments and suggestions of the following reviewers:

Paul J. Bolster, Northeastern University
Sris Chatterjee, Columbia University
Dennis Draper, University of Southern California
Alan E. Grunewald, Michigan State University
Delvin D. Hawley, University of Mississippi
Glen V. Henderson, Jr., University of Cincinnati
John S. Howe, Louisiana State University, Baton Rouge
Steven C. Isberg, University of Baltimore
Michael A. Mazzeo, Indiana University

Jim Miles, Pennsylvania State University
Thomas J. O'Brien, University of Connecticut
Don J. Rousslang, George Washington University
David S. Rystrom, Western Washington University
James A. Seifert, Marquette University
Gerald E. Smolen, University of Toledo
John D. Stowe, University of Missouri
John M. Wachowicz, Jr., University of Tennessee
Ralph A. Walkling, Ohio State University
Randy Woolridge, Pennsylvania State University

In addition, Warren Bailey of Ohio State University wrote first drafts for Chapter 5 (Options and Corporate Finance) and Chapter 33 (Hedging Corporate Risk Exposure). Professor Bailey also provided many of the end-of-chapter questions and problems, as did Joan Junkus of DePaul University. I am very grateful for their help.

I greatly appreciate the help of Caroline Carney and Ken MacLeod, my editors at Macmillan (at different times), who ably assisted in pulling together the loose ends of the book and wrapping it up. I am also deeply indebted to Chip Price, my original editor at Macmillan, who helped initiate this project and provided valuable comments and strong encouragement along the way.

I would like to thank the designer of the book, Natasha Sylvester. The development editor, Lee Marcott, served as liaison to the reviewers and coordinated the development and production of the supplements. I would also particularly like to thank the production supervisor, Ron Harris, for his tremendous patience and organizational abilities in overseeing the entire production process.

My greatest debt of all is to my wife, Diane, and my children, Tom and Kathryn. They had to bear the brunt of the countless hours I spent hunched over my computer searching for the right words and examples that would bring corporate finance to life. It's time for a break!

ACS
Pacific Palisades

Contents

PART

II

Capital Budgeting

PART
III

Long-Term Financing Strategy

PART

IV

Debt Financing

PART
VI

Working Capital Management

PART

VII

Special Topics in Corporate Finance

Introduction

There are two things, science and opinion; the
former begets knowledge, the latter ignorance.

HIPPOCRATES

Corporate finance deals with the *acquisition* and *allocation* of resources among the firm's present and potential activities and projects. The first function, also known as the *financing decision*, involves generating funds either internally or from sources external to the firm at the lowest possible cost. The second function, also known as the *investment decision*, is concerned with allocating funds over time in such a way that shareholder wealth is increased. This latter task is accomplished by undertaking activities and purchasing assets that are worth more than they cost.

Figure 1-1 shows some of the assets that companies invest in and how these assets are financed. Some of the assets—like a strong brand name or a

FIGURE 1-1
The Two Key Functions of Corporate Finance

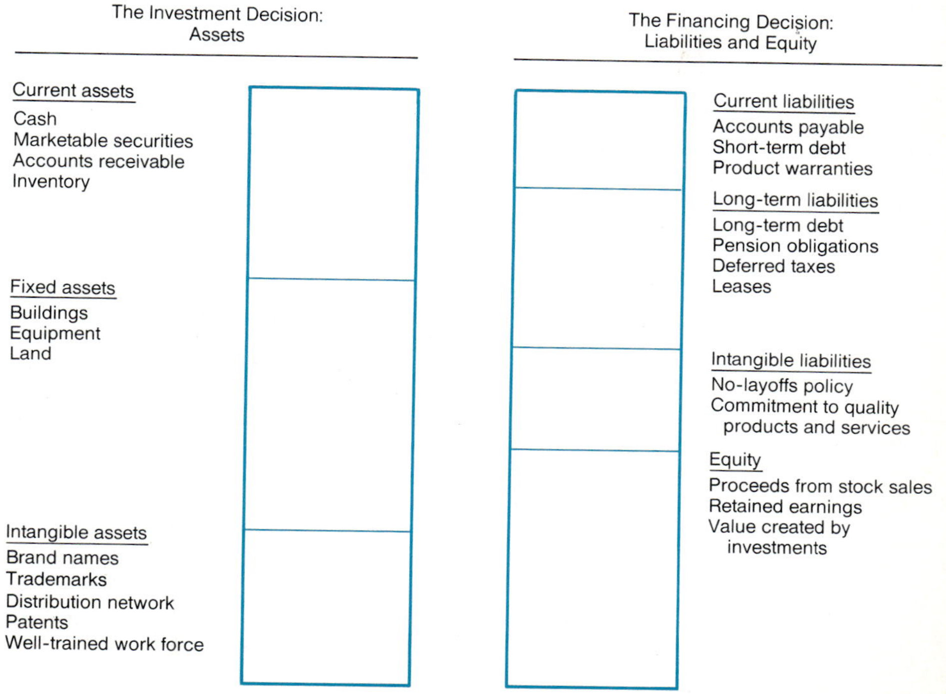

The Investment Decision: Assets	The Financing Decision: Liabilities and Equity
Current assets Cash Marketable securities Accounts receivable Inventory	Current liabilities Accounts payable Short-term debt Product warranties Long-term liabilities Long-term debt Pension obligations Deferred taxes Leases
Fixed assets Buildings Equipment Land	Intangible liabilities No-layoffs policy Commitment to quality products and services
Intangible assets Brand names Trademarks Distribution network Patents Well-trained work force	Equity Proceeds from stock sales Retained earnings Value created by investments

dedicated, well-trained work force—are intangible yet valuable all the same. Similarly, companies have intangible liabilities that help finance their assets. For example, a commitment to workers that they won't be laid off, even if business turns down, helps to create and maintain a dedicated work force.

The ultimate objective of both financial functions is to maximize the shareholders' wealth. This means making financing and investment decisions that add as much value as possible to the firm. It also means that companies must manage effectively the assets under their control. Because all corporate actions affect the value of the firm, understanding the nature of value—its creation, preservation, and destruction—is vital to all corporate executives, not just those designated as financial managers. Thus, although this book focuses on financial management, all functional areas—such as marketing, personnel management, and operations management—can benefit from the concepts and techniques presented here. In addition, despite our concentration on private-sector firms, most of the financial principles developed here are equally applicable to public-sector organizations, like hospitals, schools, and government agencies.

1.1 OBJECTIVE

The objective of this book is to help the reader make sound financial decisions, many of which involve executives in marketing, production, and other functional areas. For this purpose, we require a conceptual framework that managers can use to analyze key financial decisions. Our effort benefits greatly from the insights provided by *financial economics*—a discipline that emphasizes economic analysis to understand the basic workings of financial markets, particularly the measurement and pricing of risk and the intertemporal allocation of funds. This latter point refers to the choice faced by all individuals and institutions between investing money for future consumption and spending money today for current consumption.

By focusing on the behavior of financial markets and their participants, rather than on how to solve specific problems, we can derive fundamental principles of valuation. Using this basic theory, we can develop superior courses of action, much as a good engineer applies the basic laws of physics to design better-functioning products and processes. We can also better gauge the validity of generally accepted financial practices by seeing whether their underlying assumptions are consistent with our current knowledge. Policies that are plausible on the surface often turn out to be based on assumptions that are unrealistic in light of our understanding of how financial markets work. Moreover, rules of thumb that worked under one set of conditions, such as a low-inflation environment, may no longer work under a changed set of circumstances, such as an environment characterized by a high and variable rate of inflation.

Properly applied, the modern theory of corporate finance can provide managers with a more sensible basis for setting corporate goals and answering the questions and problems they deal with on a daily basis. For example:

- Should we overhaul our equipment or replace it?
- Do we use staff people for this project or hire outside services?
- Should we lease or buy this asset?
- Should we pay a cash dividend to our stockholders?
- Should we fund this research and development project?

- Which loan gives us the most favorable financial terms?
- Should we borrow money from a bank or issue more bonds?
- Should we raise equity capital instead of borrowing more money?
- Which division(s) should be allocated more funds?
- Which division(s) should be sold off?
- Should managers be paid higher salaries or be given bigger bonuses?
- Which manager is doing the best job?
- How should we communicate with Wall Street?
- Should we acquire this company?
- Should we stock up on inventory to get a better deal?
- What's the best way to invest the company's short-term cash?
- Should we extend more generous credit terms to our customers?

To answer these questions, we need to understand how financial markets work. The reason is simple. Firms raise capital in financial markets by selling investors claims—in the form of financial securities like stocks and bonds—to certain future cash flows. The financial markets determine the price of those claims. To the extent that managers view their role as providing the maximum returns to shareholders, which they should, all financial decisions must be grounded in some theory of how investors value, or price, financial securities and other capital assets. Unless managers know how the financial markets are likely to view particular business transactions, they may make decisions that cost the shareholders money.

1.2 BASIC CONCEPTS

You will now be presented with a series of basic principles, which together form a simple, yet elegant and powerful conceptual framework. This is just an introduction. You will see these concepts and ideas over and over again, in many different guises and circumstances. We introduce them here, at the very beginning of the book, to get you started right away thinking in a special way. Although some of the concepts we present will appear self-evident, indeed trivial, be assured that many of their implications are not at all obvious; they certainly are not always accepted in financial circles. In fact, much of what passes for financial wisdom on Wall Street and in the boardrooms of corporate America goes counter to these basic principles. This conflict stems, in part, from the previous lack of focused research. But the logic underlying the principles presented here and, more important, the empirical evidence available to support them are nearly irresistible, resulting in major changes in the way executives think about business and the decisions they make.

Our theoretical foundation begins with the simple notion that people try to maximize their well-being. Part of this well-being stems from the consumption of goods and services. All else being equal, this means that people generally prefer more wealth to less, where wealth represents the ability to consume. One way that people acquire more wealth is to defer consumption and invest the freed-up money in a company. Those who are relatively risk averse become bondholders, lending money to the company in return for a promised interest rate and repayment of the loan at an agreed-upon future date. Those who are willing to bear more risk will become shareholders, providing equity capital to the company in return for partial ownership of it. As partial owners of the firm, stockholders receive a proportional share of the firm's profits and losses. However, stockholders have only a *residual* interest in the company's earnings; bondholders and other creditors must be paid off before stockholders can claim any of the firm's earnings. If the firm fails to make its interest and principal payments on time, it is said to be in *default* and the bondholders can sue it to recover their money.

The relevance of this discussion to financial management is that the shareholders are the legal owners of the firm and management has a fiduciary obligation to act in the shareholders' best interests. Other stakeholders in the company do have rights, but these aren't coequal with the shareholders' rights. Shareholders provide the risk capital that cushions the claims of alternative stakeholders. The value of the firm could drop by as much as the value of equity capital and the company would still have enough assets to honor the claims of bondholders and noninvestor stakeholders. Allowing alternative stakeholders coequal control over capital supplied by others is equivalent to allowing one group to risk someone else's capital. This would undoubtedly impair future equity formation and produce numerous other inefficiencies.

The import of this discussion is that the primary objective of financial management is to maximize the shareholders' well-being. Because shareholders have invested their money in the expectation of being made better off financially, this objective translates into maximizing shareholder wealth. We shall see later on in this chapter that maximizing shareholder wealth is tantamount to maximizing the firm's share price.

Although it is recognized that an institution as complex as the modern corporation does not have a single, unambiguous will, the principle of shareholder wealth maximization provides a rational guide to financial decision making. However, we also examine other financial goals that reflect the relative autonomy of management and external pressures. These include maximizing earnings or earnings per share, boosting the size and degree of corporate diversification by acquiring other firms, and increasing financial flexibility by maintaining excess liquid assets and borrowing power.

Nominal Versus Real Quantities

Wealth is usually measured in terms of money, because money can be exchanged for goods and services. Indeed, if money were not accepted as a medium of exchange (e.g., Confederate dollars), it would not be money. For money is what money does. And what money does is buy goods and services. The rate at which this exchange takes place is called the *nominal* or money price of the specific good or service bought. As nominal prices change, the *purchasing power*, and hence the value, of money changes. The value of money, therefore, is determined by the level of nominal prices. Thus, inflation, which is a general rise in the nominal price level, is equivalent to a decline in the value of money.

To take account of changes in the purchasing power of money through time, we distinguish between the *nominal* or face value of money and the *real* or inflation-adjusted value of money. For example, if inflation is 5 percent per annum, the real value of a nominal dollar is declining by 5 percent annually. In other words, a dollar next year will be worth only $.95 in real terms, that is, relative to the purchasing power of a dollar today. Thus, although past, present, and future dollars all have the same nominal value, what really matters for pur-

FIGURE 1-2
Purchasing Power
of the U.S. Dollar

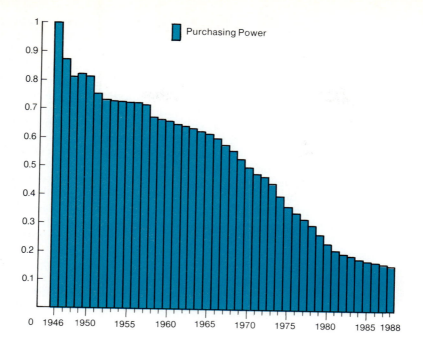

poses of economic evaluation is their real values, the differing quantities of goods and services that each can buy. Figure 1-2 shows how the purchasing power of the U.S. dollar has changed between 1946 and 1988. In effect, one dollar at the end of 1988 was worth about $.16 in 1946 dollars. This distinction between nominal and real magnitudes is crucial to understanding the relationship among prices, inflation, and interest rates.

Stripped to their essence, all financial transactions, no matter how complex, involve the exchange of goods and services today for more or less certain quantities of goods and services in the future. There are significant gains to borrowers and lenders, however, from specifying contracts in terms of money rather than directly in terms of the actual goods and services. This enables both parties to the loan agreement to avoid having to write detailed contracts specifying precise quantities and qualities of the goods or services that must be repaid. Hence, interest rates are stated in money, or nominal, terms rather than real terms. Stating contracts in money terms, however, complicates matters when inflation is present.

The **nominal interest rate** is the price quoted in lending and borrowing transactions in financial markets. It is generally expressed as the premium that must be paid when current dollars are exchanged for future dollars. For example, an interest rate of 10 percent on a one-year loan means that one dollar today is being exchanged for 1.1 dollars a year from now. What really matters, however, is the exchange rate between current and future purchasing power, as measured by the **real interest rate**.

An increase in the real interest rate means that the cost of consuming goods today has risen in terms of future goods. In other words, the *opportunity cost* of today's consumption has risen relative to future consumption. As we shall see, changes in real interest rates have enormous implications for savings and investment decisions.

The real rate of interest that people expect to receive on their investments is always positive. There are two basic reasons for this expectation. First, people generally prefer present consumption over consumption in the future. This *positive time preference* means that people value the current use of resources (goods) more highly than they do their future use. Those who have strong preferences for immediate consumption will borrow from those who are less impatient and willing to delay satisfying their wants. Because the second group also has positive time preference, the first group must pay it a positive rate of interest to gain its acquiescence in the transaction.

Even without positive time preference, however, we would still see a positive real rate, because resources can be used productively over time. Some goods, like trees and cattle, physically grow over time, whereas other goods, like wine and cheese, may improve in quality with age. Most important, resources can be converted into capital goods—goods like machinery and trucks—that produce more goods and services. Because in our world more is preferred to less, the present use of resources must have a positive price; competition among potential users will ensure that this is so.

The existence of a positive rate of interest results in what is known as the **time value of money**, the notion that a dollar today is worth more than a dollar in the future. The difference in the values of current and future dollars is determined by the rate of interest. Thus, if the interest rate is 10 percent per annum, the **present value**, or value in terms of today's dollars, of one dollar a year from now is $.91. This is because $.91 invested today at 10 percent will be worth $.91 × 1.10 = $1 one year from now. Alternatively, the **future value** of one dollar today is $1.10 a year from now.

Earnings Versus Cash Flow

The emphasis on money so far has not been misplaced. In most economies of the world, including our own, people consume by spending money to buy goods and services. The more money one has, the more one can consume. Firms benefit their shareholders, therefore, by providing them with cash, either by paying current dividends or by reinvesting the money to pay future dividends. This statement, simple as it sounds, has a profound and controversial implication— accounting profits not associated with cash flows are of no value to investors. It means, for example, that switching depreciation methods for reporting—but not tax—purposes so as to boost reported profits does not benefit shareholders because there is no effect on cash flow.

If financial markets are efficient, debates as to which accounting method to use will be irrelevant to shareholders except insofar as they may be misled concerning the firm's true cash flow. Moreover, because the value of the cash received is based on its purchasing power, the measure of a firm's performance depends on how much it increases its shareholders' purchasing power. A higher cash flow not associated with greater purchasing power does not increase the shareholders' wealth. Thus a firm generating 10 percent more cash during a time when inflation is running at a rate of 12 percent is actually suffering a diminution in its performance.

Arbitrage, Market Efficiency, and Capital Asset Pricing

Three concepts arising in financial economics have proved especially valuable in developing a theoretical foundation for the study and practice of corporate finance: arbitrage, market efficiency, and the distinction between systematic and unsystematic risk as reflected in the capital asset pricing model. Because we use these concepts throughout this book, it is worthwhile to briefly describe them.

Arbitrage.   **Arbitrage** has traditionally been defined as the purchase of securities or commodities on one market for immediate resale on another to profit from a price discrepancy. Under this definition, the positions being taken are close to riskless. More recently, the term *arbitrage* has been used to describe a broader range of financial activities. Tax arbitrage, for example, is the shifting of gains or losses from one tax jurisdiction to another or from one category of income to another to profit from differences in tax rates. Until the Tax Reform Act of 1986, a standard means of saving taxes was to convert ordinary income, then taxed at rates of up to 50 percent, to capital gains, whose top rate was 20 percent. Similarly, to the extent that multinational firms can shift export income to their operations in, say, Ireland, they can receive that income tax free because of a 15-year tax holiday provided by the Irish government. Even more important from our standpoint is the extension of arbitrage to include trading activities that involve risk. Risk arbitrage, sometimes termed *speculation*, has been used to describe the process that ensures that, in equilibrium, risk-adjusted returns on different assets are equal, unless market imperfections that hinder this adjustment process exist. In fact, it is the process of risk arbitrage, fueled by new information or differences of opinion, that ensures market efficiency.

Market Efficiency.   An **efficient financial market** is one composed of numerous well-informed individuals, with ready and cheap access to information, whose trading activities cause prices to adjust rapidly to reflect all relevant and available information. Thus, price changes at any moment must be due solely to the arrival of new information. Because new information useful for profitable trading activities arrives randomly (otherwise it would be neither new nor useful), price changes must follow a random walk.[1] In other words, in an efficient market, price changes from one period to the next are independent of past price changes and are no more predictable than is new information. Consistent with this implication, numerous studies of U.S. and overseas financial markets have shown that prices of domestic and foreign securities follow random walks. A number of studies also indicate that securities are correctly priced in that trading rules based on past prices or publicly available information do not consistently lead to profits net of transaction costs in excess of those due solely to risk taking.

The basic idea underlying market efficiency is that when Exxon announces that it's just discovered a billion-barrel oil field in the Beaufort Sea, off the northern coast of Alaska, all the smart types who had figured out that Exxon stock was worth $38 will go back to their computers and decide that it's now worth $41.25. Should you do the same and attempt to profit from this knowledge by buying Exxon stock, the odds are that by the time you placed an order with your broker, the price would have already risen to $41.25.

---

[1]In reality, asset prices follow a submartingale, which is a random walk with a drift. The drift equals the expected return on the asset.

The idea that securities and other assets are fairly priced, given their anticipated risks and returns, is intuitively appealing. In a world where hundreds of thousands of investors, including numerous professional arbitrageurs on exchange floors, are endlessly searching for marginally higher returns, it would be difficult to explain how over- or undervalued securities *could* exist for more than a few seconds or so. This is especially true today with computers and high-speed telecommunications giving investors worldwide access to nearly instantaneous price quotes and other relevant information.

Capital Asset Pricing.   It is generally agreed that investors require higher returns on riskier investments, whose return can come in the form of either a cash payment (e.g., interest or dividends) or appreciation in the value of the investment (e.g., a higher stock or bond price). The difficulty for the financial manager lies in quantifying the riskiness of an investment and establishing the trade-off between risk and expected return (i.e., the price of risk). Probably more effort has been devoted by financial economists to this issue than to any other. The outcome of this research has been to posit a specific relationship among diversification, risk, and required return, which is now formalized in the **capital asset pricing model** (CAPM).[2] Risk itself is assumed to depend on the variability of returns; the more highly variable the return is, the riskier the asset will be.

The CAPM is based on the idea that the total variability of an asset's returns can be attributed to two sources: (1) market-wide influences that affect all assets to some extent, like the level of interest rates or growth in GNP; and (2) other risks specific to a given firm, like a strike or a new patentable invention. The former type of risk is usually termed **systematic** or **market risk,** and the latter, **unsystematic** or **diversifiable risk.** It can be shown that unsystematic risk is largely irrelevant to the investor holding a well-diversified portfolio, because the effects of such disturbances can be expected to cancel out, on average, in the portfolio. On the other hand, no matter how well diversified the investment portfolio is, systematic risk, by definition, cannot be eliminated.

The distinction between systematic and unsystematic risks underlies the pricing of risk in the CAPM, as well as in the more general **arbitrage pricing theory** (APT).[3] According to both the CAPM and the APT, intelligent, risk-averse investors seek to diversify their asset holdings to eliminate the unsystematic component of risk. As a result, only the systematic component of risk will be rewarded with a risk premium. Arbitrage among securities will ensure that investors will not be paid for bearing unsystematic risks, because they can avoid these risks at no cost simply by diversifying their portfolios. In other words, the CAPM and APT assume that enough people will follow the adage "don't put all your eggs in one basket" to ensure that investors will be compensated only for bearing

[2]The bases of the CAPM were provided by Harry Markowitz, *Portfolio Selection: Efficient Diversification of Investments* (New York: Wiley, 1959); William F. Sharpe, "Capital Asset Prices: A Theory of Market Equilibrium Under Conditions of Risk," *Journal of Finance*, September 1964, pp. 425–442; and John Lintner, "The Valuation of Risk Assets and the Selection of Risky Investments in Stock Portfolios and Capital Budgets," *Review of Economics and Statistics*, February 1965, pp. 13–37. Jack Treynor also pioneered in the development of the CAPM but his paper was never published.

[3]The formal theory of arbitrage pricing was first developed in Stephen A. Ross, "The Arbitrage Theory of Capital Asset Pricing," *Journal of Economic Theory*, December 1976, pp. 341–360. It is discussed in detail in Chapter 4. Unlike the capital asset pricing model, which assumes that only one factor is priced (the market factor), the APT permits the pricing of a number of factors.

market risk. This illustrates one of the most important rules in finance: You don't get paid for doing something that is unnecessary or irrelevant. It is the equivalent of the economist's dictum that there is no free lunch.

Recognizing and Valuing Options

The recognition and valuation of options are becoming an increasingly important part of corporate finance. An option gives the holder the right—but not the obligation—to do something in the future. That something can be the right to buy or sell assets such as stocks or bonds, foreign currencies or gold, or wheat or corn at a set price and date. Options are also present in the opportunity to undertake future investments or to expand, shut down, or abandon projects already undertaken. For example, investments in research and development often yield a variety of new investment opportunities, depending on the outcome of the research. Similarly, the owner of an oil well always has the option of shutting down production if the price of oil drops too low. More financial securities are being created with explicit options built right into them. For example, convertible bonds grant holders the right to exchange them for shares of the issuing company. Even when explicit options are not present, many corporate securities contain implicit options. For example, the right to file for bankruptcy gives companies the implicit option to default on the bonds they have issued.

Options are valuable because they allow the holder to defer a decision until a later date, by which time more information will have been acquired about what is best to do. The more uncertain the future, the more valuable the ability to delay decisions will be. This implies, for example, that all else being equal, research and development (R&D) funds should be directed to projects having the widest range of possible outcomes.

Despite their importance, however, options have historically been very difficult to value because they are so complex. Then in 1973, Fischer Black and Myron Scholes pioneered a new approach to option pricing that greatly expanded our ability to value even highly complex and unusual options.[4] The Black–Scholes option pricing model is one of the great advances of modern finance.

1.3 BASIC LESSONS

Despite widespread evidence of market efficiency, many companies persist in expending real resources in attempts to provide shareholders with something, like corporate diversification, that is probably unnecessary or to fool them by manipulating accounting profits in one way or another. For instance, during the decade of rapid inflation that began in late 1973, many American companies decided to remain on the FIFO (first-in, first-out) method of inventory valuation, which results in a lower reported cost of goods sold (and hence higher reported profits), in order to "dress up" their financial statements.

Switching to the alternative method of inventory valuation, LIFO (last-in, first-out), during a period of rising prices decreases reported earnings (by showing a higher cost of goods sold) but increases corporate cash flow owing to the

[4]See Fischer Black and Myron Scholes, "The Pricing of Options and Corporate Liabilities," *Journal of Political Economy*, May–June 1973, pp. 637–654.

reduction in taxes paid. Those firms that stuck with FIFO reported higher income but suffered a decline in cash flow because of the higher taxes they had to pay. Thus, this financial "window dressing" came at the expense of shareholders. As was stressed earlier, the "economic" model of the firm holds that what matters is cash, not accounting profits. Certainly in filling out their own tax returns, corporate executives understand well enough that minimizing their reported income (the equivalent of a firm's accounting income) will maximize their share of its purchasing power. We will see the influence of taxes on corporate financial decisions throughout the text.

The basic issue is whether investors respond mechanically and unthinkingly to earnings reports or whether they exercise their collective judgment and seek to determine the underlying cash flows. The available evidence suggests that investors pay attention to accounting profits only insofar as they believe reported profits reflect real cash flows.[5] When reported earnings differ significantly from cash flows, investors disregard those reported earnings. Hence, the basic rule to follow whenever there is a conflict between the two is to "take the money and run." Not surprisingly, the stock market isn't fooled by the tricks accountants can play with inventory valuations. After all, this information is part of the public domain. To underscore this fact, publications like *Business Week* regularly present LIFO-adjusted earnings of those firms clinging to FIFO.

The Irrelevance of Financial Manipulations

There are two fundamental insights into financial management to be gained from evidence on the effects of financial window dressing. First, attempts to increase the value of a firm by purely financial measures or accounting manipulations are unlikely to succeed except under certain specific circumstances. These exceptional circumstances include capital market imperfections that don't allow prices to fully reflect all available information and asymmetries in tax regulations (like our current system of levying taxes on nominal income rather than on true economic earnings). Neither of these circumstances was present when Rapid-American Corporation replaced its low-coupon debt with higher-coupon debt and recorded a taxable gain of $30 million. Similarly, during the first six months of 1983, Aetna Life & Casualty recorded over $73 million in taxable income, nearly 40 percent of its operating income, by an accounting gimmick known as "selling loss reserves." Without getting into the technical details of these transactions, the point is that both firms created taxable income without generating any additional cash. In fact, these deals, which looked so good on the income statements, actually cost the firms cash in the form of higher taxes and transaction costs.

Incentives and Management Behavior

The second lesson is that people typically act on their own behalf, responding rationally to incentives and disincentives. Specifically, managers who sacrifice

---

[5]The classic studies providing evidence on the ability of investors to see through accounting numbers are R. Ball and P. Brown, "An Empirical Evaluation of Accounting Income Numbers," *Journal of Accounting Research*, Autumn 1968, pp. 159–178; and Robert Kaplan and Richard Roll, "Investor Evaluation of Accounting Information: Some Empirical Evidence," *Journal of Business*, April 1972, pp. 225–227.

cash flow for higher reported profits are often being judged and rewarded on the basis of those profits. This is just one example among many of an evaluation system that rewards behavior that is detrimental to the best interests of the firm's shareholders. Because corporate executives are at best only partial owners of the firms they manage, they don't bear the harmful consequences of their behavior, just the benefits (in the form of higher incomes, added perquisites, or less effort). This theme of the separation between ownership and control and the consequences of that separation is one we shall return to many times. It is known formally as the **agency conflict**, a reference to the fact that managers act as agents for absentee owners.[6]

An illustration of the potentially huge gap between management actions and shareholder preferences is the embarrassing run-up of 47 percent in the price of Gulf & Western's stock following the sudden death of its chairman, Charles Bluhdorn, in 1983. One interpretation of the stock market's reaction is that G&W shareholders felt that Bluhdorn was pursuing inappropriate policies but that his position was secure as long as he was alive. A similar embarrassment occurred in 1966 after Walt Disney died. Disney stock rose by about 25 percent in the following week.

The agency conflict also extends to the relations between stockholders and bondholders. The potential for conflict between the two classes of investors arises because managers may make dividend, financing, and investment decisions that transfer wealth from bondholders to stockholders. Such decisions create gains for stockholders and capital losses for bondholders. For example, in 1986 Colt Industries announced that it would borrow $1.4 billion to pay shareholders an $85-a-share dividend. Colt shares, which were then trading at $66.75, soared on the news. But some long-term Colt bonds tumbled as much as $200 for each $1,000 face amount on the news. The bond price drop reflected the combination of a greater risk of default—Colt's interest and principal payments rose substantially—and a smaller payoff to bondholders if default occurred—fewer assets remained to satisfy bondholder claims.

Information Asymmetry

Related to the agency problem is the fact that one party to an exchange often knows something relevant to the transaction that the other party does not know. The lesson for the financial manager is that such asymmetries of information are pervasive in financial activities, for example, in the relationship between the stockholders and the managers of a firm, between the issuer and the purchaser of a security, between the insurer and the insured, and between lender and borrower. To counter the problem of information asymmetry that, if allowed to go unchecked, could cause financial markets to cease to function, a variety of mechanisms and institutions have arisen. These include the use of investment bankers to certify the quality of the securities they issue, incentive contracts structured so that all parties to the transaction will find it in their own interest to be honest, and the use of various financial instruments and structures that reduce the costs of duplicity to the ignorant party and raise them for the knowl-

---

[6]The formal theory and implications of agency in corporate finance were first presented in Michael C. Jensen and William H. Meckling, "Theory of the Firm: Managerial Behavior, Agency Costs, and Ownership Structure," *Journal of Financial Economics*, October 1976, pp. 305–360.

edgeable party. An important aspect of many of these solutions is the development of valuable reputations, whose value would be destroyed in the event the reputable party to a transaction used inside information to exploit the ignorant party.

Anticipated Versus Unanticipated Events

Another important lesson in corporate finance is also simple to describe but has wide-ranging, though at times subtle, implications for financial decision making. As we have seen previously, in an efficient market, asset prices already incorporate expectations of factors likely to affect their values. This means that investors often react not to what actually happens but to the *difference* between what happens and what was expected to happen. Thus, for example, in 1988 when Hewlett-Packard announced a 30 percent increase in second-quarter earnings per share to $.82, from $.63 in 1987, its share price fell by 8 percent (a loss in market value—the number of shares times the price drop—of over $1.3 billion), not because investors didn't care about earnings but because the increase was less than expected. Similarly, G.D. Searle plunged $5.75 to close at $40.50 the day after the company reported a 50 percent jump in 1984 first-quarter earnings per share. According to the *Wall Street Journal*, "Investors had been expecting an even bigger increase, and their disappointment led to a flood of sell orders."[7]

This distinction between *anticipated* and *unanticipated* phenomena plays an important role in describing the market's reaction to such events as dividend and inflation announcements as well as providing some clues as to the proper objectives of management. An illustration of the latter is the following: A common piece of financial advice is to borrow during times of inflation and profit at the lender's expense by paying back the loan with cheaper money. But if nominal interest rates already reflect anticipated inflation (as we would expect them to and which seems to be the case), such a policy can be successful only if actual inflation consistently exceeds the amount predicted. This is highly unlikely in a market with numerous well-informed participants. In fact, one would have to expect the unexpected—a logical impossibility—to anticipate profiting from such a situation. An alternative rationale for borrowing during inflation, which is to protect the firm against *unexpected* inflation, may be more sensible.

The basic financial principles we have touched upon briefly so far can be summarized easily: More wealth is preferred to less wealth; sooner is better than later; less risk is preferred to more risk; and options are valuable. All the other concepts presented (including market efficiency, arbitrage, capital asset pricing, the time value of money, and the distinction between nominal and real interest rates) and conclusions reached (what matters is not the quantity of money per se but the purchasing power represented by that money; investors will pay only for value received; one can't expect to profit from or successfully protect against expected changes; the more uncertain the environment, the more valuable the opportunity to make decisions contingent on future information; and managers and investors respond in a rational manner, on average, to the economic incentives, opportunities, and information they face) are logically derived conse-

---

[7]*Wall Street Journal*, April 16, 1984, p. 55.

quences of the rational pursuit of economic self-interest, based on the preceding four principles.

Insights from Microeconomics

The financial manager must also pay heed to three fundamental rules arising out of microeconomic theory. First, and perhaps most important, is the following maxim weighing an action's costs and benefits: *Profit-making activities should be undertaken up to the point at which marginal revenue equals marginal cost.* Specifically, money should be invested in long-term assets, like new plant and equipment, and working capital items, like inventory and accounts receivable, up to the point at which the additional returns from these assets just equal the cost of the capital invested.

Related to the idea of equating marginal costs and benefits, is the notion that only **incremental cash flows** are relevant. This means, for example, that sunk costs are sunk. In other words, costs that have already been incurred, and cannot be recovered, are irrelevant in deciding what to do in the future. This advice is contrary to the common wisdom, expressed in statements like, "If we don't invest another million dollars, we'll lose the million dollars we already have tied up in the project." But investing more money to protect a poor investment that has already been made is just throwing good money after bad.

Similarly, it will not pay to invest more money to expand a good project if new returns are less than the opportunity cost of the capital employed. This rule introduces the third key concept from microeconomics, that of **opportunity cost**. The opportunity cost of an asset is the maximum return the asset could generate for the firm if it were sold or put to some other productive use. Financial decision making is most concerned with the **opportunity cost of funds**, the yield forgone on the best available investment alternative. As such, it becomes the basic criterion of financial success. This opportunity cost will vary with the riskiness of the project; the higher the project's risk is, the greater the opportunity cost will be. An investment that earns less than its opportunity cost of capital reduces shareholder wealth. For example, money invested in drilling new oil wells will be misspent if the returns on the funds are 12 percent and the cost of the funds is 16 percent.

Other resources used by firms also have opportunity costs, which must be included when evaluating projects. For example, a software development project requiring extensive computer time should be charged the opportunity cost of that time, even if the firm owns the computer. This opportunity cost could equal the profits the firm forgoes by not having extra time to lease out to others or the cost of additional computer time that must be bought by another department because the new project used up all the available time. But if the computer system has excess capacity, with no other plans for its use, then the opportunity cost will be zero.

These basic concepts and principles are used throughout this text to point out how managers, financial and otherwise, can add value to their firms. The focus is on those areas and circumstances in which financial decisions can measurably increase value, as well as on the characteristics of those investment and financing decisions most likely to benefit shareholders. The value of good financial management is enhanced in today's world because of the greater complexity of the decisions that must be made, the increase in the available financing options, and the added competition and opportunities provided by an integrated global economy.

1.4 CORPORATE OBJECTIVES

Thus far we have talked about shareholder wealth maximization without spelling out what this means in practice. Investors have a diverse set of preferences for risk and for current versus future consumption. If corporate management attempted to satisfy all these contradictory demands simultaneously, this could theoretically result in paralysis. Fortunately, this problem is more apparent than real, as indicated by the following statement: *In well-functioning capital markets, where investors are able to freely buy and sell financial securities with minimal transaction costs, the goal of shareholder wealth maximization translates into maximizing the current share price.*

Maximizing Share Price

Regardless of individual shareholders' preferences, they will be able to increase their perceived welfare by owning more valuable shares. Those who prefer increased consumption today can either sell some of their higher-priced shares or borrow against them. Shareholders who wish to save for consumption later can either hold their more valuable shares or, if they are risk averse, convert some of their increased wealth into less risky assets. What actions contribute to higher share prices? As we will see in Chapter 3, share prices are based on the present value of the future cash distributions, in the form of dividends and share repurchases, to shareholders. Hence, corporate actions that increase the present value of these cash distributions will increase share prices.

Although other objectives are often pursued by corporate management, none is as encompassing as share price maximization. No other objective so fully accounts for differences in the amounts, timing, and riskiness of future cash flows. Maximizing corporate profits or earnings per share has serious defects as a corporate goal.

Maximizing Earnings or Earnings Per Share

Total corporate profits can always be increased by issuing additional shares of common stock and investing the proceeds in safe Treasury bills. But investors are more interested in earnings per share (EPS), assuming there is no divergence between earnings and cash flow, and these could decline if the company sold more shares. Consider, for example, a company with 1 million shares outstanding that has $5 million in annual earnings or $5 per share. Suppose the firm issues an additional million shares and uses the proceeds to acquire assets that produce $3 million in income. As Table 1-1 shows, although total earnings are now $8 million, earnings per share have declined from $5 to $4. Focusing on earnings per share can avoid such earnings dilution, but the objective of maximizing earnings per share also has serious shortcomings. It ignores the crucial distinc-

TABLE 1-1 Effects of Issuing New Shares on Earnings Per Share		Before	After
	Number of shares outstanding	1,000,000	2,000,000
	Earnings	$5,000,000	$8,000,000
	Earnings per share	$\dfrac{\$5,000,000}{\$1,000,000}$ $= \$5.00$	$\dfrac{\$8,000,000}{\$2,000,000}$ $= \$4.00$

tion between earnings and cash flow, the timing of the earnings, and the riskiness of these earnings.

As discussed earlier, in the example of LIFO versus FIFO inventory valuation, managers can sometimes increase earnings at the expense of corporate cash flows. Other methods, which we will explore later on, can be used to increase earnings without having any impact on cash flows. What really matters to shareholders, of course, is an earnings increase that results in more cash flow.

Another problem with focusing on earnings or earnings per share to the exclusion of other considerations is that it pays no attention to the timing of the earnings. Often the firm must sacrifice current earnings for greater earnings in the future. Suppose, for example, that a project that costs $1 million will return $300,000 for each of the next five years. Is the trade-off worthwhile? Similarly, consider two mutually exclusive investments, one of which will pay out $.25 per share for the next five years, or $1.25 in total, and the other of which will pay out nothing for the first four years and $1.50 per share in the fifth year. Which investment is preferable? The answer in both these situations depends on the time value of money to investors, a consideration conspicuously absent from the goal of EPS maximization.

Yet another shortcoming of EPS maximization is its disregard of the riskiness of these earnings streams. One way to boost returns is to invest in riskier projects. Suppose two mutually exclusive projects cost the same but one is expected to yield an increase in EPS of $1.00 whereas the other, which is riskier, is expected to increase earnings by an average of $1.15 per share. Which project, if either, should be selected? Another way to increase projected EPS, which also involves assuming added risk, is to raise the proportion of debt in the firm's capital structure, thereby increasing the chance of bankruptcy. The correct project to select and the appropriate capital structure depends on the price of risk, which, in turn, hinges on how risk averse the shareholders are.

Of course, if capital markets did not rationally price corporate securities, managers would be hard pressed to design strategies to maximize firm values. Fortunately, as we have already seen, there is strong evidence that capital markets are relatively sophisticated in responding to publicly available information. For example, announcements of major earnings write-downs for Lockheed and Texas Instruments led to significant increases in their share prices because they resulted from decisions by the managements of both companies to cut their losses and abandon unprofitable lines of business (Lockheed's L-1011 and TI's home computers).

1.5
THE
INTERNATION-
ALIZATION OF
BUSINESS AND
FINANCE

A key theme of this book is that companies today operate within a global marketplace and can ignore this fact only at their peril. The internationalization of finance and commerce has been brought about by the great advances in transportation, communications, travel, and technology. This introduces a dramatic new commercial reality—the global market for standardized consumer and industrial products on a previously unimagined scale. It places primary emphasis on the one great thing all markets have in common—the overwhelming desire for dependable, world-class products at aggressively low prices. The international integration of markets also introduces the global competitor, making firms insecure even in their home markets. Tandon Corp., a major California-based supplier of disk drives for microcomputers, cut its U.S. work force by 39 percent in 1984 and transferred production overseas in an effort to achieve "cost effectiveness in an extremely competitive marketplace."[8] As the president of Tandon put it, "We can wait for the Japanese to put us out of business or we can be cost-effective."[9]

The transformation of the world economy has dramatic implications for business. American management is learning that the United States can no longer be viewed as a huge economy that does a bit of business with secondary economies around the world. Rather, the United States is merely one, albeit very large, economy that is part of an extremely competitive, integrated world economic system. To succeed, U.S. companies need great flexibility; they must be able to change corporate policies quickly as the world market creates new opportunities and challenges. Big Steel, which was virtually the antithesis of this modern model of business practice, paid the price for failing to adjust to the transformation of the world economy.

Today's financial reality is that money knows no national boundary. The dollar has become the world's central currency, with billions switched at the flick of an electronic blip from one global corporation to another, from one central bank to another. The international mobility of capital has benefited firms by giving them more financial options, while at the same time complicating the job of the chief financial officer by increasing its complexity.

Because we operate in an integrated world economy, all students of corporate finance should have an international orientation. Thus, a key aim of this book is to help you bring to bear on key business decisions a global perspective, manifested by questions like "Where in the *world* should we locate our plants?"; "Which *global* market segments should we seek to penetrate?"; and "Where in the *world* should we raise our financing?" This international perspective is best captured in the following quotation from an ad for J. P. Morgan, the large and successful New York bank: "J. P. Morgan is an international firm with a very important American business."

---

[8]"Tandon to Reduce U.S. Work Force, Concentrate Abroad," *Wall Street Journal*, March 8, 1984, p. 22.

[9]Ibid.

1.6
OUTLINE OF
THE BOOK

The remainder of this book elaborates on and applies the ideas set forth here. Although these ideas are interrelated, by necessity they must be discussed individually. Eventually, they must also be integrated because they are all part of a grand framework. To accomplish this objective, the book is divided into seven parts, each of which builds on the previous material. Part I presents in more detail the basic valuation concepts we have already seen. It addresses the key issue of how to value assets that produce more or less certain amounts of cash in the future. Chapter 2 discusses the time value of money and shows how to place a value on dollars (or other currencies) to be paid out or received in later years by taking into account inflation and interest rates. We use these concepts to explain the pricing of stocks and bonds in Chapter 3. Chapter 4 examines the link between risk, return, and value. Chapter 5 explains the basic concepts of option pricing and shows how options are embedded throughout corporate finance.

Once we are familiar with these principles, our next step will be to apply them to the investment or capital budgeting decision. We shall do this in Part II, where we are concerned with the most important problem facing management—finding or creating investment projects worth more than they cost. Chapter 6 presents the basics of capital budgeting, including an evaluation of four alternative investment criteria. Chapter 7 discusses the estimation of project cash flows, and Chapter 8 introduces risk into the capital budgeting process. We turn in Chapter 9 to the issue of cost of capital, the determination of how much projects must yield to make it worthwhile to invest in them. Chapter 10 discusses corporate strategy and its relationship to the capital budgeting decision, focusing on those factors that have contributed to success in the past. Chapter 11 concludes Part II by showing how firms create value for their shareholders.

Part III is concerned with developing a long-term financing strategy. Chapter 12 lays out and compares the long-term financing options that firms have, and Chapter 13 discusses the alternatives available to firms to raise long-term capital. Chapter 14 looks at how a firm's mixture of debt and equity financing—its capital structure—affects its value. The practical factors and trade-offs involved in selecting a capital structure are discussed in Chapter 15. Chapter 16 provides an overview of the financing decision as well as the many considerations that go into the design of an overall financing package. Chapter 17 deals with dividend policy and how it affects a firm's value.

Part IV takes a closer look at the long-term financing options available to the firm. Chapter 18 examines the fundamental nature of debt. The institutional features and costs associated with bonds and term loans are discussed in Chapter 19. Chapter 20 discusses the valuation of equity-linked securities, including warrants and convertibles, and Chapter 21 examines lease financing.

Part V is concerned with financial planning and the evaluation and control of operations. Chapters 22 and 23 present the basic financial statements and show how management, investors, lenders, and other interested parties can analyze these statements to check on a firm's financial well-being. Chapter 24 examines how financial managers forecast future financial statements and use these projections to develop an overall financial plan for the firm.

Part VI deals with the efficient use of the firm's current assets—its working capital—and how these assets should be financed. Chapter 25 contains an overview of working capital policy, emphasizing the relationship between this policy and overall corporate strategy. The specific components of working capital—cash and marketable securities, accounts receivable, inventory, and current liabilities—are analyzed in Chapters 26 through 29.

Part VII, comprising Chapters 30 through 33, covers special topics in financial management, including mergers and acquisitions, international corporate finance, bankruptcy and reorganization, and financial hedging techniques. These important subjects are best treated as applications of concepts and principles developed previously.

SUMMARY AND CONCLUSIONS

Financial management is concerned with the efficient allocation of resources. As such, it lies at the heart of the decision-making process, whether in a private- or public-sector organization. This chapter provides an overview of the basic concepts and principles applicable to the practice of corporate finance. It began by establishing the key objective of maximizing shareholder wealth, which translates into maximizing price per share. It then discussed many relevant considerations that lie behind the achievement of this goal, including the time value of money, the trade-off between risk and return, the distinction between nominal or money values and real or inflation-adjusted values, and the value of delaying decisions until more information becomes available.

The companion to value maximization is market efficiency, the notion that, on average, investors rationally incorporate all available information in forming judgments as to the values of different assets. To the extent that markets are efficient, managers can concentrate on developing strategies to maximize corporate value without having to worry about whether investors will misinterpret their decisions. The idea of market efficiency provides a series of fundamental insights into financial management that will prove to be of enormous value in deciding on appropriate financial actions.

REFERENCES

Ball, R., and Brown, P. "An Empirical Evaluation of Accounting Income Numbers." *Journal of Accounting Research*, Autumn 1968, pp. 159–178.

Black, Fischer, and Scholes, Myron. "The Pricing of Options and Corporate Liabilities." *Journal of Political Economy*, May–June 1973, pp. 637–654.

Jensen, Michael C., and Meckling, William H. "Theory of the Firm: Managerial Behavior, Agency Costs, and Ownership Structure." *Journal of Financial Economics*, October 1976, pp. 305–360.

Kaplan, Robert, and Roll, Richard. "Investor Evaluation of Accounting Information: Some Empirical Evidence." *Journal of Business*, April 1972, pp. 225–227.

Lintner, John. "The Valuation of Risk Assets and the Selection of Risky Investments in Stock Portfolios and Capital Budgets." *Review of Economics and Statistics*, February 1965, pp. 13–37.

Markowitz, Harry. *Portfolio Selection: Efficient Diversification of Investments*. New York: Wiley, 1959.

Ross, Stephen A. "The Arbitrage Theory of Capital Asset Pricing." *Journal of Economic Theory*, December 1976, pp. 341–360.

Sharpe, William F. "Capital Asset Prices: A Theory of Market Equilibrium Under Conditions of Risk." *Journal of Finance*, September 1964, pp. 425–442.

QUESTIONS

1. What are the principal functions of financial managers?
2. What is the distinguishing characteristic of the following assets?
   a. IBM's trademark.
   b. A patent on a new wrinkle cream.
   c. The Tropicana brand name.
   d. Avon's sales force.
3. Why do people usually prefer to receive $1 today instead of $1 next year?
4. What is the distinction between nominal and real interest rates? Why is this distinction important?
5. Why might 150 percent be considered a low interest rate in Brazil at the same time that 15 percent is a high interest rate in the United States?
6. What is the difference between earnings and cash flow?
7. What is the problem with the stock market advice to "buy low and sell high"?
8. What is the distinction between systematic and unsystematic risk? How does this distinction affect the premium that investors demand for bearing risk?
9. What is an option? Why is it valuable?
10. What option does debt give stockholders?
11. Define the agency conflict. How does it help explain the price run-up in Gulf & Western's stock when its chairman died?
12. Why did Colt Industries' bond prices drop after management announced that it would borrow $1.4 billion to pay a huge dividend to shareholders? Why did Colt's stock price soar on this news?
13. Comment on the following statement: "It makes sense to borrow during times of high inflation because you can repay the loan in cheaper dollars."
14. What is an opportunity cost? Give some examples of opportunity costs.
15. Why is shareholder wealth maximization a better objective than maximizing earnings or earnings per share?
16. In 1983 when Analog Devices announced an increase in earnings per share, from $.55 in 1982 to $.97, its share price dropped by almost 4 percent. Explain what might have triggered this decline. Is this explanation consistent with market efficiency?

The Time Value of Money

When one has had to work so hard to get money, why should he impose on himself the further hardship of trying to save it?

DON HEROLD

If you would know the value of money, go and try to borrow some.

BENJAMIN FRANKLIN

Virtually all financial decisions involve the exchange of money today for money in the future. Because money is valued not for its own sake but rather for what it will buy—its *purchasing power*—the exchange of current for future dollars is really an exchange of consumption today for consumption in the future. The rate at which this exchange takes place depends on the **time value of money**. This concept—that the value of money varies according to when it is to be received or paid out—is probably the single most important idea in all of finance. Yet it rests on the simple notion that a dollar today is worth more than a dollar tomorrow. How much more is determined by the time preference of individuals, their investment opportunities, and the amount of expected inflation. The more that people prefer current over future consumption and the more lucrative the available investments are, the more valuable will be current dollars relative to future dollars. In addition, because inflation erodes the purchasing power of money, the higher the expected rate of inflation is, the less valuable future dollars will be relative to current dollars.

Understanding the time value of money is essential to achieving the objective of shareholder wealth maximization because a host of key corporate activities—like valuing securities and other assets, assessing corporate projects, pricing potential acquisitions, deciding whether to buy or lease equipment, and making bond refunding and credit extension decisions—involve an exchange between current dollars and future dollars. To know when it is worthwhile to engage in these exchanges, you must be able to compare dollars today with dollars in the future.

The basic techniques for making these comparisons are provided in this chapter, which covers several key time value of money concepts. Sections 1 and 2 discuss the concepts of the future (or compound) value of an investment and the present value of future cash flows, respectively. Both rely on the notion of compound interest, which simply means earning interest on interest. Section 3 shows how to value an annuity, which is a stream of equal cash flows, and Section 4 does the same for a stream of uneven cash flows. Section 5 examines the determinants of interest rates, and Section 6 explores the relationship between interest rates and inflation.

2.1 FUTURE VALUE

If offered a choice between $1,000 today and $1,000 a year from now, almost all of us would take our money up front. We could then invest the money and have more than $1,000 next year. To illustrate, suppose the $1,000 could be invested at an interest rate of 10 percent per annum. How much money would you have at the end of one year? The answer can easily be found by a couple of straight-forward calculations. Because this is a common problem, however, it would be best to deal with it systematically by devising a general formula relating the **future value** of an investment—the amount to which the investment will grow during a specified time period—to the principal amount (the amount invested on which interest is earned), the interest rate, and the number of periods during which the interest is earned. This requires that we define the following terms:

$$PV = \text{principal amount at time 0, also known as present value}$$

$$r = \text{interest rate on the investment}$$

$$FV_n = \text{future value of the investment at the end of } n \text{ periods}$$

For $n = 1$, the future value equals the principal amount plus the interest on the principal, or

$$FV_1 = PV + (PV \times r)$$
$$= PV(1 + r) \tag{2.1}$$

In our example, the principal amount is $1,000, and r is 10 percent. Hence, the future value of the principal, FV_1, is the solution to

$$FV_1 = \$1,000(1 + .10)$$
$$= \$1,000(1.1)$$
$$= \$1,100$$

Therefore, if you invested $1,000 at 10 percent interest, at the end of one year, you would have $1,100.

Compound Interest

Suppose you decide to leave your funds invested for a second year. How much will your money have grown by the end of year 2? The answer depends on whether you are receiving simple or compound interest. **Simple interest** implies that you receive interest only on the principal amount of your initial investment. This means that at the end of two years your original investment will have grown to $1,200, the $1,000 principal you began with plus two annual interest payments of $100 each. Almost all investments pay compound interest, however, so from here on we assume that compounding always takes place.

The idea behind **compound interest** is that the interest earned is added periodically to the principal amount. The result is that interest is earned on interest. Returning to our example, we see that the $1,100 received at the end of year 1 becomes $1,210 at the end of year 2, as you earn $110 in interest on the $1,100 (.10 × $1,100 = $110). Of the $110, $100 represents interest earned on the original $1,000 investment, and $10 represents interest earned on the first year's interest receipt of $100. This can be depicted as

TODAY	YEAR 1	YEAR 2
$1,000———— 10%————	$1,100	
	1,100———— 10%————	$1,210

In general, the value of an investment at the end of year 2, FV_2, equals the value of the investment at the end of year 1, FV_1, plus the interest earned during year 2 on the investment, which is $FV_1 \times r$. Expressed mathematically, we have

$$FV_2 = FV_1 + FV_1 \times r$$
$$= FV_1(1 + r)$$

Applying this equation to our example, where $FV_1 = \$1,100$ and $r = 10$ percent, yields

$$FV_2 = \$1,100 \times 1.10$$
$$= \$1,210$$

From Equation 2.1 we know that $FV_1 = PV(1 + r)$. Therefore, the compounding process, whereby interest is paid on interest, can be expressed as

$$FV_2 = FV_1(1 + r)$$
$$= PV(1 + r)(1 + r)$$
$$= PV(1 + r)^2$$

Returning to our example, we have

$$FV_2 = \$1,000(1.10)^2$$
$$= \$1,000 \times 1.21$$
$$= \$1,210$$

the same as the answer using the formula $FV_2 = FV_1(1 + r)$. Similarly, the balance at the end of the third year, FV_3, is equal to

$$FV_3 = FV_2(1 + r)$$
$$= PV(1 + r)^3$$

TABLE 2-1	Year	Principal Amount	×	Interest Factor	=	Total Amount
Compound Value of $1,000 After Five Years	1	$1,000.00		1.10		$1,100.00
	2	1,100.00		1.10		1,210.00
	3	1,210.00		1.10		1,331.00
	4	1,331.00		1.10		1,464.10
	5	1,464.10		1.10		1,610.51

A general form of this equation can be written as

$$FV_n = PV(1 + r)^n \qquad (2.2)$$

where FV_n is the value of the investment at the end of n periods.

Equation 2.2 is the fundamental equation of compound interest and as such, it is the key to understanding the mathematics of finance. To illustrate its use, suppose you left your money invested for five years at 10 percent interest annually. At the end of that time, your investment should have grown to $1,000(1.1)^5$, or $1,611. The calculations are shown in Table 2-1. Without compounding, this amount would be $1,500 ($1,000 + 5 × $100). The difference of $111 between the amounts received with compound interest and simple interest illustrates the power of compounding.

An even more dramatic example of the value of compound interest involves the purchase of Manhattan Island in 1626. In what is often considered to be one of the great bargains in history, Peter Minuit bought Manhattan from the Indians for $24 in trinkets. Suppose that the Indians had taken cash, however, and invested the $24 at an annual rate of 6 percent. How much would the Indians have had in 1986, 360 years later?

According to Equation 2.2, the initial $24 would have grown to

$$FV_{360} = \$24(1.06)^{360}$$

$$= \$24(1,288,580,323)$$

$$= \$30.926 \text{ billion}$$

This translates into a price of approximately $32 per square foot for Manhattan Island, perhaps not such a bad deal for the Indians after all. Without compounding, the original $24 would have grown to only $542.40 by 1986 if invested at 6 percent, the original $24 principal plus $518.40 in interest. The latter amount equals 360 interest payments of $1.44 ($24 × .06) apiece.

The higher the interest rate is and the greater the number of compounding periods is, the larger will be the future value of a given investment. Moreover, the future value of an initial amount of money grows more rapidly over time. This is because with compounding, the principal amount on which interest is paid becomes progressively larger with time. These points are illustrated in Figure 2-1, which plots the future value of $1 over time, compounded at different interest rates; that is, it graphs $(1 + r)^n$ for different values of r and n.

FIGURE 2-1
Future Value of $1

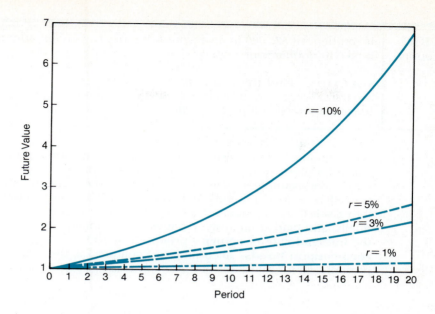

Calculating the future value of an item like the sales price of Manhattan Island can be tedious. Fortunately, there is a shortcut. The term $(1 + r)^n$ is known as the **future value interest factor**, or $FVIF_{r,n}$. Using this expression, we can rewrite Equation 2.2 as

$$FV_n = PV \times FVIF_{r,n}$$

Although a particular interest factor can be calculated directly, an easier way is to look it up in a "future value of $1" table. These tables have been constructed to provide FVIF values for various interest rates and time periods. Although electronic calculators and electronic spreadsheets have made the table-based approach obsolete for computational purposes, you should still understand the operations that calculators perform.

For example, the interest factor for the five-year, 10 percent future value illustration is presented in Appendix Table 1 at the back of the book. Just go down the period column to 5, then across this row to the 10% column to find the correct interest factor of 1.6105. Then, for any initial amount PV invested at 10 percent

$$FV_5 = PV \times 1.6105$$

Substituting in the value of $1,000 for PV yields

$$FV_5 = \$1,000 \times 1.6105$$
$$= \$1,610.50$$

the same as the value in Table 2-1, except for rounding.

APPLICATION
Savings Accounts

If you deposit $25,000 in an account that pays 8 percent annually, how long will it take to double your money?

SOLUTION   Find the $FVIF_{8,n}$ that equals 2.0. Examining Appendix Table 1 we see that $FVIF_{8,9} = 1.9990$, close enough to 2.0 for our purposes. This means that $25,000 invested at 8 percent will double in nine years to $50,000.

Equation 2.2 can also be used to find the compound interest rate that will convert a given sum of money today into a specified amount of money in the future. For example, in late 1983, Kidder, Peabody, the investment banking firm, was offering tax-free bonds that would multiply an initial investment of $10,000 into $34,000 in 13 years. All interest would be accumulated, compounded annually, and paid at maturity. What was the implicit interest rate—also known as the **internal rate of return**—promised by Kidder, Peabody on these so-called **zero-coupon bonds**? According to Equation 2.2, the relationship between the present and future values of these bonds is

$$\$34,000 = \$10,000 \times FVIF_{r,13}$$

or

$$FVIF_{r,13} = 3.4$$

where $FVIF_{r,13}$ is the compound interest factor that will convert $1 today into $3.40 in 13 years. We can see from Appendix Table 1 that $FVIF_{9,13}$ is 3.0648 and $FVIF_{10,13}$ is 3.4523. Therefore, the unknown interest rate r must be somewhat less than 10 percent. Using an electronic calculator, we find that the exact value is 9.87 percent. In other words, $1 compounded annually at 9.87 percent will grow to $3.40 in 13 years.

APPLICATION
**Benjamin
Franklin's
Bequest**

At his death in 1790, Benjamin Franklin left $4,000 each to the cities of Boston and Philadelphia on the condition that they not touch the money for 100 years. Boston's bequest ballooned to $332,000 by 1890. What was the annual interest rate at which Boston's $4,000 compounded?

SOLUTION   Applying Equation 2.2 yields

$$\$332,000 = FVIF_{r,100} \times \$4,000$$

or

$$FVIF_{r,100} = 83$$

This problem must be solved by an electronic calculator because FVIF tables typically don't provide values beyond 50 or so periods. The answer turns out to be about 4.5 percent.

Compounding Interval

Appendix Table 1 is labeled in periods rather than years because compounding can occur more frequently than once a year. Interest on savings deposits, bonds, mortgages, and other financial instruments may be paid daily, monthly, quarterly, semiannually, or for any other time period. This requires an adjustment of our future value formula to permit compounding more often than once a year. The general formula for the future value in n years when interest is paid m times a year is

$$FV_{n,m} = PV(1 + r/m)^{n \times m} \tag{2.3}$$

In the earlier example dealing with money invested at 10 percent, if compounding occurred semiannually instead of annually, the future value of $1,000 in five years would be

$$FV_{5,2} = \$1,000(1 + .10/2)^{5 \times 2}$$
$$= \$1,000(1.05)^{10}$$
$$= \$1,000(1.6289)$$
$$= \$1,628.90$$

This compares with the previous value of $1,610.50 in the case of annual compounding. With quarterly compounding, we would have $1,000(1.025)^{20}$, or $1,638.60. The more times during a year that interest is paid, the greater the future value will be at the end of a given year. This is because additional interest will be paid sooner on the interest already earned.

In each case, the future value interest factor is found by using r/m as the interest rate and $n \times m$ as the number of periods. Thus, the appropriate future value interest factor is $FVIF_{r/m,n \times m}$. With semiannual compounding over a period of five years, therefore, the correct future value interest factor is

$$FVIF_{10/2,5 \times 2} = FVIF_{5,10}$$
$$= 1.6289$$

In other words, compounding 10 percent semiannually for five years is equivalent to paying 5 percent interest compounded each period for ten periods. Similarly, with quarterly compounding over five years, which is equivalent to compounding interest at 2.5 percent for 20 periods, the correct future value interest factor is $FVIF_{2.5,20} = 1.6386$. This latter value was found with the aid of an electronic calculator because Appendix Table 1 contains future value interest factors for only integral values of the interest rate.

APPLICATION
The Purchase of Manhattan Island

In the example of the purchase of Manhattan Island, suppose the Indians had deposited the $24 they received in 1626 in a bank that paid 6 percent interest compounded semiannually, instead of annually. How much would the Indians have in 1986, 360 years later?

SOLUTION   From Equation 2.3 we have

$$FV_{360,2} = \$24(1.03)^{720}$$

$$= \$24(1,749,048,240)$$

$$= \$41.977 \text{ billion}$$

This sum contrasts with the $30.924 billion received with annual compounding. A good deal gets better!

Continuous Compounding.   In the limit, as the number of compounding periods becomes infinite (and the compounding interval becomes infinitesimally small), we have the case of **continuous compounding**. With continuous compounding, interest earned instantaneously begins earning interest itself. Equation 2.3 can be transformed into the equation for continuous compounding by letting m go to infinity. This yields[1]

$$FV_n = PVe^{r \times n} \tag{2.4}$$

where e is the base for natural logarithms 2.7183.... To see the effect of continuous compounding on the answer to the previous problem, apply Equation 2.4, substituting $1,000 for PV, 10 percent for r, and 5 for n:

$$FV_5 = \$1,000e^{.10 \times 5}$$

$$= \$1,000e^{.5}$$

$$= \$1,000 \times 1.6487$$

$$= \$1,648.70$$

As expected, the future value is greater under continuous compounding than under any other finite compounding interval.

Annual Percentage Rate.   Because of different compounding intervals, it is difficult at times to compare financial securities just by examining their quoted interest rates. For example, is it better to receive 9 percent compounded annually, 8.75 percent compounded quarterly, or 8.60 percent compounded daily? To deal with this confusing situation, there is a convention that puts all interest rate quotes on a comparable basis, by distinguishing between the *stated* or quoted rate and the **annual percentage rate** (APR). This latter rate, also known as the **effective annual rate**, is the rate that would produce the same return under annual compounding using the quoted rate.

For example, a builder might describe the new home financing he is providing as a 12 percent (12.68 annual percentage rate) 30-year mortgage (paid monthly), or a bank might advertise its deposit rate as 8 percent compounded

---

[1]The number e is defined as the limit of the expression $(1 + 1/m)^m$ as m becomes infinitely large. Similarly, the limit of the expression $(1 + r/m)^{n \times m}$ as m becomes infinitely large is $e^{r \times n}$. As m becomes larger and larger (i.e., the compounding interval becomes shorter and shorter), we approach the case of continuous compounding.

quarterly (8.24 annual percentage rate). In both cases, a stated rate is converted into an APR. To see how this is done, consider the bank deposit. According to Appendix Table 1, the future value of $1 in one year at 8 percent compounded quarterly is $1.0824 ($FVIF_{2,4} = 1.0824$). Thus, the APR is 8.24 percent because $1 compounded annually at this rate also yields $1.0824. Similarly, we can see that 12 percent compounded monthly (1 percent per month) is equivalent to 12.68 percent compounded annually ($FVIF_{1,12} = 1.1268$).

In general, we can convert a stated rate r, compounded m times per year, into its annual percentage rate using the following formula:

$$APR = (1 + r/m)^m - 1$$

$$= FVIF_{r/m,m} - 1$$

(2.5)

APPLICATION Determining the Highest Savings Rate	We can now use Equation 2.5 to answer the question of which option is the best: 9 percent compounded annually, 8.75 percent compounded quarterly, or 8.60 percent compounded daily. Because the first investment involves annual compounding, its APR is its stated rate, 9 percent:

$$APR = FVIF_{9,1} - 1$$

$$= 1.09 - 1$$

$$= 9 \text{ percent}$$

The APR for 8.75 percent interest compounded quarterly is 9.04 percent:

$$APR = FVIF_{8.75/4,4} - 1$$

$$= (1.021875)^4 - 1$$

$$= 9.04 \text{ percent} \qquad 10904 - 1 = .904$$

Finally, the APR for 8.60 percent compounded daily is 8.98 percent:

$$APR = FVIF_{8.60/365,365} - 1$$

$$= (1.0002356)^{365} - 1$$

$$= 8.98 \text{ percent}$$

The highest annual return, therefore, is provided by the investment paying 8.75 percent compounded quarterly.

2.2 **PRESENT** **VALUE**	Most financial decisions require a trade-off between money today and money in the future. To properly evaluate these trade-offs, we need a way to determine the value today or **present value** of future cash flows. We want to know how much a dollar in the future is worth in terms of today's dollar. This requires that we find the amount of money that would leave us indifferent between receiving

that amount today or one dollar in the future. The process of converting future dollars into their present values is known as **discounting**. The interest rate used to calculate the present value is known as the **discount rate**.

Opportunity Cost of Money

The exchange rate between current and future dollars is determined by the cost of waiting until the future to pay or collect money. This cost, called the **opportunity cost of money**, depends on the rate of interest at which money can be invested. To see this, suppose you can earn a riskless return of 8 percent, compounded annually. At the end of one year, therefore, you will have $1.08 for each dollar invested today. In five years, your one dollar will have grown to $1.47. Thus, you should feel equally about receiving a dollar today or $1.47 in five years, provided you can invest your money at an annual rate of 8 percent. We say that the present value of $1.47 received in five years is $1.

Alternatively, suppose you want to buy a car next year that will cost $12,000. How much will you have to deposit now at 8 percent to have enough to purchase the car in a year? If PV is the amount saved today, then in one year the deposit will have grown to PV(1.08). Setting this amount equal to the required $12,000 gives us the solution, PV = $11,111.11. This means that $11,111.11 invested today at 8 percent will be worth $12,000 in a year. In other words, the present value of $12,000 a year from now, discounted at 8 percent is $11,111.11. Equivalently, a dollar next year has a present value of $1.00/1.08, or $.9259. How much will a dollar four years from now be worth today if the discount rate is 8 percent? The answer, which is $.7350, can be found by viewing the process of discounting as follows:

TODAY	YEAR 1	YEAR 2	YEAR 3	YEAR 4
			.9259——8%——1.00	
		.8573——8%——.9259		
	.7938——8%——.8573			
.7350——8%——.7938				

We can rearrange terms in Equation 2.2 to find the general relationship between future dollars, also known as future cash flows, and their present values (dollars today):

$$PV = FV_n \times \frac{1}{(1 + r)^n} \qquad (2.6)$$

The $1/(1 + r)^n$ term in Equation 2.6 is known as the **present value interest factor,** or $PVIF_{r,n}$. Fortunately, PVIF values, like FVIF values, are available in tables like Appendix Table 2, for various combinations of r and n. For example, Appendix Table 2 shows that the present value of $1.00 in seven years, discounted at 9 percent, is $.5470.

APPLICATION
Carl Lindner's Gift

Because 1983 was such a good year for American Financial Corporation, its principal owner, Carl Lindner, announced at a lavish Christmas party for his employees that he was giving a "special one-time gift of $1,000 to each and every person employed with us today, provided they are still employed with us in five years." Despite the applause, it was clear that at least some of the employees were less than thrilled with the offer. How much was the $1,000 worth at the time of the announcement, given that the riskless interest rate on five-year Treasury bonds was about 12 percent?

SOLUTION   From Appendix Table 2 we see that $\text{PVIF}_{12,5} = .5674$. Thus, the present value of $1,000 to be received in five years, discounted at 12 percent, is $567.40.

As the discount rate increases, the opportunity cost of receiving future dollars goes up and their present value goes down. Similarly, the further into the future that money is to be received, the less valuable it is today. These aspects are illustrated in Figure 2-2. For a relatively high discount rate, or for money to be received in the distant future, the present value is likely to be minimal. For example, $1 due in ten years will be worth about $.74 if discounted at 3 percent, but its present value will drop to less than $.25 if the discount rate is increased to 15 percent. Similarly, $1 to be received in five years and discounted at 4 percent is worth $.82 today, but that same dollar due in 50 years, and also discounted at 4 percent, is worth only $.14 today. When discounted at 15 percent, a dollar in 50 years is essentially worthless today.

Discounting Interval

The present value formula must be revised when discounting takes place more often than once a year. This can be done along the same lines as for the calculation of future values. Equation 2.6 becomes

$$\text{PV} = \text{FV}_n \times \frac{1}{(1 + r/m)^{n \times m}} \tag{2.7}$$

where m is the number of discounting periods per year.

FIGURE 2-2
Present Value of $1

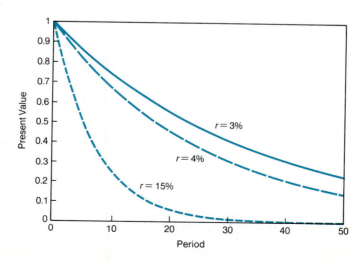

To illustrate, the present value of $1 due in five years, discounted at 8 percent, discounted quarterly, is

$$PV = \$1 \times \frac{1}{(1 + .08/4)^{5 \times 4}}$$

$$= \$1 \times \frac{1}{(1.02)^{20}}$$

$$= \$.6730$$

This contrasts with a present value of $.6806 with annual discounting. It is evident that the shorter the discounting period is, the higher will be the effective yield on an investment and, therefore, the lower the present value of a future cash flow. For a given interest rate, a future cash flow will attain its minimum present value under continuous discounting.

With **continuous discounting**, in which m goes to infinity, we can see from Equation 2.4 that the interest factor becomes e^{-rn} or

$$PV = FV_n \, e^{-rn} \tag{2.8}$$

According to Equation 2.8, the present value of $1 due in five years and continuously discounted at a rate of 8 percent is[2]

$$PV = \$1e^{-.08 \times 5}$$

$$= \$1e^{-.40}$$

$$= \$1 \times .6703$$

$$= \$.6703$$

As expected, this value is smaller than with annual or semiannual discounting. In fact, it is less than that achieved under any other form of discounting.

**2.3
VALUING
ANNUITIES**

An **annuity** is a series of equal cash flows per period for a specified number of periods. If the payments occur at the beginning of each period, we have an **annuity due**. Examples include some lease arrangements and annuity savings plans. Far more common in finance is the **ordinary** (or **deferred**) **annuity**, which involves payments made at the end of each period. Henceforward, all annuities referred to in this book will be ordinary annuities. Semiannual coupons on bonds, mortgages requiring equal monthly payments over the life of the loan, and the retirement of bonds and preferred stock by means of equal annual installments to a sinking fund are examples of ordinary annuities.

---

[2]The negative exponent (e.g., e^{-40}) refers to the reciprocal of the term with the exponent; that is, $e^{-40} = 1/e^{40}$.

FIGURE 2-3
Calculating the
Future Value
of a Three-Year
$1,000 Annuity
Compounded at
9 Percent

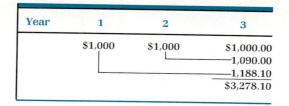

Year	1	2	3
	$1,000	$1,000	$1,000.00
			1,090.00
			1,188.10
			$3,278.10

Future Value of an Annuity

If you were to receive a three-year annuity of $1,000 annually, and you deposited each payment in a 9 percent account, how much would you have at the end of three years? The answer is illustrated in Figure 2-3. The first $1,000 is invested at the end of year 1 and thus is compounded over two years, the $1,000 received at the end of year 2 earns interest for one year, and the third payment earns no interest at all. From Appendix Table 1, we can find the future values of the $1,000 received at the end of years 1, 2, and 3 as $1,188.10, $1,090, and $1,000, respectively. Because the future value of an annuity is just the sum of the future values of each of the payments, the value in this case is $3,278.10.

The mathematical formula for the future value of an annuity lasting n periods, FVA_n, with payments at the end of each period, a periodic receipt of L dollars, and compounded at a rate of r is

$$\text{FVA}_n = \begin{pmatrix} \text{Future value} \\ \text{of annuity} \\ \text{payment in} \\ \text{period 1} \end{pmatrix} + \begin{pmatrix} \text{Future value} \\ \text{of annuity} \\ \text{payment in} \\ \text{period 2} \end{pmatrix} + \cdots + \begin{pmatrix} \text{Future value} \\ \text{of annuity} \\ \text{payment in} \\ \text{period } n-1 \end{pmatrix} + \begin{pmatrix} \text{Future} \\ \text{value of} \\ \text{annuity} \\ \text{payment in} \\ \text{period } n \end{pmatrix}$$

$$= L(1+r)^{n-1} + L(1+r)^{n-2} + \cdots + L(1+r)^1 + L(1+r)^0$$

$$= L[(1+r)^{n-1} + (1+r)^{n-2} + \cdots + (1+r)^1 + 1]$$

$$= L(\text{FVIF}_{r,n-1} + \text{FVIF}_{r,n-2} + \cdots + \text{FVIF}_{r,1} + 1)$$

$$= L \sum_{t=1}^{n} \text{FVIF}_{r,n-t}$$

$$= L \times \text{FVIFA}_{r,n} \tag{2.9}$$

where $\sum_{t=1}^{n}$ means the summation of the first to the nth terms.[3] The term $\text{FVIFA}_{r,n}$

in Equation 2.9 is the **future value interest factor for an annuity**. It can be calculated directly with the following formula, which is itself based on the formula for the sum of a geometric progression:

---

[3] Note that the final term in the annuity sum, $(1+r)^0$, is set equal to 1; any number raised to the power 0 equals 1.

$$FVIFA_{r,n} = \sum_{t=1}^{n} (1 + r)^{t-1}$$

$$= \frac{(1 + r)^n - 1}{r}$$

Alternatively, we can see from Equation 2.9 that the future value interest factor for an annuity is just the sum of the future value interest factors from period 0 through period $n - 1$, or

$$FVIFA_{r,n} = \sum_{t=1}^{n} FVIF_{r,n-t} \qquad (2.10)$$

So, for example, the future value interest factor for a three-year annuity at 9 percent, $FVIFA_{9,3}$, is the sum of the future value interest factors for periods 0, 1, and 2. Referring to Appendix Table 1 for these future value interest factors, we get $FVIFA_{9,3} = 1 + 1.0900 + 1.1881 = 3.2781$. Note that the FVIF for period 0, $(1.09)^0$, is just 1.

An even easier approach is to look up the future value annuity factor in a table like Appendix Table 3. Entries in this table can be derived from the entries in Appendix Table 1 by applying Equation 2.10. To solve our three-year, $1,000 annuity problem, simply refer to Appendix Table 3, find the interest factor for a three-period annuity compounded at 9 percent, and multiply the factor, which is 3.2781, by $1,000. The answer, $3,278.10, is the same as the brute force solution we derived earlier.

APPLICATION
Saving for
Retirement

Suppose you plan to retire at age 60. If you make 30 equal annual deposits of $5,000 to a tax-free Keogh plan, starting at age 31, how much will be waiting for you at retirement if the annual rate of interest is 7 percent? Alternatively, at a 7 percent interest rate, how much will you have to deposit each year in your tax-free fund to have $1 million at retirement?

SOLUTION   From Appendix Table 3 we see that $FVIFA_{7,30} = 94.460$. Thus, the value of the annuity in 30 years will be $94.460 \times \$5,000 = \$472,300$. The amount you will have to deposit each year for 30 years to have $1 million available at retirement can be found by rearranging the terms of Equation 2.9 to get

$$L = \frac{FVA_n}{FVIFA_{r,n}}$$

$$= \frac{\$1,000,000}{94.460}$$

$$= \$10,586.49$$

Thus, the future value of a 30-year, $10,586.49 annuity is $1,000,000.

Present Value of an Annuity

The present value of an annuity is just the sum of the present values of each of the individual payments. This is because the present value of a sum equals the sum of the present values. Thus, to find the present value of the previously discussed three-year, $1,000 annuity, discounted at 9 percent, all we need to do is calculate the present values of $1,000 received at the end of one year, two years, and three years. These values, which are $917.40, $841.70, and $772.20, respectively, sum to $2,531.30. The details are shown in Table 2-2.

Expressed algebraically, with PVA_n defined as the present value of an annual annuity of R dollars lasting n years, with payments at the end of each year, the general formula is

$$PVA_n = \begin{array}{c} \text{Present value} \\ \text{of annuity} \\ \text{payment in} \\ \text{period 1} \end{array} + \begin{array}{c} \text{Present value} \\ \text{of annuity} \\ \text{payment in} \\ \text{period 2} \end{array} + \cdots + \begin{array}{c} \text{Present value} \\ \text{of annuity} \\ \text{payment in} \\ \text{period } n \end{array}$$

$$= \frac{L}{(1 + r)} + \frac{L}{(1 + r)^2} + \cdots + \frac{L}{(1 + r)^n}$$

$$= L[1/(1 + r) + 1/(1 + r)^2 + \cdots + 1/(1 + r)^n]$$

$$= L(PVIF_{r,1} + PVIF_{r,2} + \cdots + PVIF_{r,n})$$

$$= L \times PVIFA_{r,n} \tag{2.11}$$

Values of $PVIFA_{r,n}$ can be calculated using the following formula:

$$PVIFA_{r,n} = \sum_{t=1}^{n} \frac{1}{(1 + r)^t} = \frac{(1 + r)^n - 1}{r(1 + r)^n}$$

Alternatively, they can be calculated by adding up the individual present value interest factors according to Equation 2.11. To save time, tables that already perform these calculations, like Appendix Table 4, are available for determining $PVIFA_{r,n}$ for a variety of interest rates and time periods. According to Appendix Table 4, the present value interest factor for a three-year, 9 percent annuity is 2.5313. Multiplying this factor by $1,000 gives us $2,531.30, an amount identical to the number we calculated by summing the individual present values.

TABLE 2-2 Present Value of a Three-Year $1,000 Annuity Discounted at 9%	Year	Annuity ×	Present Value Factor (9%) =	Present Value
	1	$1,000	.9174	$917.40
	2	1,000	.8417	841.70
	3	1,000	.7722	772.20
			Total	$2,531.30

APPLICATION
Reader's Digest's
Grand Prize

In early 1986, *Reader's Digest* ran a contest with a $2 million grand prize, paid in 20 annual installments of $100,000 each, with the first check paid at the end of 1986. If interest rates were 7 percent at the time, how much did it cost *Reader's Digest* to fund the grand prize?

SOLUTION   Using Equation 2.11 and Appendix Table 4, we see that the present value of an annuity of $100,000 for 20 years is

$$\text{PVA}_{20} = \$100,000 \times \text{PVIFA}_{7,20}$$
$$= \$100,000 \times 10.5940$$
$$= \$1,059,400$$

It cost *Reader's Digest* $1,059,400 to fund the $2 million grand prize. The publicized payout was almost twice its actual value!

Annuity tables can also be used to evaluate and compare contracts whose terms involve equal payments through time.

APPLICATION
Valuing Athletes'
Contracts

Suppose Magic Johnson of the L.A. Lakers basketball team is promised $1 million per year for 25 years at the same time that Larry Bird of the Boston Celtics is promised $1.5 million a year for the next 10 years. The press reports that Magic Johnson has received a "$25 million" contract, whereas Larry Bird has received a "$15 million" contract. Who has the more valuable contract?

SOLUTION   We can't compare these contracts until we know the opportunity cost of money, that is, the interest rate at which these future sums are to be discounted to their present values. Suppose the discount rate is 10 percent. From Appendix Table 4 we find that $\text{PVIFA}_{10,10} = 6.1446$ and $\text{PVIFA}_{10,25} = 9.0770$. Thus, Larry Bird's $15 million contract is worth $1,500,000 \times 6.1446 = $9,216,900, whereas Magic Johnson's $25 million contract is worth $1,000,000 \times 9.0770 = $9,077,000. Larry Bird has the better contract. Suppose, though, that interest rates drop to 8 percent. In this case, Larry Bird's contract is worth $1,500,000 \times 6.7101 = $10,065,150, less than the value of Magic Johnson's contract, which is $1,000,000 \times 10.6748 = $10,674,800.

We can rearrange Equation 2.11 to solve for the periodic payments given the present value of the annuity. This type of problem frequently arises in setting up schedules for pension plan benefits, educational funds, and mortgage payments. Suppose, for example, that you have saved $25,000 to attend graduate school starting next year. Your degree program will last four years. If you can invest your funds at an 8 percent rate of interest, how much money can you withdraw in equal annual installments, starting in one year, so that at the end of four years your investment account will have a zero balance? Dividing both sides of Equation 2.11 by $\text{PVIFA}_{r,n}$ yields

$$L = \frac{PVA_n}{PVIFA_{r,n}} \qquad (2.12)$$

According to Appendix Table 4, the present value interest factor for our problem, $PVIFA_{8,4}$, equals 3.3121. Substituting this value in Equation 2.12 gives us the answer: With a $25,000 initial investment, you can spend $7,548.08 each year for four years, with nothing left over at the end of that time.

APPLICATION
Pricing Magazine
Subscriptions

PC World offers the following subscription terms: 1 year, $17; 3 years, $44. If the interest rate is 6 percent, should you order a one-year or a three-year subscription?

SOLUTION   Buying three one-year subscriptions is equivalent to paying $17 up front and then buying a two-year annuity paying $17 annually. (Because the first payment is due at the beginning of the year, this is the same as a three-year annuity due.) Therefore, the cost in present value terms of three one-year subscriptions is

$$PV = \$17 + \$17 \times PVIFA_{6,2}$$
$$= \$17 + \$17 \times 1.8334$$
$$= \$48.17$$

Thus, the three-year subscription, with a present value of $44, is a better deal, provided you intend to order *PC World* for the next three years anyway.

Loan amortization problems can also be solved using Equation 2.12. Suppose a firm borrows $150,000 for five years at an interest rate of 10 percent compounded annually. The loan plus interest are to be repaid in five equal installments beginning at the end of year 1. What will its annual payments be? Again using Equation 2.12, we can see that the annual annuity payment L will be

$$L = \frac{\$150,000}{PVIFA_{10,5}}$$
$$= \frac{\$150,000}{3.7908}$$
$$= \$39,569.62$$

Table 2-3 shows the **loan amortization schedule**, which breaks down each yearly payment into its interest and principal repayment components. The interest component equals the interest rate times the unpaid principal, and the principal reduction equals the payment on the loan less the interest payment. For example, the interest payment in year 3 equals 10 percent of the outstanding loan balance of $98,403.80 at the end of year 2, or $.10 \times \$98,403.80 = \$9,840.38$.

TABLE 2-3	Year	Payment	Interest Payment	Principal Reduction	Remaining Principal
Loan Amortization Schedule	1	$39,569.62	$15,000.00	$24,569.62	$125,430.38
	2	39,569.62	12,543.04	27,026.58	98,403.80
	3	39,569.62	9,840.38	29,729.24	68,674.56
	4	39,569.62	6,867.46	32,702.16	35,972.40
	5	39,569.62	3,597.24	35,972.38	.02
		$197,848.10	$47,848.12	$149,999.98	

The remaining $29,729.24 of the loan payment ($39,569.62 − 9,840.38 = $29,729.24) goes to reduce the principal amount of the loan. Hence, the unpaid principal at the end of year 3 is $98,403.80 − 29,729.24 = $68,674.56. The interest portion decreases over time in line with the decline in the outstanding loan balance. The $.02 balance is due to rounding error. This type of loan amortization is similar to the amortization of a home mortgage loan, although the latter is amortized on a monthly rather than yearly basis.

Alternatively, knowing that the yearly loan payment is $39,569.62, we can calculate the interest rate on the loan, by rearranging the terms of Equation 2.11 to solve for $PVIFA_{r,n}$:

$$PVIFA_{r,n} = PVA_n/L \tag{2.13}$$

Substituting in the values $PVA_5 = \$150,000$ and $L = \$39,569.62$ in Equation 2.13 yields $PVIFA_{r,5} = 3.7908$. Examining Appendix Table 4, we see that a five-year present value annuity factor of 3.7908 corresponds to an interest rate of 10 percent. This is, of course, the same interest rate we used in solving for the annual loan repayments of $39,569.62.

Annuity Period

If the discounting or compounding interval for the annuity is less than a year, as in the case of semiannual bond interest payments, then the present and future value annuity formulas must be revised.

Let $FVA_{n,m}$ be the future value of an n-year annuity compounded m times a year and $FVIFA_{r,n,m}$ the future value interest factor for this annuity, where r is the stated annual interest rate. Similarly, let $PVA_{n,m}$ be the present value of this annuity and $PVIFA_{r,n,m}$ the present value interest factor. Then, the revised versions of Equations 2.9 and 2.11, respectively, are

$$FVA_{n,m} = L \times FVIFA_{r,n,m} \tag{2.14}$$

and

$$PVA_{n,m} = L \times PVIFA_{r,n,m} \tag{2.15}$$

where L is the periodic annuity payment.[4] Based on Equations 2.3 and 2.7, the present and future value interest factors can be found in the annuity tables under r/m for the interest rate and $n \times m$ for the number of periods. In other words, $\text{FVIFA}_{r,n,m} = \text{FVIFA}_{r/m,n \times m}$ and $\text{PVIFA}_{r,n,m} = \text{PVIFA}_{r/m,n \times m}$.

APPLICATION
Valuing a Lease

Suppose a firm has signed a two-year agreement to lease 10,000 square feet of space for $50,000 monthly. What is the present value of this lease contract if the relevant interest rate is 12 percent?

SOLUTION According to Appendix Table 4, the present value interest factor for an interest rate of 1 percent per period (month) for 24 periods (months) is 21.2434. Applying this factor to Equation 2.15 yields a present value for the lease equal to $1,062,170. By contrast, if the rentals were due at the end of each year instead of each month, the present value would be $600,000 × $\text{PVIFA}_{12,2}$ = $600,000 × 1.6901 or $1,014,060, a difference of $48,110.

APPLICATION
Valuing a Low-Interest Rate Auto Loan

General Motors has just announced that it will offer low interest rates on selected models to spur sales. For a $14,000 loan, to be repaid in 36 monthly installments, a 7 percent annual interest rate is available. Alternatively, GM is offering a rebate of $750 per car. If the market interest rate on loans of this type is 12 percent, should customers accept the rebate or GM's special financing package?

SOLUTION Customer savings on GM's low-cost financing can be found by first calculating the monthly payment based on the 7 percent interest rate and then valuing that annuity based on a 12 percent interest rate. The difference between the $14,000 loan amount and the cost of repaying that loan (which is the market value of that annuity) equals the value of the financing package to customers.

1. The monthly amortization on a $14,000 loan is the solution to

$$L = \frac{\$14,000}{\text{PVIFA}_{7/12,36}}$$

$$= \frac{\$14,000}{32.3865}$$

$$= \$432.28$$

The actual value of $\text{PVIFA}_{7/12,36}$ was found using a calculator.

---

[4]For Equations 2.14 and 2.15 to be correct, the annuity payment period must equal the compounding period.

2. The market value of a monthly annuity of $432.28 for 36 months when the market rate of interest is 12 percent annually (1 percent monthly) is the solution to

$$PVA_{1,36} = \$432.28 \times PVIFA_{1,36}$$

$$= \$432.28 \times 30.1075$$

$$= \$13,014.87$$

Thus, the true cost to GM customers of repaying the $14,000 loan at 7 percent when the market rate of interest is 12 percent equals $13,014.87. They save the difference of $985.13. Because this amount exceeds the rebate, GM's customers should take the special financing package.

Equation 2.15 can also be used to find the interest rate on a loan, given the periodic amortization of the loan:

$$PVIFA_{r,n,m} = PVA_{n,m}/L \qquad (2.16)$$

Knowing $PVA_{n,m}$, and L, we can find the periodic interest rate by using the PVIFA table to find the corresponding interest rate.

APPLICATION
Determining the Interest Rate on a Loan

If the monthly payment on a five-year loan of $100,000 is $2,224.45, what is the rate of interest on the loan?

SOLUTION   Applying Equation 2.16 we have

$$PVIFA_{r,60} = 100,000/2,224.45$$

$$= 44.9549$$

From Appendix Table 4, we see that $PVIFA_{1,60} = 44.9550$. Hence, the stated annual interest rate on the loan is 12 percent, with an APR of 12.68 percent.

Perpetuities

Most annuities, such as a 30-year, 12 percent mortgage, have a finite life. Some annuities, however, are, for all practical purposes, perpetuities. With a **perpetuity**, payments go on forever, generating an infinite series. We can calculate the formula for the present value of a perpetuity of one dollar per annum by letting the final period n in Equation 2.11 go to infinity. This yields a present value interest factor for the perpetuity equal to $1/r$. A perpetuity of R dollars a year, therefore, has a present value PVA*, where

$$PVA^* = L/r \qquad (2.17)$$

The classic example of a perpetuity is the *British Consol,* an instrument created by the Bank of England and used during the eighteenth and nineteenth centuries to consolidate past debts (hence the term consol). Consols have no maturity date and bear the obligation of the British government to pay a fixed coupon in perpetuity. Suppose a consol pays £50 per annum and the required yield is 10 percent. Using Equation 2.17, we can calculate its price as £50/.10 = £500. Alternatively, if we were quoted a price of £500 for a consol paying £50 annually, we could easily solve for the required yield of 10 percent. In general, a perpetuity valued at PVA* and carrying an annual coupon of *L* has a yield of

$$r = L/\text{PVA}^*$$

(2.18)

Equation 2.18 is often used to calculate the yield on preferred stock, another example of a perpetuity. (Unlike common stock, the dividends on preferred stock remain the same from one year to the next.) Thus, preferred stock selling at a price of $73 per share and paying an annual dividend of $6.25 will yield 6.25/73, or 8.56 percent per annum.

2.4 PRESENT VALUE OF AN UNEVEN SERIES OF CASH FLOWS

Although a number of financial decisions assume equal cash flows in each period, they are the exception rather than the norm. Dividend payments on common stock investments vary over time, primarily because the underlying investments made by corporations on behalf of their shareholders do not have fixed payouts. Firms deciding whether to invest in new plant and equipment or in a new advertising campaign must estimate the present values of the uneven cash flow streams they will generate.

For example, suppose an investment in a new machine having a life of six years is expected to produce the future income stream depicted in Table 2-4. Initially, the machine should produce a cash inflow of about $500,000 annually. Over time, however, the machine will require increasing amounts of maintenance and downtime, causing its returns to drop year by year. Assuming a discount rate of 12 percent, we can calculate the present value of investing in this new machine by using a straightforward rule: *The present value of a stream of future cash flows is equal to the sum of the present values of its individual components.* As shown in Table 2-4, all we need do is multiply each year's cash flow by the appropriate present value interest factor and then sum these individual values

TABLE 2-4
Present Value of Cash Inflows

Year	Cash Inflow	×	Present Value Factor (12%)	=	Present Value
1	$500,000		.8929		$446,450
2	470,000		.7972		374,684
3	420,000		.7118		298,956
4	350,000		.6355		222,425
5	260,000		.5674		147,524
6	200,000		.5066		101,320
				Total	$1,591,359

TABLE 2-5
Present Value of Major League Baseball's Television Contract Signed in 1983

Year	Payment (millions)	×	Present Value Factor (12%)	=	Present Value
1983	$40*		.8929		$35.7
1984	135		.7972		107.6
1985	155		.7118		110.3
1986	160		.6355		101.7
1987	180		.5674		102.1
1988	215		.5066		108.9
1989	240		.4523		108.6
Total	$1,125			Total	$674.9

SOURCE: Figures are from the *Wall Street Journal*, January 27, 1984, p. 8.
*Payment for the last quarter of 1983.

to get the overall present value, which for the machine is projected to equal $1,591,359.

Another application of present value analysis involves trying to place a value on the multimillion dollar sports contracts often reported in the media. Because only the undiscounted sum is usually announced, this has the effect of overstating the real value of the contracts. In early 1983, for example, major league baseball signed a long-term contract selling television broadcasting rights to its games. The contract, which ran through 1989, was reportedly worth $1.125 billion. As shown in Table 2-5, however, the payout structure under the contract reveals a much lower present value. The present values of the year-by-year payments, received at the end of each calendar year, are calculated using the 12 percent return required in early 1983 on seven-year riskless Treasury bills.

The present value figures in Table 2-5 indicate that the network people structured the contract in such a way that the present value of each year's payment was approximately the same. It is also evident that the true value of the contract was almost half a billion dollars (actually $450 million) less than the amount reported.

In general, the formula for the present value of a series of uneven cash flows is

$$
\begin{array}{l}
\text{Present value} \\
\text{of a sum of} \\
\text{cash flows}
\end{array}
=
\begin{array}{l}
\text{Present value} \\
\text{of cash flow} \\
\text{in period 1}
\end{array}
+
\begin{array}{l}
\text{Present value} \\
\text{of cash flow} \\
\text{in period 2}
\end{array}
+ \cdots +
\begin{array}{l}
\text{Present value} \\
\text{of cash flow} \\
\text{in period } n
\end{array}
$$

$$
PV = \frac{C_1}{(1 + r)} + \frac{C_2}{(1 + r)^2} + \cdots + \frac{C_n}{(1 + r)^n}
$$

$$
= \sum_{t=1}^{n} \frac{C_t}{(1 + r)^t} \tag{2.19}
$$

where C_t is the cash flow at the end of period n. Equation 2.19 is called the **discounted cash flow** (DCF) formula. It can be used to find the current value of any asset or investment, whether it be a stock or a bond, a new piece of machinery, a patent on a novel genetic engineering technique, or a multiyear contract for a top athlete.

APPLICATION
Pricing an
Acquisition

Multicorp has offered to buy Unicorp for $8 million, to be paid as follows: $1 million at the close of the deal, $200,000 annually for the next 20 years, and, as inflation protection, lump sums of $.5 million, $1 million, and $1.5 million payable, respectively, five, ten, and 20 years after the sale. If interest rates are at 14 percent, what is the present value of this $8 million offer?

SOLUTION   This offer is the sum of an annuity plus unequal cash flows and can be valued as follows (in $ millions):

$$PV = 1 + .5 \times PVIF_{14,5} + 1 \times PVIF_{14,10} + 1.5 \times PVIF_{14,20}$$

$$+ .2 \times PVIFA_{14,20}$$

$$= 1 + .5 \times .5194 + 1 \times .2697 + 1.5 \times .0728 + .2 \times 6.6231$$

$$= \$2,963,200$$

Multicorp's undiscounted offer of $8 million is worth slightly less than $3 million to the owners of Unicorp.

2.5
DETERMINANTS
OF THE
OPPORTUNITY
COST OF
MONEY

Up to this point, we have taken the interest rates used in the various formulas and examples as given. Yet, it is clear from reading the financial press or watching the news that interest rates—which, we saw earlier, are based on the **opportunity cost of money**—are highly volatile. What determines the level of interest rates and changes in that level?

To understand the determinants of interest rates, it is necessary to understand the economic function of interest rates. The rate of interest represents the price of shifting the use of money—more specifically, the claim on goods and services represented by money—from one time period to another. Borrowers want more buying power today than their income provides, and so they agree to give up some of their future income to get it. Lenders give up income today in return for higher income in the future. The market interest rate represents the amount of future income that will change hands between borrower and lender.

What matters, of course, to both borrower and lender is the **real interest rate**. For lenders, the real rate equals the rate of increase in wealth they expect to achieve when they save and invest their current income. Alternatively, borrowers view the real rate as the expected reduction in wealth they face when they choose to consume goods now instead of saving and investing. In this sense, the real interest rate is an opportunity cost; it represents the relative cost or price of current consumption in terms of forgone future consumption. Consequently, the real rate of interest influences the proportion of present resources devoted to producing goods that will be consumed today instead of durable goods (capital goods) that will provide consumption goods or services in the future.

This discussion suggests—and research supports the view—that four basic factors determine the opportunity cost of money, given a constant level of risk:

1. *The productivity of capital in the economy.* Investors have the option of investing in physical assets like capital goods or real estate that produce a stream of consumption goods and services or in financial assets denominated in dollars. In equilibrium, the dollar return from investing in capital assets (converting the consumer goods or services into their dollar values) must equal the dollar return from investing in financial assets like bank deposits and corporate securities, as measured by the interest rate; otherwise, investors would have an arbitrage opportunity.

For example, if financial assets earn 8 percent and tangible assets yield 10 percent with no increase in risk, investors will sell their financial assets and acquire capital assets. The net result of this activity will be to drive down the return on capital goods and raise the return on financial assets. This process will continue until the expected return on both investments are identical.

Unless investors are consistently fooled, over time the average return on financial assets should be about the same as the return on physical assets. This helps explain why, in our previous example, the $24 for which the Indians sold Manhattan in 1626, thereby converting a physical asset (land) into a financial asset, would be worth about as much today as the land comprising it is worth. Specifically, assuming that 6 percent were the average return on financial assets over that period, we would expect land to appreciate at a rate of about 6 percent annually as well. If, instead, land were appreciating at a rate of, say, 8 percent annually, investors would sell off their financial assets and buy land. The reduced demand for financial assets would drive up the return—the interest rate—required to induce investors to hold these assets, and the increased demand for land would drive down the expected return on land. In equilibrium, therefore, this arbitrage process will ensure that expected returns on land and securities of equivalent risk are about the same.

As capital investments produce greater quantities of goods and services—perhaps because of technological innovations—thereby raising the return on capital assets, the expected yield on financial assets must also rise. Another way to understand the link between the opportunity cost of money and the physical productivity of capital is to realize that an increase in the productivity of capital increases the opportunity cost of consuming today relative to consuming in the future. The result is a higher interest rate.

2. *The impatience of consumers.* Most people would prefer to buy a new car, a new house, or new clothing today rather than wait until later. A person who invests in stocks and bonds or capital assets, however, must defer some present consumption. To induce this sacrifice, the investor must be rewarded with a positive return; that is, the value of the money received in the future must exceed the value surrendered today. The more impatient consumers are, the more they must be compensated for delaying their current consumption. In other words, part of the interest received on an investment is a return for waiting. The notion that patience is a virtue and is rewarded is elevated to the status of basic financial doctrine here.

3. *Expected inflation.* The topic of expected inflation is so important that the next section has been set aside to discuss it. For now, it is useful to recall

that the return on financial assets must equal the return on capital goods translated into dollars. In Chapter 1 we saw that inflation reflects a rise in the general level of prices. Inflation means, therefore, that the dollar prices of the consumption goods produced will rise. Thus, the return on capital goods will consist of two elements: (1) the expected increase in the quantity of consumption goods and (2) the expected increase in the price of consumer goods. For example, if the physical productivity of capital is 4 percent, then $1 invested today should yield goods worth $1.04 in one year. But if prices are also rising, at the rate of 5 percent, then goods worth $1 today will sell for $1.05 next year. Thus, goods worth $1.04 next year without inflation will sell for $1.04 × 1.05 = $1.09 with 5 percent inflation. The result is a return of 9 percent in money terms.

To make the return on investing in financial assets comparable to the return on the capital goods, the interest rate must include the expected amount of price inflation. So if the interest rate with no inflation would be 4 percent but 5 percent inflation is expected, the market interest rate will be about 9 percent.

4. *Taxes.* Taxes work the same way as inflation. If interest payments are tax deductible, borrowers know that this will reduce the amount of future income they will have to surrender. The after-tax cost to borrowers declines as tax rates rise. Borrowers will pay higher interest rates as tax rates rise because their after-tax cost will be no greater. For example, suppose a borrower is in the 20 percent tax bracket. Then the after-tax cost of a 10 percent interest rate is 8 percent (.80 × .10 = .08). But if the borrower's tax rate rises to 50 percent, he can afford to pay up to 16 percent interest without his after-tax cost of borrowing being any greater (.50 × .16 = .08). In general, if r_B and r_A are the before- and after-tax interest rates, respectively, and t_b is the borrower's tax rate, then

$$r_A = r_B(1 - t_b)$$

Lenders reason along similar lines. If tax rates rise, they need a higher before-tax interest rate to get the same after-tax income. Because both suppliers and demanders of funds are amenable to higher interest rates when taxes rise, interest rates rise. Some evidence on the effect of taxes on interest rates is provided by the spread between the interest rate on taxable bonds and the interest rate on tax-exempt bonds. A drop in tax rates tends to narrow this spread, whereas a rise in tax rates widens it. In particular, if r_T is the interest rate on taxable bonds and r_{TE} is the interest rate on tax-exempt bonds, then for an investor to be indifferent between the two types of bonds, the after-tax returns must be the same, or

$$r_{TE} = r_T(1 - t_p)$$

where t_p is the investor's personal tax rate. As t_p rises, $r_T = r_{TE}/(1 - t_p)$ must also rise, increasing the value of $r_T - r_{TE}$. This can be seen in Table 2-6, which shows how the before-tax interest rate has to rise in line with an investor's tax bracket to offer the same after-tax return as a tax-free investment does. For example, an investor in the 40 percent tax bracket must earn 10 percent on a taxable investment to forgo a tax-exempt return of 6 percent.

We now shall look more closely at the crucial relationship between inflation and interest rates. This relationship has received far more attention since the bout with high inflation during the 1970s.

TABLE 2-6	Tax-free				Tax Bracket*			
How Much	Yield (%)	20%	30%	40%	50%	60%	70%	80%
Taxable Bonds								
Must Earn to	4	5.00	5.71	6.67	8.00	10.00	13.33	20.00
Keep Up with	5	6.25	7.14	8.33	10.00	12.50	16.67	25.00
Tax-free Yields	6	7.50	8.57	10.00	12.00	15.00	20.00	30.00
	7	8.75	10.00	11.67	14.00	17.50	23.33	35.00

*In some nations, such as Sweden, marginal tax rates exceed 80 percent.

2.6 INTEREST RATES AND INFLATION

Thus far, we have talked as if current dollars and future dollars are identical, aside from the date. But this is clearly not the case when inflation exists. For example, between 1967 and 1983, the U.S. price level tripled, meaning that what could be bought for $1 in 1967 cost $3 in 1983. This pales in comparison, however, to the situation in Bolivia in 1984, when prices zoomed 2,700 percent. This meant that goods costing one peso at the start of the year cost 28 pesos at the end of the year. Thus a person who received one Bolivian peso at the end of 1984 was able to buy only one twenty-eighth as much as she could at the beginning of the year. Inflation accelerated in 1985; in January 1985 alone Bolivian inflation was 80 percent, a compound annual inflation rate of almost 116,000 percent:

$$\text{Annual inflation rate} = [(1 + \text{Monthly inflation rate})^{12} - 1] \times 100\%$$

$$= [(1.80)^{12} - 1] \times 100\%$$

$$= 115,600\%$$

APPLICATION
Estimating Stock Market Performance

After closing at nearly 1000 in early 1966 and going nowhere for 16 years, the Dow-Jones Industrial Average (DJIA) of stock prices began its spurt to record highs in August 1982. It closed at 1900 in late June 1986. However, during this 20-year period, the annual rate of inflation averaged about 5 percent. What was the inflation-adjusted value of the Dow in late June 1986?

SOLUTION   With 5 percent inflation an item costing $1 in 1966 would cost $1 \times (1.05)^{20}$, or $2.6533, in 1986. Alternatively, one 1986 dollar would be worth only $1/2.6533 = \$.3769$ in terms of 1966 dollars. Thus, the value of the DJIA, 1900 when expressed in 1986 dollars, was only $1900 \times .3769 = 716$ in terms of 1966 dollars, almost 30 percent below its 1966 peak.

In general, the purchasing power of $100 at time n relative to its purchasing power at time 0 can be calculated as

$$\text{Purchasing power of \$100 at time } n \text{ relative to its purchasing power at time 0} = \frac{\$100}{(1 + \text{Annual rate of inflation})^{n}}$$

Surely the erosion in the purchasing power of money due to inflation must affect the present value of future cash flows. As investors and managers, we are concerned with how we should modify the present value and future value formulas presented in this chapter to take inflation into account.

Surprisingly, no modifications are necessary. The formulas in this chapter already take expected inflation into account, along with the investment opportunities and consumption preferences facing individuals. This is because the interest or discount rates used include an adjustment for the expected amount of inflation over the life of the loan or the investment.

The Fisher Effect

American economist Irving Fisher proposed the following relationship between the *nominal* or actual interest rate *r*, the *real* or inflation-adjusted rate of interest *a*, and the amount of expected inflation *i*:[5]

$$\begin{matrix} \text{Nominal required} \\ \text{loan repayment} \end{matrix} = \begin{matrix} \text{Real required} \\ \text{loan repayment} \end{matrix} \times \begin{matrix} \text{Adjustment for} \\ \text{expected inflation} \end{matrix}$$

$$1 + r = (1 + a)(1 + i) \tag{2.20}$$

Multiplying through and subtracting 1 from both sides yields

$$\begin{matrix} \text{Nominal required} \\ \text{interest rate} \end{matrix} = \begin{matrix} \text{Real required} \\ \text{interest rate} \end{matrix} + \begin{matrix} \text{Expected} \\ \text{inflation} \end{matrix} + \begin{matrix} \text{Cross-product} \\ \text{term} \end{matrix}$$

$$r = a + i + ai \tag{2.21}$$

A commonly used version of Equation 2.21 drops the interest–inflation cross-product term ai to become $r = a + i$. The cross-product term reflects the adjustment of the nominal interest payment for the effects of inflation. If expected inflation is relatively low, this number will be insignificant, because a is usually on the order of 2 percent to 4 percent. However, with higher expected inflation, the approximation $r = a + i$ works less well.

According to the **Fisher effect**, as the relationship in Equation 2.21 is called, borrowers and lenders alike factor expected inflation into the nominal interest rate, the rate at which they are willing to exchange present for future dollars. What matters to both parties to a loan agreement, of course, is the real rate of interest—the rate at which current goods are being converted into future goods. The lender is concerned with how many more goods can be obtained in the future by forgoing consumption today, whereas the borrower wants to know what must be sacrificed in the future to obtain more goods today.

Equation 2.21 says, for example, that if the agreed-upon real interest rate is 3 percent and a 10 percent rate of inflation is expected, the nominal interest rate will be 13.3 percent—the 3 percent required real return and the 10.3 percent adjustment for inflation. The logic behind this result is that $1 next year will have the purchasing power of $.90 in terms of today's dollars. Thus, the borrower must pay the lender $.10 as compensation for the erosion in the purchasing power of the $1 principal, $.03 as interest to provide a 3 percent real return, plus

[5]Irving Fisher, *The Theory of Interest* (New York: Augustus M. Kelley, 1965). Reprinted from the 1930 edition.

$.003 to compensate for erosion in the purchasing power of the $.03 interest payment.

Let's look again at the example just presented to see how the Fisher effect helps preserve the investor's purchasing power. With a real return of 3 percent, $100 invested today yields $103 next year with no inflation. With 10 percent inflation, however, the amount of money received next year must be increased by 10 percent to yield a 3 percent increase in purchasing power. This means that $100 invested today must yield $103 × 1.10 = $113.30—a nominal return of 13.3 percent—for the real return to equal 3 percent. The purchasing power of $113.30 next year in terms of the purchasing power provided by this year's dollars equals $113.30/1.10 = $103. This represents a real return of 3 percent.

Note that Equation 2.21 does not guarantee the real rate will be 3 percent. The nominal rate of 13.3 percent compensates only for *expected* inflation. After the fact, if actual inflation is greater than 10 percent, the real interest rate will be less than 3 percent; alternatively, if inflation is less than 10 percent, the real rate will exceed 3 percent.

The historical evidence suggests that the Fisher effect is a reasonable approximation of reality and that most of the variation in nominal interest rates is due to changing expectations of inflation. Figure 2-4 illustrates the relationship between inflation and 90-day U.S. Treasury bill rates for the period 1955 to 1988. Figure 2-5 shows the same relationship with inflation for 20-year Treasury bonds over the period 1961 to 1986. In both graphs, real returns are shown by the gap between the interest rate on the security and the annual rise in the Consumer Price Index, a commonly accepted measure of inflation.

It is evident from the graphs that most of the increase in market interest rates since the mid-1960s resulted from rising inflationary expectations. From 1959 to 1965, annual inflation averaged 1.5 percent and real interest rates averaged about 2 percent. In contrast, when inflation soared in the 1970s, averaging nearly 8 percent from 1973 to 1980, real rates were actually negative during two

FIGURE 2-4
U.S. Treasury Bill Rate Versus Inflation: 1955–1988

FIGURE 2-5
Real Rates of Return: Twenty-Year Treasury Bond Versus Inflation

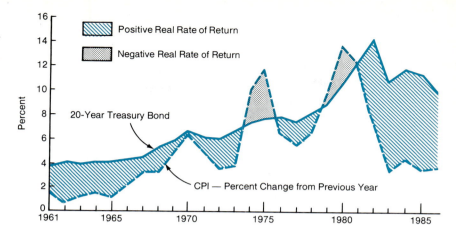

periods—1973 to 1975 and 1979 to 1980. Although investors were earning very high nominal interest rates, inflation was more than offsetting those returns. The negative real rates indicate that the market was initially caught off guard by the acceleration in inflation following the quadrupling of oil prices in late 1973 and again in 1979, when oil prices again jumped. But inflationary expectations adjusted to the rise in prices and interest rates quickly followed prices north.

The decline in inflation during the early 1980s led to a sharp drop in nominal interest rates. But both Figures 2-4 and 2-5 indicate that real interest rates during this period were at historically high levels as inflation fell more than did nominal interest rates. One explanation for these high real returns is that investors could not decide whether the deceleration in the inflation rate during the early 1980s was permanent. So they tried to protect their returns by demanding a significant yield premium over inflation.

The relevant consideration from all this for the investor or borrower is that the nominal rate already incorporates expected inflation, and hence, no further adjustment is necessary or warranted. After the fact, of course, inflation may be more or less than expected, leading to a lower or higher real rate than originally anticipated. But this is irrelevant at the time the borrowing or lending decision is made. Decisions today can be based only on the information currently available. Unexpected changes in inflation or other financial variables are unpredictable by definition and, therefore, are unable to influence our current decisions. Inflation risk can, of course, affect the required rate of return. The Fisher effect does not take inflation uncertainty into account. But Figures 2-4 and 2-5 provide striking evidence of just how infrequently the market is fooled and how quickly expectations and interest rates adjust to new information.

A piece of advice that often passes for financial wisdom is that during times of inflation you should be a borrower. But the Fisher effect says that expected inflation is already built into the cost of borrowing. Hence, borrowers will win only if inflation is *higher* than expected; they will lose if inflation is *lower* than expected.

APPLICATION
Craig Hall's Texas
Real Estate
Investments

In 1981, at the depth of the industrial recession in the Midwest and the height of the oil boom in the Southwest, Craig Hall joined the exodus from Michigan to Texas. He brought with him an inflation-based business strategy developed during the 1970s, when real estate prices were going nowhere but up. His strategy was simple: to borrow as much as possible for as long as possible and count on inflation to enable him to repay the loans with cheaper dollars. His Gospellike faith in the inevitability of high inflation and rising property values led him to pay premium prices for properties and to finance them at interest rates averaging 16 percent. He became the nation's largest private real estate syndicator, with lenders and investors clamoring to get in on his deals. But the cooling of inflation, along with the drop in oil prices, meant that real estate price rises were not there to bail him out. Mr. Hall shared his problems with many of the Texas S&Ls that had lent him over $600 million.

APPLICATION
Speculating
on American
Farmland

During the late 1970s many American farmers were convinced that inflation, combined with continuing Soviet agricultural failures, would keep farmland prices rising. Lenders encouraged farmers to borrow against their appreciating land. In the early 1980s, however, inflation abated, harvests came in at record levels, and crop prices and land values fell. Farmers who borrowed to buy more land when interest rates were 15 percent and inflation about 12 percent found that they could not service those debts when inflation dropped to the 2–3 percent range. The farmers who borrowed so much money on the expectation of higher inflation and rapidly appreciating farmland lost when inflation turned out to be lower than expected. They shared their misery with many of the banks that lent them the money.

The *expected* real interest rate exerts a powerful influence on financial decisions. An increase in the real rate of interest reduces the present value of claims to future income streams, even though these future values remain constant. This means that the owners of such claims will find that their wealth declines as real interest rates rise. The opposite occurs when the real rate of interest falls. Future values are worth more in current dollars, and this leads to an increase in wealth for owners of bonds, stocks, and other assets.

**SUMMARY AND
CONCLUSIONS**

In this chapter, we saw that money has a time value that depends on the productivity of capital, the desire for present versus future consumption, and the amount of expected inflation over the term of the loan or investment. The greater each of these factors, the more valuable current dollars will be relative to future dollars, or equivalently, the less valuable future dollars will be relative to today's dollars.

Financial decisions often require converting current dollars into future dollars or future dollars into their present value. Formulas were developed to speed up the necessary calculations. The most important of these formulas, which form the basis for the *mathematics of finance*, are summarized as follows:

Future value. $FV_n = PV(1 + r)^n$, where FV_n is the future value of a principal amount PV compounded at a rate r for n periods. The term $(1 + r)^n$ is known as the *future value interest factor*, or $FVIF_{r,n}$.

Present value. $PV = FV_n/(1 + r)^n$, where the terms are the same as above. All we are doing here is transforming a future dollar amount into its present value. The term $1/(1 + r)^n$ is known as the *present value interest factor*, or $PVIF_{r,n}$; it is just the reciprocal of $FVIF_{r,n}$.

Future value of an annuity. An annuity is the payment or receipt of equal amounts of L dollars per period for a specified number of periods. The future value of an annuity lasting n periods and compounded at a rate of r per period is

$$FVA_n = L \sum_{t=1}^{n} (1 + r)^{n-t}$$

The term $\sum_{t=1}^{n} (1 + r)^{n-t}$ is referred to as the *future value interest factor for an annuity*, or $FVIFA_{r,n}$.

Present value of an annuity. The present value of an annuity of L dollars per period for n periods, defined as PVA_n, is the solution to

$$PVA_n = L \sum_{t=1}^{n} 1/(1 + r)^t$$

The term $\sum_{t=1}^{n} 1/(1 + r)^t$ is known as the *present value interest factor for an annuity*, or $PVIFA_{r,n}$.

Values for each of these interest factors can be found in tables like those contained in the appendix at the back of this book. Using these interest factors, we can solve a variety of problems, including valuing stocks and bonds, developing loan amortization schedules, and determining the worth of undertaking particular investment projects.

REFERENCES

Fisher, Irving. *The Theory of Interest*. New York: Augustus M. Kelley, 1965. Reprinted from the 1930 edition.

Hirschleifer, Jack. "On the Theory of Optimal Investment Decision." *Journal of Political Economy*, August 1958, pp. 329–352.

QUESTIONS

1. What effect will an interest rate increase have on the value today of a loan repayment to be made in one year?
   a. Will the percentage change in value brought about by a rise in the interest rate be greater for a payment due in one year or one due in five years? Explain.
   b. Will an increase in the interest rate make the borrower better off or worse off? How about the lender? Explain.

2. Suppose the compounding interval is shortened.
   a. Will this increase or decrease the present value of a future payment? Explain.
   b. What will happen to the future value of money invested today? Explain.
3. Because of overbuilding, commercial office towers are offering a year of free rent to tenants who sign a five-year lease. Would you expect the "free" year to be the first year or the fifth year? Why?
4. Suppose two side-by-side office towers are identical to each other. However, one is fully leased at rates fixed for the next 20 years, whereas the other is also fully leased but its rates are renegotiated at the end of each year. At a time of rising office rents, explain which is likely to be the more valuable property.
5. Professional football teams often require season ticket holders to pay for their tickets by June 1, even though the football season doesn't start until September 1. Why might this policy exist?
6. A typical piece of advice is to be a borrower during a time of inflation. Comment on this advice.
7. Suppose borrowers, but not lenders, factor inflation into their financial decisions. Will the Fisher effect hold? Explain.
8. As the chief financial officer, you are responsible for funding your company's pensions. Because your company is fairly new, none of the employees has retired yet. You have invested primarily in fixed-rate, long-term bonds. Employee pensions are based on their earnings at the time they retire.
   a. What does a rise in interest rates do to the value of your bond portfolio?
   b. What will the interest rate increase do to your expected cost of funding these pensions? Consider the different effects of a nominal interest rate rise due to an increase in the real interest rate and one due to an increase in the anticipated rate of inflation.
9. Communist countries do not charge interest on the capital they supply to their industries.
   a. Explain how this policy will introduce distortions in the capital allocation process.
   b. Are the distortions likely to be greater for projects with short-term payoffs or those with longer-term payoffs? Explain.
10. Discuss some of the factors that determine the level of interest rates.
11. Usury laws in many states prohibit the charging of interest rates in excess of a set amount (say, 18 percent). What is rapid inflation likely to do to loan-sharking activity (supplying money at rates in excess of the usury rate)? Explain.

PROBLEMS

1. John Doe plans to invest his life savings, $10,000, in his company's stock.
   a. If the value of the shares increases by 5 percent a year, how much will John have in 20 years at retirement?
   b. If the value of the shares increases by 15 percent a year, how much will he have in 20 years?
2. The parents of a newborn girl decide to put aside $5,000 today for her college education.
   a. If the rate on the savings account is 6 percent, how much will she have in her college fund when she's ten years old?
   b. How much will she have in the fund at age 18?
   c. Do you think this will be enough for her education? Explain.
3. How long will it take your money to double if you invest it at 5 percent? At 15 percent?
4. Suppose you invest $500,000 in a five-year certificate of deposit that pays 12 percent compounded annually.
   a. How much will the CD be worth at its maturity?
   b. How much will the CD be worth if interest is compounded quarterly? Monthly? Continuously?

Pg 80

5. Sterling Character decides to put aside a sum of mon~~ey~~ operation. She needs $10,000.
   a. If the operation is scheduled for five years in the fut~~ure, how much should he~~ set aside today (assume an 8 percent rate of return
   b. If Sterling could get a 12 percent return on his inve~~stment, how much should he~~ set aside?
   c. If the rate were 12 percent and the operation is resc~~heduled for ten years in the~~ future, how much should he set aside today?

6. In comparing money market funds, you decide to invest ~~in a~~ fund paying 8 percent compounded daily or the Don Wette~~_____ percent~~ compounded quarterly. Which will you choose?

7. On March 15, 1979, a Manhattan executive bought a three-story penthouse apartment overlooking Central Park for $750,000. Six years later, in 1985, the executive sold the apartment for $3 million, a record amount for a real estate transaction of its kind.
   a. Calculate the annual rate of return on this investment.
   b. In the same six-year period, the annual return on the Dow-Jones Industrial Average was 11 percent. Can such a discrepancy in return on investment persist? Why or why not?

8. In 1936, Dizzy Dean—the great St. Louis Cardinals pitcher—was paid an annual salary of $27,500. If inflation between 1936 and 1988 averaged an annual rate of 4 percent, how much would his salary be worth in 1988 dollars?

9. In 1982, Merrill Lynch introduced a new type of security, the Treasury Investment Growth Receipt (TIGR). This entitles the holder to the coupon interest payment from a Treasury bond that is due on one particular date.
   a. On March 15, 1990, how much would you pay for the TIGR representing $1,000 coupon interest payable on March 15, 2000, if the current rate on such investments is 12 percent?
   b. How much would you pay for a similar TIGR due on March 15, 2006? Assume a current rate on such investments of 12 percent as well.
   c. If the annual rate of inflation were 6 percent, what would be the purchasing power of the 2006 TIGR in terms of 1990 dollars?

10. You have been promised a 10 percent share in the profits of your biotechnology firm. The firm expects to show its first profit, $1 million, in three years.
    a. How much is this promise worth today if interest rates are 6 percent?
    b. How much is it worth today if interest is compounded monthly? Daily? Continuously?

11. You have recently purchased shares of stock in the Q-Mart Corporation. Currently, the dividend per share is $1.75. If you expect dividends to grow by 12 percent a year, what will your dividend payment be seven years from today?

12. In 1985, the New York State lottery awarded a prize of $40 million to be received in 20 annual payments of $2 million each, with the first payment due at year end. If interest rates in 1985 were 10 percent, how much was the lottery worth to the winner(s)?

13. The pension plan at your new company will set aside 25 percent of your annual salary of $32,000 every year until you retire in 25 years. Interest rates are currently 8 percent.
    a. How much can you expect to have at retirement?
    b. If your company's plan begins setting aside this amount for you after five years of employment, how much can you expect to have at retirement?

14. The usual legal settlement for an industrial accident is the present value of the employee's lifetime earnings. If you make $50,000 a year, and expect to work for 30 more years, what would your settlement be (assume a discount rate of 10 percent)?

15. During a late-night television commercial, the Kwan-tzu Metalcraft Company offers its hardware set for the unbelievably low price of $200, or at its easy payment plan of $9 down and $9.50 a month for 25 months. What is the finance rate charged by Kwan-tzu on its easy payment plan?

16. You are considering a student loan of $10,000 at 4 percent interest. Repayment on the loan will commence one year from now and will consist of six equal yearly installments.
    a. How much principal will you owe after two payments?
    b. How much principal will you owe after four payments?

17. The monthly rent on your apartment is $900. If you pay 20 percent down, how expensive a house can you buy if you get a 30-year mortgage at an annual rate of 11 percent? Your mortgage payments per month should equal your rent.

18. In 1986, a newly hired executive for AT&T opened a tax-exempt Individual Retirement Account (IRA) to which she plans to contribute at year end $2,500 a year from now until she retires at the age of 70 in 2031. From this fund, the retired executive plans to draw an annual income of $200,000 for 20 years, from 2032 through 2052. Assuming that she leaves nothing to her estate, will the IRA fund be sufficient to cover her retirement plans? (Use an annual interest rate of 12 percent.)

19. The Perpetual Care Memorial Garden will maintain a garden plot in perpetuity for a customer for $50 a year. If the payments are indeed perpetual, with the first one due immediately, what is the value of this maintenance agreement as of today? (Use an annual interest rate of 8 percent.)

20. An individual graduates from college and begins work at age 22. If she has an annual income of $35,000, pays 7.15 percent of this income into Social Security, and retires at age 65 with Social Security benefits of $8,300 annually, how long must she live before the present value of these benefits equals the value of her contributions? Assume a discount rate of 8 percent per year and that all payments and benefits occur at the end of the year.

21. The Security Atlantic Bancorp. is buying an office building for its staff in downtown Manhattan for $45,000,000. The terms of the sale offered by Olympic Real Estate Co., the seller of the property, call for four annual payments of $7.8 million each, with the first payment occurring at the end of year 1, and one "balloon" payment of $45,000,000 at the end of year 5.
    a. What is the annual mortgage rate charged by Olympic?
    b. Suppose, instead, that the terms offered by Olympic Real Estate Co. call for annual payments of $7.8 million for four years and a "balloon" payment of $13.8 million in year 5. If the annual mortgage rate on comparable properties is 9 percent, what is the true price of the building?

22. You are considering a one-year investment in McDonald's common stock. You expect the stock to pay a quarterly dividend of $.325 per share and to be able to sell the stock at year end for $75 a share. If investments of this kind generally yield a rate of return of 8 percent annually, how much should you be willing to pay for McDonald's stock?

23. The Pennco Oil Co. must decide whether it is financially feasible to open an oil well off the coast of China. The drilling and rigging cost for the well is $5,000,000. The well is expected to yield 585,000 barrels of oil a year at a net profit to Pennco of $5 a barrel for four years. The well will then be effectively depleted but must be capped and secured at a cost of $4,000,000. Pennco requires an annual rate of return of 14 percent on its investment projects. Should Pennco open the well? (Assume all of a year's production occurs at the end of the year.)

24. As winner of a lottery, you can choose one of the following prizes:
    a. $1,000,000 now.
    b. $1,700,000 at the end of five years.
    c. $135,000 a year forever, starting at year end.
    d. $200,000 for each of the next ten years, starting in one year.
    e. $75,000 at year end and increasing by 6 percent a year forever.
    If the interest rate is 9 percent, which is the most valuable prize?

25. Chrysler has just announced that to spur sales it will offer free financing on selected models. How much will a zero-interest $15,000 loan, to be repaid in 30 equal monthly

installments, be worth to customers if the market rate on loans of this type is 12 percent (1 percent monthly)?

26. GM's special financing package was valued at $985.13 in the chapter. Show that you would receive the same answer if you valued the difference between the monthly payment of $432.28 on the GM financing package and the monthly payment on a 36-month loan of $13,250 (the $14,000 price less the $750 rebate) at the market rate of 12 percent. (*Hint*: Determine the monthly payment on a $13,250 loan. Subtract from that the monthly payment of $432.28 and take the present value of that 36-month annuity, discounted at 12 percent.)

27. Your grandparents took pity on you and decided to finance four years of your college expenses. For this purpose, they created a trust fund worth $140,000, which earns 10 percent (ignore taxes).

    a. How much can you withdraw annually, beginning at the end of the first year, so that the fund will provide a level amount of cash in each of the four years? Assume that any cash left in the trust after four years will revert to your grandparents.

    b. Alas! What about inflation? If you spend the same amount of cash each year for four years, your living standard would decline by the rate of inflation. To maintain the same standard of living, your spending must increase each year by the rate of inflation (i.e., you must spend the same real amount of dollars each year). Assuming that the inflation rate is 4 percent annually, how much cash can you withdraw at the end of each of the next four years so that you maintain the same standard of living (and, of course, exhaust all the funds in the trust)?

28. Commercial Credit is advertising that for low payments of just $94.35 a month, for 48 months, you can have $3,000 today.

    a. What is the monthly rate on Commercial Credit's loan offer?

    b. What is the APR on this loan?

29. Suppose you are quoted an annual percentage rate of 8.75 percent on a 15-year, fixed-rate, $150,000 mortgage. The loan will be repaid in 180 monthly installments, with the first payment due one month from now (assuming that the loan is approved and granted today).

    a. What is the monthly payment for the loan?

    b. Suppose two years from now 15-year mortgages plummet to 5 percent and you want to refinance the loan. If there is no penalty for early repayment, how much will you have to pay the mortgage company to settle the loan?

Institutional Features and Pricing of Stocks and Bonds

We should all be concerned about the future because we will have to spend the rest of our lives there.

CHARLES F. KETTERING

Firms finance new projects, acquisitions, and working capital requirements by issuing claims against the income generated by these investments. These claims include bonds, preferred and common stock, and other long-term securities. The return to these claims is in the form of dividends, interest, and principal repayments. The common characteristic of these securities is that they promise to pay more or less certain amounts of cash in the future. Hence, the concepts developed in the previous chapter to analyze the time value of money can be used to value stocks and bonds. Bonds can be valued as annuities; certain preferred stock are perpetuities; and common stock involve streams of uneven cash flows.

Knowing how the values of corporate securities are determined is important to a firm's managers and owners, as well as to investors. Current and prospective investors need to compare their valuation of a firm's securities with actual market prices in order to decide whether now is the time to buy low or sell high. Equally important, managers responsible for maximizing the wealth of their stockholders must understand how their investment and financing decisions are likely to affect the price of the firm's common stock. As we saw in Chapter 1, the objective of shareholder wealth maximization translates into maximizing share price.

Moreover, because the value of a firm's common stock equals the value of the firm minus the cost of satisfying the claims represented by the firm's debt and preferred stock, it is important for managers, as well as investors, to know how these other securities are valued.

Section 1 discusses the general approach to asset valuation, and Sections 3, 5, and 7 apply this approach to the valuation of bonds, preferred shares, and common stock, respectively. Preceding each of these latter sections is a discussion of the basic characteristics of the security.

3.1
ASSET
VALUATION

The price or value of a financial asset like a stock or a bond is determined by the future cash flows that the owner expects to obtain from that asset. These cash flows take the form of future interest or dividend payments plus the amount the owner receives on sale of the asset. Ultimately, of course, investors are really concerned with the quantity of goods and services they can purchase with that stream of future cash. *In effect, people who buy stocks and bonds are trading off current consumption for increased future consumption.* As we saw in Chapter 2, the terms of that trade-off are dictated by the opportunity cost of money.

An investor's *opportunity cost of money* depends on the next best investment opportunity available. Investors who want to maximize their wealth should never accept a lower return on an asset than could be obtained elsewhere. *If each investor faces virtually identical investment opportunities in the market, they all will have the same minimum required return.* This is why the existence of easily accessible, organized markets for the purchase and sale of assets is so important.

Capital Markets and Asset Valuation

In the United States and in many other countries with well-developed capital markets—markets in which people trade current dollars (pounds, marks, francs, and the like) for claims to future dollars (pounds, marks, francs)—opportunities to invest exist for a wide range of financial assets with varying amounts of risk. *The returns on these traded assets establish, for each degree of risk, the minimum return that an investor should accept on a particular investment.* Because people are generally risk averse—that is, all else being equal they prefer less risk to more—the higher the risk is, the higher the required return will be. Chapter 4 explores in more detail the relation between risk and return.

The assumption that each investor faces essentially the same set of investment opportunities has a very important implication for corporate finance: *Two individuals, no matter how different their consumption preferences or wealth, will always use the same discount rate to value the future cash flows associated with a particular asset.* Therefore, managers do not have to worry about different shareholders assigning different present values to the same investment project; the market establishes a single discount rate—which equals the required risk-adjusted return—to be used for all investments having the same risk. Similarly, two people who agree on the future cash flows and risk characteristics of a specific stock or bond will always assign it the same value.

Even if investors have different personal discount rates, because their attitudes toward risk or the time-value of money differ, they will still agree to use the market discount rate to value an asset's future cash flows. Consider an investor who demands an 18 percent return on an asset, in contrast with the market's required return of 13 percent. If the asset yields an expected return of 15 percent, the investor should still buy it. As we will see shortly, an asset that yields more than the market rate will be worth more than it costs. This means that an investor who demands a higher return can acquire the asset at the lower price and then sell it to another investor at a gain. Alternatively, someone who uses a lower personal discount rate to value assets should not accept any investment yielding less than the market's required return on assets of similar risk. For example, an investor who demands a 10 percent return should not purchase an asset yielding 12 percent if the market discount rate is 13 percent. The reason is that the investor can always buy another asset having the same risk but a 13 percent return.

What matters is not what an asset is worth to the investor but what the asset is worth in the marketplace. If you think an asset is overpriced you can always sell it, whereas if you think an asset is underpriced you can always buy it.

The net effect, therefore, of having easy and low-cost access to an organized capital market is that the price of an asset will equal the present value of its expected future cash flows and the discount rate will be determined by the rate of return in the market for investments with comparable risk. This means, for example, that the required return on an investment with riskless future cash flows will equal the interest rate on safe securities like United States Treasury bonds. Riskier cash flows will be discounted at progressively higher interest rates.

The proposition that all investors should apply the same discount rate in valuing assets depends crucially on the existence of a *perfectly competitive capital market*. This is a capital market with essentially no barriers to entry, minimal trading costs, and costless access to economically relevant information.[1] Although no market fulfills all these requirements, financial markets in the United States and several other countries are sufficiently good approximations that most asset prices appear to be set *as if* they were being traded in a perfectly competitive market. Except where otherwise mentioned, therefore, we assume in the remainder of this text that securities are being priced in perfectly competitive capital markets. Most financial economists would agree that this is a good description of reality.

Market Efficiency and Asset Valuation

The view that securities markets are highly competitive implies that any security clearly identified as a superior investment—one yielding more than the minimum required return—will have its price bid up by astute investors. This process will continue until its price reaches a level at which future risk-adjusted returns would be normal. Conversely, securities expected to provide below-average returns will be sold off until their prices decline sufficiently to yield acceptable returns again. The adjustment of security prices to their perceived worth will be almost instantaneous; just as nature abhors a vacuum, so too investors hate an unexploited profit opportunity. Nearly as quickly as air rushes in to fill a vacuum, investors will rush to earn arbitrage profits by buying underpriced securities and selling overpriced ones. The very act of taking advantage of this opportunity will ensure its evanescent nature.

This is the **efficient market hypothesis** (EMH), the idea that security prices tend to reflect everything known about the prospects of individual companies and the economies in which they operate. This hypothesis goes against the grain of most professional investors, who indignantly reject its central verdict: *Nobody*

---

[1]If these conditions are violated—because there are significant trading costs or because not all investors have access to the same investments—investors will hold different portfolios of risky assets. In that case, investors may face different risk–return trade-offs and, hence, may value risk and the opportunity cost of their funds differently.

really knows how to beat the stock market, or any other financial market for that matter. Despite its controversial nature, the EMH explains the single most obvious mystery about financial markets—that thousands of highly professional, hardworking, and clearly intelligent stock pickers are continually confounded by the market.

There are three levels of market efficiency: (1) a *weakly efficient* market, in which present prices reflect all information contained in the record of past prices; (2) a *semistrongly efficient* market, in which prices reflect all publicly available information; and (3) a *strongly efficient* market, in which present prices reflect all information, both privately held or insider information and publicly available information.[2] Each level is nested within the next level. For example, a semistrongly efficient market is also weakly efficient because the past price history is part of the public record.

Money managers, of course, live by convincing investors that they can beat the market by picking the right stocks. But their performance contradicts this claim: The boring old Standard & Poor's 500 index outperformed 87 percent of all money managers in the decade 1970 to 1979.[3] And for the decade ending in 1982, the S&P 500 beat two thirds of the managers.[4] Most financial economists view this as convincing support for the efficient market hypothesis. Figure 3-1 shows that this performance has continued in recent years. As of the end of the first quarter of 1987, the S&P 500 convincingly beat money managers and mutual funds over the previous quarter, one year, three years, and five years. The primary reason for this poor performance by hands-on management is that active managers cost a lot. To cover these costs and beat the S&P 500, you have to beat the market by about 2 percent annually. It is evident from the data that managers who can do that are hard to find.

Recent evidence has suggested some superior investors systematically beat the market. Although this could be due to luck, it seems unlikely to be the case. Indeed, it would be surprising if among the millions of people who try their hand at beating the market, none would succeed. Some investors must be able to perceive patterns where others see only chaos or must be able to forecast trends where others see nothing.

More troubling is the discovery of some further anomalies—facts that appear to be inconsistent with the EMH. The most significant anomaly is the discovery by Rolf Banz and Marc Reinganum of the "small-firm effect"—that even after adjusting for risk, stocks of small companies yield enormous returns, on the order of 20 percent annually.[5] Other anomalies include the "January effect" (the finding that about half the excess returns of small firms is due to their superior performance in January), the "weekend effect" (the persistent tendency for stock returns on Monday to be negative), the apparently superior long-run

---

[2]These three categories are discussed in Eugene F. Fama, "Efficient Capital Markets: A Review of Theory and Empirical Markets," *Journal of Finance*, May 1970, pp. 383–417.

[3]Standard & Poor's 500 index is a value-weighted index of the prices of 500 stocks, covering 400 industrial companies, and 20 transportation, 40 utility, and 40 financial stocks.

[4]These numbers were compiled by SEI Funds Evaluation Services and reported in Randall Smith, "S&P 500 Index Bests Money Managers in '83, Sharpening Debate on Investment Tactics," *Wall Street Journal*, January 20, 1984, p. 27.

[5]See Rolf W. Banz, "The Relationship Between Return and the Market Value of Common Stocks," *Journal of Financial Economics*, March 1981, pp. 3–18; and Marc R. Reinganum, "Misspecification of Capital Asset Pricing: Empirical Anomalies Based on Earnings Yields and Market Values," *Journal of Financial Economics*, March 1981, pp. 19–46.

FIGURE 3-1
The Allure of Invest-
ing in the S&P
Index

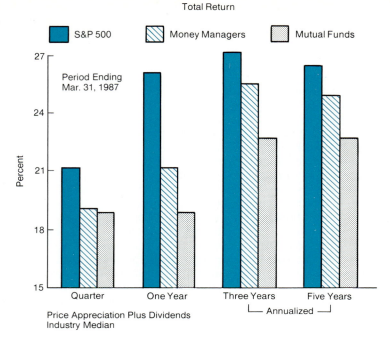

performance of the *Value Line Investment Survey*, and the huge discounts from
net asset values on some closed-end funds.[6]

Many, if not all, of these anomalies may be due to inadequate measures of
risk or failure to account for sizable transaction costs and liquidity problems
associated with buying and selling securities with limited markets. Even if superior investors exist, it could be a real mistake to act as though you or your
investment adviser are among them: As a rule, financial managers should make
decisions based on the assumption of market efficiency.

Black Monday and Market Efficiency

More recently, the volatility of stock prices since Black Monday (October 19, 1987)
has caused many people to question the efficiency and rationality of the stock
pricing process. How can a market in which share prices can drop 23 percent
in one day, wiping out over a trillion dollars in market value, be considered
efficient? Is it conceivable, if prices are set by rational people on the basis of all
economically relevant information, that IBM stock could be worth $135 on Friday
and only $102 on the following Monday? It still has the same plant and equip-
ment, the same work force and customers, and the same patents and products.

Obviously, this controversial issue has no clear-cut answers. Some would

[6]See the special issue of the *Journal of Financial Economics*, June 1983, for a discussion of
many of these anomalous effects.

consider such stock price volatility prima facie evidence of market inefficiency. Note, however, that much of a company's value is based on the health of the economy in which it operates: Healthy economies make companies more valuable and vice versa. IBM's plant and equipment and patents may be unchanged after a drop in economic growth, but if customers don't buy as many computers, the cash generated by these assets and hence their value will drop. As we will see in this chapter, the value of corporate assets largely determines the value of a firm's stock. Thus, a big shift in investors' expectations regarding the future course of the economy can cause a dramatic change in stock prices.

Before Black Monday, indications were growing that U.S. economic policy was adrift. The growing budget and trade deficits, the rise in interest rates (owing in large measure to growing fears of inflation), the drop in the value of the dollar, and discord among U.S. trading partners in their attempts to coordinate monetary policy, along with the threats of higher taxes, protectionist trade legislation, and legislation designed to limit corporate acquisition and restructuring activity, combined to make investors more nervous about the future health of the U.S. economy.

Moreover, the same government fiscal irresponsibility that put America's international trade balance into a deep hole also created the need for a scapegoat to bear the brunt of the resulting frustrations. Scapegoats were quickly found and attacked: the strong dollar and America's trading partners.

Investors appeared to have efficiently interpreted the negative consequences of these destructive macroeconomic policies. Between August 26, 1987 and October 16, 1987 (a Friday), the Dow-Jones Industrial Average, a commonly used measure of stock market values, dropped almost 476 points. On Friday, October 16 alone, the Dow dived 108 points (reports of an Iranian attack on a U.S.-flagged oil tanker didn't help any). It dropped another 508 points on Black Monday. The triggering event over the weekend that caused the market to drop so far and so fast on Monday is debatable. The mystery though is more likely to be why the drop occurred in one day instead of spreading out over time, rather than why it occurred in the first place.

One possible explanation for the suddenness of the market decline is that over the weekend, U.S. Treasury Secretary James Baker publicly threatened to talk down the U.S. dollar against the West German mark, hoping to punish the Germans for their decision to raise interest rates in order to stave off inflation. Some have argued that Baker's threat was the proverbial straw that broke the camel's back, signaling to foreign and American investors that the United States would renege on its promise to stabilize the value of the dollar.

Another possible explanation for Black Monday is that investors learned during the previous week that the market was more volatile than they had believed. The market had dropped a highly unusual 9.6 percent the previous week and investors may have concluded over the weekend that market volatility had reached unprecedented levels. As we will see in Chapter 4, a large rise in perceived market volatility leads to an increase in the required return on stocks and hence to a drop in stock prices.[7]

[7]This explanation for Black Monday is suggested by Hayne E. Leland, "On the Stock Market Crash and Portfolio Insurance," working paper, University of California, Berkeley, December 21, 1987.

Market Efficiency and "True Values"

Despite various questions and doubts about the rationality of the stock pricing process, the existence of market efficiency is supported (even though it cannot be proved) by numerous empirical studies. Some of this evidence has already been cited; other evidence that supports the EMH is cited in later chapters. The EMH is also consistent with evidence on the wealth-maximizing behavior of investors. For these reasons, this text will use the efficiency of financial markets as a working hypothesis.

One more point must be clarified before discussing bond and stock pricing in an efficient market: To say that securities are correctly priced does not mean that the securities reflect the maximum possible value—often called the *true value*—of the corporate assets that underlie them. Corporate assets, and therefore the financial claims issued against them, will attain their maximum value only if the firm turns out products efficiently, safely, and in keeping with its customers' desires. Indeed, as we will see in Chapter 30, when corporate managers are viewed—rightly or wrongly—as bunglers or wastrels, corporate raiders perceive an opportunity for creating value by taking over the company and restructuring it. However, only in an ideal world would bad management be instantly and costlessly replaced before assets are squandered. The time lag and the costs associated with corporate takeovers permit a gap between a company's potential value and its current market value. The more efficient the market is for corporate control, the smaller this gap will be.

3.2 CHARACTERISTICS OF CORPORATE DEBT	When a firm borrows money, it promises to repay the principal amount of the borrowing plus interest according to a schedule described in the debt contract. If the payments are not made on time and in the amounts specified in the contract, the debtholders can take a variety of actions to collect their due. This includes, but is not limited to, forcing the firm into bankruptcy and eventually liquidation. If default occurs, lenders will have a priority claim on the firm's assets. This means that common and preferred stockholders will receive a portion of the liquidation proceeds only after all creditors have been paid in full.

In Chapters 18 to 21, we will study the various types and features of corporate debt claims. The following is a brief introduction to the major characteristics of corporate debt.

Maturity

Debt that must be paid back in less than one year is considered to be short-term debt and is carried on the books as a current liability. By convention, debt having a maturity greater than one year is considered long-term debt and is carried as a noncurrent liability. Firms borrow money for periods ranging from overnight to a hundred years and more.

Repayment Provision

The manner in which debt must be repaid varies from one issue to the next, but typically long-term debt is repaid steadily over time. In the case of a bond, which is a long-term debt security that can be traded, this can be done by means of a

sinking fund or **serial maturities**. A sinking fund requires the firm to pay a certain amount of cash into a fund that is then used to repurchase the bonds. A **serial bond** differs from a bond with a sinking fund in that bondholders know in advance which bonds will be repurchased and when. Both sinking funds and serial maturities allow the firm to avoid a large final payment, known as a **balloon payment**. In this way, there is less risk for both the bondholder and the firm.

Most corporate bonds are issued with a **call provision**; that is, the firm has the right to repay and retire the debt at will. The call privilege is valuable because it gives the firm the option to replace its high-interest debt with less expensive debt in the event of a decline in interest rates. This process is known as **refunding**. Because the gain to the firm comes at the investor's expense (the investor loses a high-yielding bond), firms must pay for the call privilege. This is usually done by means of a higher required yield and a **call premium**, a penalty fee for calling the bonds.

Security

Bonds vary in the degree of security they afford investors. A **mortgage bond** is secured by specific corporate assets, whereas a **debenture** is unsecured. Holders of debentures must look to the firm's earning power for security. In the event of default, secured debtholders have first claim to the mortgaged assets. Debenture holders share equally with other creditors in the cash generated by unmortgaged assets but have only a residual right to mortgaged assets.

Seniority

Subordinated debentures rank behind **senior debt** with respect to their claim on assets. In the event of default, subordinated claims are paid off only after all other creditor claims are fully satisfied. Lenders are considered to be senior unless their loans are specifically subordinated.

Floating-Rate Versus Fixed-Rate Debt

Most long-term debt is issued with a fixed coupon or interest payment. But because the coupon amount is fixed in nominal terms, the present value of these future cash flows fluctuates in line with interest rate fluctuations.

In recent years, the greater volatility in interest rates—due primarily to inflation uncertainty—has led investors to demand floating- or variable-rate debt. Usually the rates on floating-rate debt are adjusted every three to six months.

Currency and Jurisdiction

Debt can be denominated in either the domestic currency or a foreign currency. The foreign currency borrowing option is frequently used by multinational firms. Moreover, the advent of the Eurocurrency market—a Eurocurrency being any currency held on deposit outside its country of origin—means that the choice of currency to be borrowed can be separated from the choice of the country in which the borrowing takes place. For example, General Motors borrows dollars both in New York and in London. Similarly, Nestle can borrow Swiss francs in Zurich or in Frankfurt.

**3.3
PRICING
BONDS**

A **bond** is a specific type of long-term debt security. Like any other corporate creditor, bondholders lend money to a company. In return for this loan, the company promises to pay to the bond's owner a series of fixed interest or coupon payments until the bond matures. At maturity, the bondholder also receives a specified principal sum called the **face value**, or **par value**. The **coupon interest rate** on the bond equals the annual coupon amount divided by the bond's face value. Alternatively, the actual coupon or interest payment is just the face value multiplied by the coupon rate. Thus, an 8 percent coupon bond with a face value of $1,000 will pay $80 of interest each year (.08 × $1,000).

Once issued, bonds are traded in a **secondary** market by securities dealers. Prices of corporate bonds traded on the New York Stock Exchange appear in a table called *New York Exchange Bonds*, which is published daily in the *Wall Street Journal*. Exhibit 3-1 contains an excerpt from *New York Exchange Bonds* for February 17, 1989. The first column names the issuer (e.g., Illinois Bell). The second shows the coupon rate and the year of maturity, with an "s" for ease of pronunciation. Thus, the 8s 04 for Illinois Bell's bonds reads "eights of four," or 8 percent bonds due in 2004. The third column gives the current yield, the yield obtained by dividing the coupon by the latest price. With a price of 87 and a coupon rate of 8 percent, Illinois Bell's bonds yield 8/87 = 9.2 percent. The fourth column gives the volume of trading, in thousands of dollars. The last two columns give the closing price of the day, along with the change in the closing price from the previous close. Bond price quotations are given per hundred dollars of face value. Thus, a price of $100 is par. Each one-hundredth of par is called a *point*. We can see that Illinois Bell's "eights of four" closed at $87, down 5/8 points, or $.625, from the day before.

The price of a bond is just the present value of the future cash flows associated with it—the coupon payments plus the face value. As we shall see, if the required return on the bond is unequal to the bond's coupon rate, the market price of the bond will differ from its face value.

Consider the following example. At the end of 1983, a Ford Motor Company bond maturing in 1994 had a face value of $1,000 and a coupon rate of 9.25 percent. This means that if you buy this bond, Ford promises to pay you interest of $92.50 (.0925 × $1,000) each year through 1994. In that final year, you will receive the $1,000 par value, in addition to the last $92.50 in interest. As of the beginning of 1984, therefore, the future cash flows from the Ford bond consist of two parts: an 11-year annuity, from year-end 1984 to year-end 1994, of $92.50 annually; and a future value of $1,000 at the end of 1994.

To determine the market value in late 1983 of Ford Motor's "9.25s of 94" bond, we need to find its required return. At that time, the return provided by similar bonds maturing in 1994 was 12 percent. Hence, for each period t, the present value of the coupon payment is $\$92.50/(1.12)^t$. The present value in late 1983 of all the bond cash flows, therefore, discounted at 12 percent, is

$$B = \$92.50 \sum_{t=1}^{11} 1/(1.12)^t + \$1,000/(1.12)^{11}$$

$$= \$92.50 \times \text{PVIFA}_{12,11} + \$1,000 \times \text{PVIF}_{12,11}$$

$$= \$92.50 \times 5.9377 + \$1,000 \times .2875$$

$$= \$836.74$$

Exhibit 3-1

NEW YORK EXCHANGE BONDS

Bonds	Cur Yld	Vol	Close	Net Chg.
ConEd 4⅜92W	5.1	16	85⅝	+ ⅝
ConEd 9⅜00	9.5	50	98⅞	+ 2¼
ConEd 7.9s02	9.2	56	85¾	+ ¼
ConEd 7¾03	9.2	6	84⅜	+ ⅜
ConEd 8.4s03	9.4	16	89½	...
ConEd 9⅛04	9.7	8	93⅝	...
CnNG 8¼94	8.6	1	95½	...
CnPw 7⅝99	9.1	6	83½	...
CnPw 8⅛01	9.5	4	85½	+ ⅜
CnPw 9s06	10.1	3	89¼	− ¼
Ct IC zr89	...	5	92 13/16	+ 1/16
CtlInf 9s06f	cv	55	12½	− ½
CtlDat 12¾91	12.5	55	101⅞	...
CtlDat 8½11	cv	9	95½	+ 1¾
CoopCo 8⅝05	cv	109	63½	+ ½
CrayRs 6⅛11	cv	20	94½	− ½
CrdF zr90s	...	30	83⅜	...
CritAc 13⅛14	12.4	6	105½	+ 3⅜
Datpnt 8⅞06	cv	8	57	+ ⅛
DaytH 10¾13	10.8	20	99½	− ½
DetEd 9s99	9.8	5	92	+ ½
DetEd 9⅞04	10.2	5	96½	− ⅜
DetEd 11⅞00	11.4	7	103¾	− ¼
Dow 8⅞2000	9.5	3	93⅞	− ⅝
Dow 8½s06	9.6	2	88¼	− ¼
duPnt 8.45s04	9.4	5	89⅝	...
duPnt 8½06	9.4	10	90⅛	+ ⅛
duPnt dc6s01	8.2	241	72⅞	...
duPnt 12⅞92	12.6	10	102⅛	...
duPnt 7½93	8.1	110	92½	+ ⅛
DukeP 7⅜01	8.9	1	83	+ 1⅝
DukeP 7¾03	9.3	5	83⅝	+ ⅛
DukeP 8⅛03	9.5	5	85¾	− ½
DukeP 9¾04	9.8	2	99¾	...
DukeP 9⅜08	9.8	10	96	+ ¾
DukeP 10⅛09	10.0	9	101	...
DuqL 8¾00	9.8	5	89¼	+ ⅛
DuqL 10⅛09	10.0	8	101½	+ 1¼
EKod 8⅝16	10.1	140	85⅝	+ ⅛
Eaton 7⅞03	9.6	25	82⅛	...
Enron 10¾98	10.6	25	101	+ ½
Ens 10s01	cv	18	101½	− 1
EnvSys 6¾11	cv	7	47½	+ 2⅜
Exxon 6s97	7.4	127	80⅝	− ¼
Exxon 6½98	7.9	32	82½	− ⅛
Fairfd 14¼89	14.7	193	97	− 2
FlowGn 14.30s04	14.3	92	100	+ 1
FrdC 8⅜01	9.3	10	89¾	...
FrdC 7⅞89	7.9	10	99 5/16	+ 1/32
FrdC 8⅜02	9.4	10	88⅝	+ [illegible]

Quotations as of 4 p.m. Eastern Time
Thursday, February 16, 1989

Volume $30,890,000

SALES SINCE JANUARY 1
(000 omitted)

1989	1988	1987
$996,770	$1,074,455	$1,394,221

	Domestic Thu.	Domestic Wed.	All Issues Thu.	All Issues Wed.
Issues traded	616	625	623	634
Advances	269	197	269	199
Declines	198	272	205	276
Unchanged	149	156	149	159
New highs	13	11	13	11
New lows	9	24	10	25

Dow Jones Bond Averages

−1988− High	−1988− Low	−1989− High	−1989− Low		−1989− Close	−1989− Chg.	−1989− %Yld	−1988− Close	−1988− Chg.
91.25	86.92	89.62	88.35	20 Bonds	88.80	−0.14	10.01	90.56	−0.01
91.88	86.05	89.74	87.94	10 Utilities	88.78	−0.25	10.00	91.05	−0.04
90.64	86.96	89.76	88.61	10 Industrials	88.83	−0.03	10.02	90.06	+0.01

Bonds	Cur Yld	Vol	Close	Net Chg.
GMA 10⅜95	10.3	145	101⅛	+ ⅛
GMA 9¼93	9.4	220	98¼	...
GMA 8½91	8.7	20	98⅛	...
GMA 8⅞96	9.3	162	95	...
GMA 8s90	8.2	29	98⅛	− ⅛
GMA 8⅛92	8.5	35	95⅝	+ ½
GMA 8s93J	8.5	100	93¾	+ ¼
GMA 8s93O	8.6	25	93½	+ ⅛
GMA 7¼90	7.5	15	96¼	+ ⅛
GMA 8s94	8.7	175	92	...
GM 8⅝s05	9.6	2	90	− ¼
GTE 9⅜99	9.6	8	98⅛	− 1
GTCal 8⅞96	9.3	7	95⅛	...
Genrad 7¼11	cv	2	74	...
GaPw 8⅞00	9.7	10	91⅜	+ ⅜
GaPw 7⅜01	9.1	5	81⅛	− 1½
GaPw 8⅛01	9.4	5	86½	+ 2
GaPw 8⅝04	9.8	15	88	+ 1
GaPw 11⅝00	11.3	30	103¼	...
GaPw 11¾05	11.5	24	102¼	− ¼
GaPw 9⅞06	10.3	12	95½	− 1
GaPw 9⅝08	10.1	15	95⅛	− ⅛
GaPw 10½09	10.5	60	99⅞	− ⅜
GaPw 11s09	10.9	1	101¼	+ ¼
GaPw 13⅛12	12.5	10	104¾	+ ⅛
GaPw 10s16J	10.5	16	95½	...
GaPw 10s16A	10.4	29	95⅞	− ⅛

Bonds	Cur Yld	Vol	Close	Net Chg.
Humn 13¾13	12.4	62	110½	− 1
viHuntIR 9⅞04f	...	4	5½	+ ⅛
IBM Cr 7⅛89	7.2	104	99 1/16	− 1/16
IBM Cr 8s90	8.1	8	98¼	...
IBM Cr 8⅜90	8.5	15	98⅛	− ⅛
ICN 12⅞98	14.5	40	89	...
IllBel 7⅝06	9.2	25	82⅝	+ ¼
IllBel 8s04	9.2	5	87	− ⅝

EXPLANATORY NOTES
(For New York and American Bonds)

Yield is current yield.

cv-Convertible bond. cf-Certificates. dc-Deep discount. ec-European currency units. f-Dealt in flat. il-Italian lire. kd-Danish kroner. m-Matured bonds, negotiability impaired by maturity. na-No accrual. r-Registered. rp-Reduced principal. st-Stamped. t-Floating rate. wd-When distributed. ww-With warrants. x-Ex interest. xw-Without warrants. zr-Zero coupon.

vj-In bankruptcy or receivership or being reorganized under the Bankruptcy Act, or securities assumed by such companies.

If 12 percent is the correct discount rate—the rate of return required by investors to hold the bond—then $836.74 must also be the price in late 1983 of this Ford Motor Company bond. In the jargon of Wall Street, Ford's bond has been *priced to yield 12 percent to maturity*. This yield is not the same as the current yield shown earlier in the case of the Illinois Bell bonds. The relevant yield for bond pricing is the yield to maturity. Henceforth, all yields referred to are yields to maturity.

APPLICATION
Pricing a Government Bond

A government bond pays $100 in interest at the end of each year and $1,000 at maturity two years from now. If the yield to maturity is 10 percent, what is its current price?

SOLUTION Because the coupon rate and yield to maturity are the same, the bond must sell at par value:

$$B = \$100/1.10 + \$1{,}100/(1.10)^2$$

$$= \$90.91 + \$909.09$$

$$= \$1,000$$

If the required yield on the bond drops to 5 percent, at what price will the bond sell for?

SOLUTION

$$B = \$100/1.05 + \$1,100/(1.05)^2$$

$$= \$95.24 + \$997.73$$

$$= \$1,092.97$$

The drop in interest rates has increased the present value of the bond's future cash flows, thereby raising the price of the bond.

Yields, Coupon Rates, and Bond Prices

The Ford bond example illustrates an important point in bond pricing: *If its coupon rate is below the required yield, a bond will sell at less than face value.* The Ford bond is said to be selling at a 16.33 percent *discount* from its par value. Alternatively, as shown in the government bond illustration, if the required yield is less than the coupon rate, the bond will be selling at a *premium* above its par value. A bond yielding its coupon rate will sell at par. Thus, if the required return on Ford's 9.25 percent bond is exactly 9.25 percent, the price of the bond will be $1,000.

The general formula for the current price of a bond is

$$\begin{matrix} \text{Current bond} \\ \text{price} \end{matrix} = \begin{matrix} \text{Present value of} \\ \text{coupon payments} \end{matrix} + \begin{matrix} \text{Present value of} \\ \text{the face value} \end{matrix}$$

$$B = C/(1 + r) + C/(1 + r)^2 + \cdots + (C + F)/(1 + r)^n$$

$$= \sum_{t=1}^{n} C/(1 + r)^t + F/(1 + r)^n$$

$$= C \times \text{PVIFA}_{r,n} + F \times \text{PVIF}_{r,n} \tag{3.1}$$

where

$$B = \text{current price of the bond}$$

$$C = \text{annual coupon amount}$$

$$F = \text{face or par value of the bond}$$

$$r = \text{required yield on the bond}$$

$$n = \text{number of years until maturity}$$

Given the present price of a bond, we can use Equation 3.1 instead to solve for the bond's **yield to maturity** or **internal rate of return**. The internal rate of return on a bond or any other asset is the discount rate that equates the present value of the future cash flows—which for a bond would be the interest payments and principal repayment—to the current market price of the asset. In the case of the Ford bond, the yield to maturity was 12 percent.

Equation 3.1 indicates that as r increases, bond prices decline. Conversely, a fall in interest rates will lead to a rise in bond prices. The rationale for these price movements is as follows. If the bond were priced at par, it would yield exactly the coupon rate, say, 8 percent. But if interest rates have risen above the coupon rate to, say, 10 percent, investors in the secondary market will not want to pay full price for bonds yielding 8 percent when they can buy new ones yielding 10 percent. They will be interested in buying bonds in the secondary market only if they can earn a return comparable to that available on new issues. Because the coupon payments and the face value are fixed on bonds selling in the secondary market, the only way to increase the bond's yield to maturity is to reduce its current price below its face value. In this way, the lower coupon rate will be offset by the capital gain on redemption of the bond, in which the capital gain is the difference between the bond's par value and its purchase price. Similarly, a decrease in the required yield will lead to a rise in the market price. In this case, the higher coupon rate will be offset by the capital loss on the bond at redemption.

The basic point is that bond prices—indeed, security prices in general—fluctuate inversely to the interest rate. Thus, when interest rates rise, bond prices go down, and when interest rates fall, bond prices go up. The inverse relationship between interest rates and stock and bond prices is shown in Figure 3-2, which depicts the positive effect on asset values of the steep decline in interest rates over the period from January 1985 to April 1986.

FIGURE 3-2
The Inverse Relationship Between Interest Rates and Asset Prices

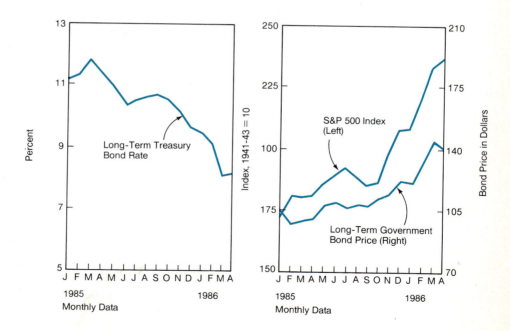

1985   Monthly Data   1986

1985   Monthly Data   1986

Semiannual Compounding

In calculating the value of the Ford 9.25 percent 1994 bonds, we assumed the interest is paid annually. Although some bonds do pay interest only once a year, most pay interest every six months. Thus, instead of receiving $92.50 every year, the purchaser of a Ford bond would receive $46.25 twice a year. We also assumed that the required 12 percent yield was an annually compounded rate, whereas most bonds are priced on a semiannually compounded basis.

The general formula for pricing a bond with semiannual compounding is as follows:

$$B = C/2 \times \text{PVIFA}_{r/2,2n} + F \times \text{PVIF}_{r/2,2n} \tag{3.2}$$

where C is the annual coupon payment and r is the annual interest rate. To find the price of Ford's 9.25 percent bond with semiannual compounding, substitute $92.50 for C, $1,000 for F, 11 years for n, and 12 percent for r in Equation 3.2:

$$B = \$46.25 \times \text{PVIFA}_{6,22} + \$1,000 \times \text{PVIF}_{6,22}$$
$$= \$46.25 \times 12.0416 + \$1,000 \times .2775$$
$$= \$834.42$$

This number compares with a value of $836.74 with annual compounding. The difference of $2.32 between these two numbers occurs because the annual percentage rate under semiannual compounding exceeds 12 percent, thereby discounting more heavily the future redemption value of $1,000. In particular, the annual percentage rate under semiannual compounding equals $(1.06)^2 - 1 = 12.37$ percent.

APPLICATION
Pricing a Bond

What is the highest price you should be willing to pay for an 8 percent coupon bond with interest paid semiannually, with a face value of $1,000, which has five years to maturity, if your required yield-to-maturity is 10 percent?

SOLUTION   The bond pays interest of $40 every six months. According to Equation 3.2, the price of the bond is

$$B = \$40 \times \text{PVIFA}_{5,10} + \$1,000 \times \text{PVIF}_{5,10}$$
$$= \$40 \times 7.7217 + \$1,000 \times .6139$$
$$= \$922.77$$

You should be unwilling to pay more than $922.77 for this bond.

3.4 CHARACTER- ISTICS OF PREFERRED STOCK

From a legal standpoint, preferred stock is part of equity; but from a practical standpoint, preferred is a hybrid security, combining characteristics of common stock and debt. It appears in the equity portion of the balance sheet, and so from the standpoint of lenders, it is equity capital. As are coupon payments on long-term debt, however, dividends paid to preferred shareholders are fixed in advance and take preference over payment of common stock dividends (hence the security's name). But unlike interest payments, preferred dividends are discretionary; their omission does not constitute an event of default. The only restriction is that the firm cannot pay dividends on common stock until all the preferred dividends owed to date have been paid.

Preferred stock has a number of distinguishing features, some of which are common to virtually all issues of preferred stock, whereas others are relatively rare. We review these features by examining the preferred stock shown on Atlantic Richfield's balance sheet as of year-end 1983. Table 3-1 shows that at that time Atlantic Richfield had three issues of preferred stock outstanding.

Par Value and Dividend Payments

Preferred stock may be issued with or without a par or face value. All three Atlantic Richfield preferred issues have par values, the Series B at $100 and the other two at $1 apiece. This par value bears no necessary relation to the issuing price, although the two numbers are frequently the same. The preferred dividend is often stated as a percentage of par. For example, the Atlantic Richfield Series B preferred pays a 3.75 percent dividend, and par is $100. The annual dividend on this preferred issue is therefore $3.75. Alternatively, the dividend could be stated as a dollar amount. This is the case for Atlantic Richfield's $3.00 and $2.80 cumulative convertible preferred issues, which pay annual per share dividends of $3.00 and $2.80, respectively.

Cumulative Provision. Atlantic Richfield's preferred issues, like most preferred stock, all bear the word *cumulative* in their names. This means that unpaid dividends are carried forward from year to year. Until this obligation is cleared, the firm cannot pay any dividends on common stock. For example, suppose

TABLE 3-1 Preferred Stock of Atlantic Richfield Company	
Cumulative preferred stock, 3.75% Series B, par $100	
Shares authorized	352,000
Shares issued	352,000
Aggregate value in voluntary liquidation (thousands)	$35,728
$3.00 cumulative convertible preference stock, par $1	
Shares authorized	407,992
Shares issued	285,330
Aggregate value in voluntary liquidation (thousands)	$22,826
$2.80 cumulative convertible preference stock, par $1	
Shares authorized	5,952,389
Shares issued	2,431,496
Aggregate value in voluntary liquidation (thousands)	$170,205

Atlantic Richfield has skipped dividends for the past three years on its 3.75 percent Series B, par $100 preferred. The company is now $11.25 per share in arrears on its preferred dividends ($100 × .0375 × 3). Before it can legally pay any common stock dividends, it must pay preferred stockholders $11.25 for each share held. The cumulative provision is an important protective feature for owners of preferred. Without it, the firm could pay large, infrequent common stock dividends and in between pay no preferred dividends.

When a firm in financial difficulty has skipped several preferred dividend payments under a cumulative provision, it may seek to exchange new securities for the preferred stock arrearages. In the previous example, Atlantic Richfield may offer preferred stockholders $11.25 or more in new common stock in lieu of the missed dividends.

Claim on Income and Assets

The claim of preferred stock to the firm's income is intermediate between common stock and debt. Preferred stock has priority over common stock with respect to the firm's income, because preferred dividends must be paid before common stock dividends. But creditor claims against the firm's income must be settled completely before any preferred dividends are paid.

In the event of bankruptcy, preferred stock is senior to common stock but subordinate to all debt. Creditors must be paid fully before preferred or common stockholders receive anything. Any money left over from the sale of the firm's assets is then used to settle preferred stock claims. The value of these claims in liquidation is usually stated on the firm's balance sheet. For example, in the event of liquidation, holders of Atlantic Richfield's par $100 preferred are entitled to $101.50 for each share they own, a total of $35.728 million. Atlantic Richfield also would owe aggregate amounts of $22.8 million and $170.2 million, respectively, to the holders of the $3.00 and $2.80 cumulative preferred stock. Common stockholders receive what remains after the claims of creditors and preferred stockholders are fully satisfied.

Rights of Preferred Stockholders

Preferred stock often contains protective covenants whose purpose is to preserve the priority of its claims to the firm's income and assets. For example, dividends on common stock may be restricted to amounts that maintain a specified working capital position (current assets minus current liabilities) or a minimum level of retained earnings. In addition, preferred stockholders usually seek some control over the sale of new securities of equal or higher seniority.

Voting Rights.   Preferred stockholders often have voting rights contingent on the firm's not abiding by the provisions of its agreement with them. For example, the New York Stock Exchange lists only preferred stocks that provide contingent voting rights after the firm has skipped the equivalent of six quarterly preferred dividends. In such an event, the preferred stockholders may have the right to elect one third of the members of the board of directors.

Convertibility.   Many issues of preferred stock are convertible into common stock at the option of the holder. For example, Atlantic Richfield's $3.00 and $2.80

cumulative preferred stock are convertible into 6.8 and 2.4 shares of common stock, respectively. Convertibility is valued by holders because it allows them to benefit from unexpected appreciation of the common stock. This feature, therefore, reduces the required size of the preferred dividend.

Retirement of Preferred Stock

Although preferred stock has no fixed maturity date, firms generally make provisions for its retirement. As with most bond issues, almost all preferred issues contain a **call** provision that gives the firm the right to buy back the preferred stock at a price specified when it is first issued. For example, Atlantic Richfield has the option of redeeming its 3.75 percent Series B, par $100 preferred at a per share price of $101.50. This option is valuable because it enables the firm to replace its preferred stock with a less expensive security in the event that interest rates decline.

Some preferred issues have a **sinking fund** provision that requires the firm to set aside money to retire a certain number of shares annually. The money is used either to buy back the preferred stock in the market (if the market price is below the call price) or to call the stock (if the market price exceeds the call price).

Tax Status

Unlike interest payments, preferred and common dividends are not tax deductible. However, dividends received from domestic corporations are 70 percent tax-free to corporate investors, whereas interest income is fully taxed. Thus, an insurance company that receives a dividend of $100 would have to pay corporate tax on only $30 of that income. If it is in the 34 percent bracket, its tax on the $100 dividend will be just $10.20 ($30 × .34). Because of this tax advantage, most preferred stock is held by corporations in lieu of holding debt securities, whose interest receipts are fully taxed.

3.5 PREFERRED STOCK VALUATION

The market value of a share of preferred equals the present value of future dividend payments plus the redemption price, if the issue is called or retired. Mathematically, the formula for the value of preferred stock is

$$
\begin{array}{rcl}
\text{Value of} & & \text{Present value} & & \text{Present value} \\
\text{preferred} & = & \text{of preferred} & + & \text{of redemption} \\
\text{stock} & & \text{dividends} & & \text{price}
\end{array}
$$

$$V_0 = \sum_{t=1}^{n} PD_t/(1 + k_p)^t + V_n/(1 + k_p)^n \qquad (3.3)$$

where

V_0 = value today of a preferred share

PD_t = expected preferred dividend in year t

$$V_n = \text{redemption price}$$

$$k_p = \text{required rate of return on preferred stock}$$

$$n = \text{maturity of the preferred stock}$$

The required return on preferred stock usually differs from the required return on the company's bonds because of differences in risk, hence, the use of k_p instead of r.

Given the different claims to the firm's income, preferred stock is typically riskier than a bond but less risky than common stock. Therefore, the rate at which preferred dividends are discounted should ordinarily lie somewhere between the firm's cost of debt and the required return on its common stock. However, because of the tax advantage to corporate investors, preferred stock often carries a lower yield than do bonds, despite its greater riskiness.

If there is no maturity date, and future dividends are expected to be constant, the preferred can be treated as a perpetuity and Equation 3.3 will reduce to

$$V_0 = PD/k_p \qquad \textbf{(3.4)}$$

where PD is the yearly preferred dividend.

As an illustration of Equation 3.4, Aetna Life has a preferred issue outstanding paying an annual dividend of $5.18 per share with no likelihood of redemption. In late 1983, the price of Aetna's preferred was $55.70. Using Equation 3.4, we can estimate the required yield by investors on Aetna's preferred as follows:

$$\$55.70 = \$5.18/k_p$$

or

$$k_p = 5.18/55.70 = 9.3 \text{ percent}$$

Thus, the required yield on Aetna's preferred stock issue at the end of 1983 was approximately 9.3 percent.

APPLICATION
Pricing Preferred Stock

An investor is considering the purchase of a preferred share. The share will pay $5 per year in perpetuity.

a. If the current required return on this issue of preferred is 10 percent, what is the maximum price the investor should pay for the share?

SOLUTION According to Equation 3.4, the maximum price is

$$V_0 = \$5/.10 = \$50$$

b. Suppose the issuing company has the right to repurchase the issue at a price of $30 in five years. How will this change your estimate of the maximum price an investor should pay for the share?

SOLUTION   If the required return remains at 10 percent and the company can repurchase the share in five years, it will do so. In such a case, the shareholder would receive

$$V_0 = \sum_{t=1}^{5} 5/(1.10)^t + 30/(1.10)^5$$

$$= 5 \times \text{PVIFA}_{10,5} + 30 \times \text{PVIF}_{10,5}$$

$$= 5 \times 3.7908 + 30 \times .6209$$

$$= \$37.58$$

The call provision reduces the value of the preferred stock.

3.6 CHARACTERISTICS OF COMMON STOCK FINANCING

The common stockholders of a corporation are its owners. As such, they are entitled to a proportional share of what remains of the firm's income and assets after the claims of debtholders and preferred stockholders have been fully met. Their liability, however, is limited to the amount of their initial investment.

Consider Table 3-2, which shows the shareholders' equity section of Atlantic Richfield's balance sheet as of year-end 1983. It indicates that Atlantic Richfield had issued 249,753,102 shares of common stock out of a maximum possible total of 300,000,000 shares authorized by stockholders. The authorized number of shares is specified in the company's corporate charter and can be changed only by amending the charter. Amending the charter is not difficult, but it requires the approval of current stockholders, which takes time. For this reason, management usually prefers to have available a certain number of authorized but unissued shares to provide flexibility in situations such as an acquisition attempt. In the case of Atlantic Richfield, management can issue an additional 50,246,898 shares without the stockholders' approval.

When authorized shares of common stock are sold, they become **issued stock**. Issued stock held by the public is described as *outstanding*. Sometimes a firm buys back part of its issued stock and holds it as **Treasury stock**. Atlantic Richfield's equity account indicates that it is not holding any Treasury stock.

TABLE 3-2 Shareholders' Equity for Atlantic Richfield (thousands)		
Capital stock		$662,299
Capital in excess of par value of stock		1,317,153
Retained earnings		8,968,548
Foreign currency translation		(59,862)
		$10,888,138
Note: Common stock, par $2.50		
Shares authorized		300,000,000
Shares issued		249,753,102

Issued shares are recorded at their **par value**, a number selected by management, which is $2.50 a share for Atlantic Richfield. Thus, the total par value of Atlantic Richfield's common stock is

$$\frac{\text{Par value of}}{\text{common stock}} = \frac{\text{Number of shares}}{\text{outstanding}} \times \text{Par value}$$

$$\$624{,}382{,}755 = 249{,}753{,}102 \times \$2.50$$

This number is less than the balance in the capital stock account because this account includes preferred stock at par as well as common stock. Par value has little economic significance aside from the fact that a purchaser who paid less than par would be liable for the difference between par and the issue price in the event the firm went bankrupt. For example, if an investor bought 10,000 shares of Atlantic Richfield stock at $2.00 per share, $.50 below par, the investor would have to put up an additional $5,000 ($.50 × 10,000) if Atlantic Richfield later went bankrupt. This contingent liability effectively precludes firms from issuing stock at below par and is why par value is generally set at a very low figure. Firms can also issue "no par" stock, in which case the stock is listed on the balance sheet at an arbitrarily chosen price.

The difference between the price at which new stock is sold to the public and par value is entered on the balance sheet in an account called *additional paid-in capital* or something similar. The corresponding account for Atlantic Richfield has the descriptive title *capital in excess of par value of stock*. Its balance of $1,317,153,000 means that over the years, Atlantic Richfield has sold stock to the public at prices that yielded revenues in excess of par value in that amount. If Atlantic Richfield sold an additional 1 million shares at $45 apiece, the common stock account would rise by 1,000,000 × $2.50 = $2,500,000 and the additional paid-in capital account would rise by 1,000,000 × ($45 − $2.50) = $42,500,000.

By far the most important source of equity financing for Atlantic Richfield, as for most firms that have been in business for a long time, is retained earnings. In Atlantic Richfield's case, retained earnings have supplied almost $9 billion in equity capital.

Stockholder Rights

As the ultimate owners of the firm, stockholders have certain rights and privileges. The most important ones are the claim on the firm's income and assets, voting rights, and the preemptive right.

Claim on Income. As owners of the firm, common stockholders have the right to the residual income after all creditors and preferred stockholders have been paid. They have the right to a proportionate share of any of these residual earnings that the board of directors decides to distribute in the form of dividends. However, the board is not required to declare dividends and can choose instead to retain the firm's earnings in the business. Thus the position of the common stockholder sharply contrasts with that of a creditor. The firm has a contractual obligation, which can be enforced in a court of law, to pay interest and principal to creditors; common stockholders desiring dividends have no such recourse to the law if the board decides not to distribute the firm's profits.

Claim on Assets.   In the event of liquidation, common stockholders are last in line. They receive only what is left over after the claims of all other creditors have been fully satisfied. In effect, common equity is used to provide a cushion against possible losses in liquidation for the other claimants of the firm. This adds to the riskiness of common stock.

Voting Rights.   As owners of the firm, common stockholders have ultimate control of the firm's affairs, including the right to vote on appointments to the board of directors and charter changes. Voting for directors and charter changes takes place at the annual meeting. Each share of stock confers one vote; thus the owner of 100 shares has 100 votes. Stockholders can vote in person, or by *proxy*, which involves transferring their right to vote to a second party.

    In theory, stockholders control the firm by electing directors who then select the corporate management. The reality, however, is often quite different, with management, rather than shareholders, selecting the board of directors and the shareholders ratifying management's slate. In practice, therefore, the stockholders of most corporations are limited in the amount of control they can exert over management, even when management controls only a small fraction of the shares outstanding. This is especially true when ownership is widely dispersed and diluted.

Preemptive Right.   The preemptive right grants stockholders the right to maintain their pro-rata share in the firm's earning and assets by purchasing new common stock in the same proportion as their current ownership.[8] For example, a stockholder who owns 5 percent of a firm is entitled to purchase 50,000 shares of a new issue of 1 million shares. The preemptive right protects the investors' ownership and control positions in the firm. Certificates called **rights** are issued to shareholders, giving them the option to buy the requisite number of shares during a specified period, usually about two to four weeks. These rights can be exercised, allowed to expire, or sold in the market. In Chapter 13, we examine the mechanics of a rights offering to raise additional equity capital.

3.7 COMMON STOCK VALUATION

Owners of common stock, like investors in any other asset, are interested in more cash for more future consumption. The current price per share of common stock, therefore, is based on the future cash flows expected to accrue to the shareholder. These cash flows are in the form of dividends paid, plus (minus) any capital gain (loss) on sale of the stock. Increasingly frequent sources of capital gains on stock are share repurchases by the issuer and purchases by potential acquirers. For a one-year holding period, the expected rate of return k is

$$\frac{\text{Expected return}}{\text{on common stock}} = \frac{\text{Dividend}}{\text{yield}} + \frac{\text{Rate of price}}{\text{appreciation}}$$

$$k = DIV_1/P_0 + (P_1 - P_0)/P_0$$

$$= (DIV_1 + P_1 - P_0)/P_0 \tag{3.5}$$

[8]Preemptive rights are not common in the United States, but they are common in other countries, such as Great Britain.

where

$$DIV_1 = \text{expected dividend per share during the coming year}$$

$$P_0 = \text{current price per share}$$

$$P_1 = \text{expected price at the end of the year}$$

The expected return k, more commonly called the **required rate of return** or the **cost of equity capital**, is the rate at which the market capitalizes or discounts future cash flows from the stock. It is based on (1) the time value of money, and (2) the risk associated with the particular stock. Chapter 4 explains how risk influences the cost of equity capital.

To illustrate the application of Equation 3.5, suppose General Motors (GM) stock is currently selling for $50.00. GM is expected to pay a $2.50 dividend at the end of the year, at which time its share price is expected to be $56.00. Then the expected return to an owner of GM stock for the coming year is

$$k = (\$2.50 + \$56.00 - \$50.00)/\$50.00$$

$$= 17 \text{ percent}$$

Alternatively, given investors' price and dividend forecasts and their required rate of return, we can compute the price today:

$$P_0 = (DIV_1 + P_1)/(1 + k) \tag{3.6}$$

For General Motors, a predicted dividend of $2.50 and end-of-year price of $56.00, along with a 17 percent required return, should result in a current market price of

$$P_0 = (\$2.50 + \$56.00)/1.17$$

$$= \$50.00$$

Can any other price exist in a competitive market? The answer is an unambiguous *no*. Consider what would happen if P_0 were below $50.00. Given investors' dividend and price appreciation expectations, the expected yield on GM stock will exceed the required return of 17 percent. Investors will start buying more shares of GM to earn this higher return, thereby driving up its current price and driving down its return. This arbitrage process will continue until the expected return on GM stock just equals its required return of 17 percent. As we saw above, this point is reached when $P_0 = \$50.00$. The reverse would occur if GM stock were priced above $50.00, thus yielding less than 17 percent. Investors would switch their funds to other investments promising higher returns, in the process forcing down the price of GM shares. As before, equilibrium would occur when $P_0 = \$50.00$.

APPLICATION
Pricing Common Stock

A stock selling for $12.50 is expected to pay $.50 in dividends this year and has an expected rate of return of 8 percent. What is the expected price at the end of a year?

SOLUTION   Rearranging Equation 3.6 to express P_1 in terms of the other variables leads to

$$P_1 = (1 + k)P_0 - DIV_1$$

Substituting in the values .08 for k, \$12.50 for P_0, and \$.50 for DIV_1 yields

$$P_1 = (1.08) \times \$12.50 - \$.50$$

$$= \$13$$

In a sense, these formulas beg the question, for they leave unanswered the question of what determines next year's price. According to Equation 3.6,

$$P_1 = (DIV_2 + P_2)/(1 + k) \tag{3.7}$$

where DIV_2 and P_2 are the expected dividend and price, respectively, at the end of the second year. This means that in forecasting P_1 investors are looking at the following year's price and dividend. Substituting Equation 3.7 for P_1 in Equation 3.6 allows us to express P_0 in terms of DIV_1, DIV_2, and P_2:

$$P_0 = DIV_1/(1 + k) + P_1/(1 + k)$$

$$= DIV_1/(1 + k) + (DIV_2 + P_2)/(1 + k)^2 \tag{3.8}$$

If GM shareholders expect a dividend of \$2.80 in the second year and a year-end price of \$62.70, this would imply a price today of

$$P_0 = \$2.50/1.17 + (\$2.80 + \$62.70)/(1.17)^2$$

$$= \$50.00$$

the same as previously estimated. It can easily be seen that P_1 must also maintain its estimated value of \$56.00. Any inconsistency in prices would result in a profitable arbitrage opportunity.

We could continue this process indefinitely, each time substituting $(DIV_{t+1} + P_{t+1})/(1 + k)$ for P_t, where DIV_t is the projected dividend in period t. Projecting out n years gives us a general stock valuation formula

$$P_0 = DIV_1/(1 + k) + DIV_2/(1 + k)^2 + \cdots + (DIV_n + P_n)/(1 + k)^n$$

$$= \sum_{t=1}^{n} DIV_t/(1 + k)^t + P_n/(1 + k)^n \tag{3.9}$$

Because the validity of Equation 3.9 does not depend on any specific value of n, we can allow n to become arbitrarily large. As n approaches infinity, the term $1/(1 + k)^n$ approaches zero. Hence, the present value of P_n will approach zero. This leads to a formula expressed solely in terms of future expected dividends and the required rate of return:

$$P_0 = \sum_{t=1}^{\infty} \text{DIV}_t/(1 + k)^t \tag{3.10}$$

Dividends and Stock Valuation

The logic behind valuing a stock on the basis of its future dividends alone, including a liquidating dividend if the firm is sold to another firm or dissolved and any share repurchases (which can be treated as dividends), is that these are the only cash flows provided by the stock. Although the return to any individual investor consists of dividends plus the final sale price, the return to investors in the aggregate consists solely of dividends plus any share repurchases. Equation 3.10 is consistent, therefore, with the rule that the value of an asset is the present value of the future cash flows generated by that asset.

The implication is that a stock that is never expected to pay a dividend will be worthless. How does this statement square with the evidence of Digital Equipment Corporation (DEC), a highly valued company that has never paid a cash dividend? Actually, there is no contradiction once you realize that the current price depends on *future* expected dividends. DEC has been a rapidly growing firm (its sales grew at an incredible average annual rate of 36 percent during the decade 1972–1981; after some problems in the early 1980s, DEC sales averaged annual growth of 22 percent from 1983 through 1987) with numerous opportunities to reinvest its profits internally. As we will see later on, shareholders are likely to benefit by earning their returns in the form of untaxed capital gains (until realized by sale of the appreciated stock) rather than receiving taxed dividends. Eventually, these growth opportunities will diminish and DEC will have cash on hand in excess of that needed for investment purposes. The market clearly expects that when this happens, DEC will begin to pay dividends (or repurchase its shares). In the meantime, DEC is building up an investment base on which it is earning a rate of return that is at least equal to the rate its shareholders would earn if they were to receive dividends.

Constant Dividend Growth

We can develop a simplified version of Equation 3.10 by assuming that dividends will grow at a constant rate g: $\text{DIV}_{t+1} = \text{DIV}_t(1 + g) = \text{DIV}_1(1 + g)^{t-1}$. By substituting the value $\text{DIV}_1(1 + g)^{t-1}$ for DIV_t in Equation 3.10, the present value of the dividend series becomes an infinite geometric series whose sum is the current price P_0:

$$P_0 = \sum_{t=1}^{\infty} \text{DIV}_t/(1 + k)^t$$

$$= \sum_{t=1}^{\infty} \text{DIV}_1(1 + g)^{t-1}/(1 + k)^t$$

$$= \text{DIV}_1/(k - g) \tag{3.11}$$

The final term, $DIV_1/(k - g)$, is just the sum of the infinite geometric series and is derived from the formula for the sum of such a series.[9] It is important to realize that Equation 3.11 says only that dividends are *expected* to grow at a constant annual rate of g; year-to-year deviations are always possible and, in fact, are almost guaranteed to occur. Those deviations that do occur, however, will be around the constant-growth path g. Another implicit assumption underlying Equation 3.11 is that the required rate of return k must be constant over time. Moreover, k must always exceed g; otherwise, the present value would be infinite. Because we don't see infinite stock prices, this assumption is satisfied.

Although it is clearly unrealistic to assume that the expected dividend growth rate and required return are forever constant, Equation 3.11 is one of the most useful valuation formulas in finance. It often provides good price approximations, even though its assumptions abstract from reality.

To illustrate its application, suppose that IBM will almost certainly pay a dividend of $4.50 during the coming year and that this dividend is expected to grow at a compound annual rate of 12 percent. Figure 3-3 shows the time pattern of dividends under this scenario and the present value of this dividend stream over the next 15 years, assuming that IBM stock bears a required return of 15

FIGURE 3-3

Projected IBM Dividend Stream (actual value and present value)

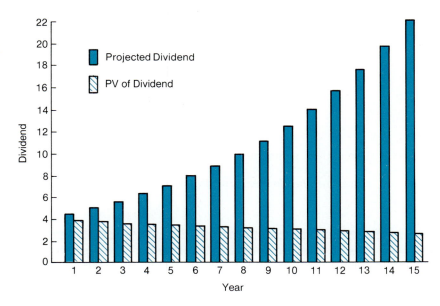

[9]To derive Equation 3.11, note that the formula for the sum of an infinite geometric series a, ar, ar^2, ..., ar^n, ..., where $0 < r < 1$ is $a/(1 - r)$. In this case, $a = DIV_1/(1 + k)$ and $r = (1 + g)/(1 + k)$. Substituting these terms into the formula $a/(1 - r)$ yields

$$P_0 = \frac{DIV_1/(1 + k)}{1 - (1 + g)/(1 + k)} = \frac{DIV_1/(1 + k)}{(k - g)/(1 + k)} = DIV_1/(k - g)$$

percent. Given these assumptions, then, according to Equation 3.11, IBM's stock price today will be

$$P_0 = \$4.50/(.15 - .12)$$
$$= \$150.00$$

We can also use Equation 3.11 to derive an estimate of the market's required return on the stock, using just the current dividend yield DIV_1/P_0 and the expected dividend growth rate:

$$k = DIV_1/P_0 + g \qquad (3.12)$$

Thus, if you buy a stock for $50 that is expected to pay a dividend next year of $2.50 and the dividend growth rate is anticipated to be about 8 percent, then your expected rate of return will be 13 percent:

$$k = 2.50/50 + .08$$
$$= 13 \text{ percent}$$

This expected return comprises a 5 percent dividend yield ($DIV_1/P_0 = .05$) and a capital gains yield of 8 percent. The capital gains figure is based on the expected dividend increase of 8 percent annually. Next year, for example, the projected dividend is $2.70 ($2.50 × 1.08), which will result in an expected value for P_1 of $54:

$$P_1 = DIV_2/(k - g)$$
$$= \$2.70/(.13 - .08)$$
$$= \$54$$

The capital gains yield, therefore, is 4/50 = 8 percent. This example illustrates an important principle: *In a constant-dividend growth situation, the price of the stock and the dividend can be expected to increase at the same rate.*

APPLICATION
Valuing Common Stock with Different Dividend Growth Rates

A stock with an expected rate of return of 15 percent will pay a $2 dividend this year. If this dividend is paid in perpetuity, what will be the value of the stock?

SOLUTION In this case, we use the formula to value a perpetuity:

$$P_0 = DIV_1/k$$
$$= \$2/.15$$
$$= \$13.33$$

If this dividend is expected to grow by 10 percent a year in perpetuity, what is the theoretical value of the stock?

SOLUTION   Applying Equation 3.11, we have

$$P_0 = \$2/(.15 - .10)$$
$$= \$40$$

Earnings Per Share and Common Stock Valuation

Our analysis is based on the assumption that the current stock price incorporates the market's best estimate of the discounted amount of future cash dividends paid by the firm to present and future investors. Because cash distributions to investors must come from the firm's cash flows, the forecast of future dividends must necessarily entail an assessment by the market as to the amounts, timing, and riskiness of corporate cash flows. Consequently, there is a direct link between an investor's return on investing in a company's stock and the cash flows generated by that firm.

If dividends, and ultimately, cash flows are what matter, why then do investors and security analysts spend so much time trying to project future company earnings? The answer is straightforward: Corporate earnings provide the bulk of cash flows for the firm. As a result, although there can be temporary deviations, the long-run dividend growth rate cannot exceed the rate at which earnings per share grow. In assessing future corporate cash flows, therefore, investors focus on the firm's past performance, its competitive position, its financial flexibility, and other information, like top management's competence, that bear on the firm's ability to generate these future earnings. These earnings are those that accurately reflect a firm's true profitability. In Chapter 22 we examine those accounting conventions, like historical cost depreciation and the first-in, first-out (FIFO) inventory valuation method, that distort the relationship between accounting earnings and true profitability.

The belief that the stock market is efficient does not mean a firm should not supply it with additional information that does not appear to be reflected in the firm's stock price. A good illustration of this point is the case of IBM. In a radical departure from the company's customary tight-lipped policy, IBM presented a detailed— and upbeat—appraisal of its prospects at a December 1983 meeting of financial analysts. This followed a somewhat mysterious decline in IBM's stock price that began in mid-October. IBM claimed there was no connection between the meeting and the drop in its stock price; but one security analyst said, "I can only speculate that the company felt that for the stock to reflect its great growth, momentum, and earnings prospects, management had to put more numbers on the table."[10] Whatever the reason for holding the meeting, the net result was that the price of IBM stock jumped $5 a share right afterwards.

The Price–Earnings Ratio and the Dividend Growth Model

Wall Street pays a great deal of attention to the price–earnings ratio, P_0/E_1, the ratio of the price today to anticipated earnings per share for the coming year.

[10]"How IBM Changed the Market's Mind," *Fortune*, January 9, 1984, p. 117.

The constant-dividend growth formula, on the other hand, focuses on the price–dividend ratio $P_0/\mathrm{DIV}_1 = 1/(k - g)$. The relation between the two ratios is formed if, as is customary, the firm sets its target dividend payout rate—the fraction of its earnings paid out as dividends—equal to a constant b; that is, $\mathrm{DIV}_t = bE_t$, where E_t is earnings per share for year t. With a constant dividend payout rate, therefore, both dividends and earnings per share will grow at the same annual rate g. Substituting bE_1 for DIV_1 in Equation 3.11 yields

$$P_0 = \mathrm{DIV}_1/(k - g)$$
$$= bE_1/(k - g)$$

or

$$P_0/E_1 = b/(k - g) \tag{3.13}$$

According to Equation 3.13, the P/E for a firm is affected by the expected growth in earnings per share, the dividend payout ratio, and the required rate of return on the stock.

APPLICATION
Determining a
Stock's P/E Ratio

Suppose a stock's earnings per share for the current year are projected at $5 and are expected to grow at a rate of 11 percent annually. The company pays out 40 percent of earnings as dividends. Hence, the expected year-end dividend is .4 $\times$ $5 = $2. The required return on this stock is 13.5 percent. According to the dividend growth model, this stock should be worth

$$P_0 = \$2/(.135 - .11)$$
$$= \$80$$

The price–earnings ratio is $80/5 = 16$, which is consistent with Equation 3.13:

$$P_0/E_1 = .4/(.135 - .11) = 16$$

Is a high P/E good or bad? The answer depends on why the P/E is high. According to Equation 3.13, a high P/E could be due to low current earnings, which would generally be bad, or to a high payout ratio, which could be either good (if it indicates substantial cash flow), bad (if it is due to a dearth of good investment opportunities), or neutral (if caused by the firm's raising outside capital instead of retaining earnings). It could also be due to high expected growth in earnings or a low required return on equity capital, either of which would be a favorable sign. A low P/E can be similarly interpreted.

These factors, in turn, are influenced by the firm's investment prospects and their associated risks and returns. The more investment opportunities that are available to the firm, the more earnings it is likely to retain and the lower its payout ratio will be. **Retained earnings** are the earnings left over after dividends are paid. As retained earnings per share increase, earnings per share E will grow, and the amount of dividends paid per share can also grow. The rate at which E grows depends on the increase in retained earnings and the firm's **return on equity** (ROE).

As usually defined, the firm's ROE is the ratio of earnings per share to the total net worth, also called **book value of equity** (assets minus liabilities), per share. But for the following discussion the appropriate ROE figure is the additional, or *incremental*, return per dollar of *new* investment undertaken; that is, ROE represents the return on an additional dollar of equity investment.

If the firm's ROE is a constant R, then each dollar of equity yields R dollars in earnings annually, of which a fraction $1 - b$ is reinvested in the company. Thus, the growth in net worth per share equals the return on equity times the fraction of earnings retained for reinvestment purposes.

With a constant return on equity, the rate of increase in earnings per share will also equal the rate of increase in equity per share, or

$$\text{Earnings growth rate} = (1 - b)R$$

If dividends are a constant fraction of earnings, dividends must also grow at this rate. Consequently,

$$\frac{\text{Dividend}}{\text{growth rate}} = \frac{\text{Earnings}}{\text{growth rate}}$$

$$g = (1 - b)R$$

For example, suppose that IBM's payout ratio is 40 percent and its return on equity is 20 percent. With an earnings retention rate of 60 percent, net worth per share of IBM stock will grow at a rate of $.6 \times .2 = .12$ or 12 percent annually. With the ROE and payout ratio assumed constant, earnings per share and dividends will also grow at a constant rate of 12 percent per annum.

APPLICATION
Estimating
Growth in
Earnings Per
Share

The stock of HiFlier has a current price of $40, a projected first-year dividend of $2, and a required rate of return of 15 percent.

a. If 60 percent of earnings are paid out as dividends, what is the expected growth rate of HiFlier's earnings?

SOLUTION

$$P_0 = \text{DIV}_1/(k - g)$$

$$40 = 2/(.15 - g)$$

or

$$g = 10 \text{ percent}$$

If dividends are growing at 10 percent and they represent a constant 60 percent of earnings, then earnings are also growing at 10 percent.

b. If the book value of HiFlier's equity is currently $20 per share, what will it be in two years?

SOLUTION   The book value in two years will equal the sum of the current book value plus two years' worth of retained earnings. This year, HiFlier's dividend will be $2. Because this represents 60 percent of earnings, this year's earnings must be $2/.6 = $3.33. Thus, retained earnings will equal .40 × $3.33 = $1.33. Next year's earnings will be 10 percent greater than this year's earnings or $3.33 × 1.1 = $3.66. Thus, next year's increase in retained earnings will be .40 × $3.66 = $1.46. Book value in two years will, therefore, equal $20 + $1.33 + $1.46 = $22.79.

c. What is HiFlier's return on equity on its reinvested earnings?

SOLUTION   As just shown, $g = (1 - b)R$. Solving for R, the return on equity, yields $R = g/(1 - b)$. Substituting in the numbers for HiFlier yields $R = .10/.4 = 25$ percent. Hence, HiFlier's ROE on reinvested earnings is 25 percent.

The preceding discussion indicates that the price of a company's stock can be separated into the value created by the earnings on the firm's already existing investments—its assets in place—and the value created by the presence of future growth opportunities. The latter value is termed by Stewart Myers the **present value of growth opportunities** (PVGO).[11] If there were no growth opportunities, the firm would pay out all its earnings as dividends, b would equal 1, and g would be 0. In that case the firm's stock price would be

$$P_0 = E_1/k$$

This means that HiFlier's stock would be worth

$$\$3.33/.15 = \$22.20$$

if the company had no growth opportunities.

With growth opportunities, the price of the firm's stock can be expressed as follows:

$$\begin{array}{lll} \text{Price} \\ \text{today} \end{array} = \begin{array}{l} \text{Present value} \\ \text{of earnings on} \\ \text{assets in place} \end{array} + \begin{array}{l} \text{Present value} \\ \text{of growth} \\ \text{opportunities} \end{array}$$

$$P_0 = E_1/k \qquad\qquad + \text{PVGO}$$

In the case of HiFlier's stock, the company reinvests 40 percent of its earnings at a permanent return on equity of 25 percent. The first year's reinvested earnings are $1.33. With a 25 percent ROE, this investment generates .25 × $1.33 = $.333 in cash annually, beginning in year 2. Because this is a perpetuity, it has a present value as of year 1 equal to

$$\text{PV} = .333/.15$$

$$= \$2.22$$

[11]Stewart Myers, "Determinants of Corporate Borrowing," *Journal of Financial Economics*, vol. 5, 1977, pp. 147–175.

Because the company has to invest $1.33 to realize this return, the value of the investment in year 1 net of its cost is $2.22 − $1.33 = $.89. Everything is the same in year 2 except that HiFlier will invest 10 percent more at the same 25 percent return. Hence, the value of the opportunity to invest in year 2 is worth 10 percent more than it was in year 1, or 1.10 × $.89 = $.979, and so on. Each year, HiFlier's opportunity to invest in that year is worth 10 percent more.

Note that HiFlier's growth opportunities are analogous to a stock that pays a dividend which starts at $.89 and grows at a rate of 10 percent annually. Thus, the present value of the stream of growth opportunities available to HiFlier can be found using the constant-dividend growth formula:

$$\text{PVGO} = \$.89/(.15 - .10)$$

$$= \$17.80$$

Everything now adds up for HiFlier:

$$\begin{array}{c} \text{Price} \\ \text{today} \end{array} = \begin{array}{c} \text{Present value} \\ \text{of earnings on} \\ \text{assets in place} \end{array} + \begin{array}{c} \text{Present value} \\ \text{of growth} \\ \text{opportunities} \end{array}$$

$$P_0 = E_1/k \qquad + \text{PVGO}$$

$$= \$22.20 \qquad + \$17.80$$

$$= \$40.00$$

FIGURE 3-4
Valuing HiFlier's
Stock: Separating
out the Value of
Earnings on Assets
in Place from the
Present Value of
Growth
Opportunities

Year	0	1	2	3	4
Earnings on assets in place	3.33	3.33	3.33	3.33	3.33 ...
Year 1 growth opportunity					
Cash flows		−1.33	.333	.333	.333 ...
Present value of future earnings (as of year 1)		2.22			
Year 1 special dividend		.89			
Year 2 growth opportunity					
Cash flows			−1.467	.366	.366 ...
Present value of future earnings (as of year 2)			2.446		
Year 2 dividend			.979		
Year 3 growth opportunity					
Cash flows				−1.613	.403 ...
Present value of future earnings (as of year 3)				2.689	
Year 3 dividend				1.076	
				.	
				.	
Year t dividend				$.89(1.10)^{t-1}$	

$$\begin{array}{ll} \text{Present value of earnings on assets in place} & = \quad 3.33/.15 \\ & = \quad \$22.20 \\ \text{Present value of earnings from growth opportunities} & = \quad .89/(.15 - .10) \\ & \quad \underline{\$17.80} \\ \text{Total present value} & = \quad \$40.00 \end{array}$$

Another way to value HiFlier's shares, which leads to the same $40 price, is to assume that the company sells off its stream of investment opportunities rather than financing them internally. In this way, HiFlier can pay a regular dividend of $3.33 annually plus a special dividend each year that equals the proceeds from selling off its growth opportunities. This process is shown in Figure 3-4.

In Chapters 6–11, we study in more detail how to value a firm's future investment opportunities and the factors that valuation depends on. Of course, in addition to affecting the future returns to shareholders, the firm's investment choices also affect the required return on equity k. This is because different investments usually have different degrees of risk. Because investors are risk averse, they demand higher returns for bearing higher risks. The nature of risk and the way in which risk affects the required return k is explored in Chapter 4. For now, bear in mind that although risk has its reward, it also has its cost.

Accounting Earnings Versus Cash Flows

Although we have been using the terms *cash flow* and *earnings* as though they are interchangeable, they are not. Accounting earnings or profits may differ significantly from cash flows. Because it is cash that matters, it is important to disentangle the two.

Accounting profits equal the difference between revenues and costs, where these items are matched as closely as possible. For example, new investments are capitalized on the balance sheet and then written off, or depreciated, as the investment generates revenues. By contrast, cash flow analysis proceeds by examining the firm's *sources* and *uses* of funds. Sources of cash include revenues from operations, and the sale of assets and additional securities. Uses of funds include out-of-pocket costs, taxes, dividends, payments on debt, increases in working capital, and new investment. Noncash costs like depreciation or amortization of goodwill are not a use of funds.

Net cash flow in excess of that needed to undertake all profitable investment opportunities is sometimes known as **free cash flow**. It is out of this free cash flow that dividends are paid. Hence, in analyzing a firm's dividend-paying ability, the focus should be on estimating free cash flow per share and projecting its likely growth over time.

The two important points to remember are that (1) dividends are paid out of cash flow, not earnings; and (2) in estimating future cash flows available for paying dividends, you must subtract the investments required to generate those future cash flows.

APPLICATION
Earnings Versus Cash Flow

Two identical companies have cash revenues of $1 million and cash expenses of $500,000 for the year. Both pay corporate income tax at the rate of 35 percent of profits and both can claim noncash depreciation of $200,000.

a. Alpha Company wants to maximize book earnings and decides to ignore the depreciation allowance. What will its after-tax earnings be? What will its after-tax cash flow be?

SOLUTION

Alpha Company

Revenues	$1,000,000
Cash expense	− 500,000
Earnings before tax	$500,000
Cash flow before tax	500,000
Tax	− 175,000
Earnings after tax	$325,000
Cash flow after tax	$325,000

b. Beta Company decides to utilize the depreciation allowance. What will its after-tax earnings and after-tax cash flow be?

SOLUTION

Beta Company

Revenues	$1,000,000
Cash expense	− 500,000
Noncash expense	− 200,000
Earnings before tax	$300,000
Cash flow before tax	500,000
Tax	− 105,000
Earnings after tax	$195,000
Cash flow after tax	$395,000

c. In light of your results, which company is operating correctly?

SOLUTION Although Alpha is maximizing "earnings," true profit is measured by cash flow, and Beta is correctly maximizing this. By taking the depreciation charge, the company is saving $70,000 (.35 × $200,000) in tax, which boosts cash flow by the same amount.

Above-Average Growth

In the long run, no firm can grow more rapidly than the economy in which it operates, whether this be the domestic or the world economy. This means a sustainable real, or inflation-adjusted, long-run dividend growth rate of perhaps 3 to 4 percent. Thus, a 15 percent annual real dividend growth rate should be regarded as a temporary deviation from the long-run growth path.

Applying the constant-growth formula to the stock of a rapidly growing firm without allowing for the temporary nature of this growth will lead to overvaluation. For example, suppose that over the past five years a firm's dividend growth rate has averaged 10 percent in real terms. (If the rate of inflation during this period averaged, say, 8 percent, then the nominal growth rate would have been about 18 percent.) Suppose that a zero rate of inflation is forecast for the foreseeable future, or alternatively, assume that all the following numbers are stated in real terms. If the firm is expected to pay a $2 dividend next year and its required return is 12 percent, then the assumption that this rapid growth will continue in perpetuity implies a stock value of

$$P_0 = \$2/(.12 - .10)$$

$$= \$100$$

If dividend growth had been 20 percent instead and this growth rate was expected to persist in the future, the estimated value of the stock would be infinity, or $-\$25$ dollars, depending on whether Equation 3.10 or 3.11 were used. Regardless of which formula is used or whether real dividend growth of 10 percent or 20 percent is assumed, the answer would be nonsense because it is based on a growth rate that is impossible to sustain forever. (The previous assumption of a 12 percent nominal growth rate in dividends for IBM translates into a real growth rate of about 5 percent if the anticipated long-run inflation rate is approximately 7 percent.)

The point is that all high-flying firms are eventually brought back to earth, and this must be explicitly taken into account when estimating stock values. For example, assume that the growth rate for a firm's dividends will be 20 percent for the next five years, after which it is expected to drop to a more normal rate of 4 percent. How should you go about estimating the current value of the firm's stock in this type of situation? The general approach to follow is first to calculate the present value of the dividends during the period of rapid growth, then calculate the price of the stock at the end of this period, take its present value, and finally add together the two present value components.

To implement this approach and illustrate its application, it is necessary to define and assign values to the following terms:

g_r = dividend growth rate during period of rapid growth = 20 percent

n = number of years rapid growth is expected to continue = 5

g = long-run growth rate following period of rapid growth = 4 percent

k = required return on common stock = 13 percent

DIV_0 = dividend at time 0 = \$1.50

We can now value the stock of this company by using the following four-step procedure:

1. *Calculate the present value of dividends received during the period of rapid growth.* With a constant-dividend growth rate for the next five years, the expected value of DIV_t for any of the next five years will equal $\text{DIV}_0(1 + g_r)^t$. Discounting this dividend at the cost of equity capital k yields a present value of DIV_t, call it $\text{PV}(\text{DIV}_t)$, of

$$\text{PV}(\text{DIV}_t) = \text{DIV}_0(1 + g_r)^t/(1 + k)^t$$

$$= \$1.50(1.2)^t/(1.13)^t$$

$$= \$1.50 \times \text{FVIF}_{20,t} \times \text{PVIF}_{13,t}, \text{ for } t = 1, \ldots, 5$$

Note that $(1.2)^t = \text{FVIF}_{20,t}$ and $1/(1.13)^t = \text{PVIF}_{13,t}$. As shown in Table 3-3, the sum of the present values of these dividends is \$9.01.

2. *Calculate the price of the stock at the end of the period of rapid growth.* At the end of the fifth year, dividends are expected to grow at a more normal

	Year	Dividend	×	Present Value Factor (13%)	=	Present Value
TABLE 3-3 Present Value of Dividends: Rapid Growth Period	1	$1.80		.8850		$1.59
	2	2.16		.7832		1.69
	3	2.59		.6931		1.80
	4	3.11		.6133		1.91
	5	3.73		.5428		2.02
					Total	$9.01

rate of 4 percent. This allows us to calculate P_5 by applying the constant-dividend growth formula:

$$P_5 = \text{DIV}_6/(k - g)$$
$$= \text{DIV}_0(1 + g_r)^5(1 + g)/(k - g)$$
$$= \$1.50(1.2)^5(1.04)/(.13 - .04)$$
$$= \$43.13$$

3. *Find the present value of this stock price.* This requires calculating

$$\text{PV}(P_5) = P_5/(1 + k)^5$$
$$= \$43.13/(1.13)^5$$
$$= \$43.13 \times \text{PVIF}_{13,5}$$
$$= \$43.13 \times .5428$$
$$= \$23.41$$

4. *Sum the two present values.*

$$P_0 = \$9.01 + \$23.41$$
$$= \$32.42$$

The general mathematical formula for computing the current stock price in the case of temporary above-average dividend growth is

$$\text{Current stock price} = \text{Present value of dividends during period of above-average growth} + \text{Present value of stock price at end of above-average growth period}$$

$$P_0 = \sum_{t=1}^{n} \text{DIV}_t/(1 + k)^t + P_n/(1 + k)^n$$

$$= \sum_{t=1}^{n} \frac{DIV_0(1 + g_r)^t}{(1 + k)^t} + \frac{DIV_0(1 + g_r)^n(1 + g)}{(k - g)(1 + k)^n}$$

$$= \sum_{t=1}^{n} DIV_0(1 + g_r)^t \times PVIF_{k,t}$$

$$+ \frac{DIV_0(1 + g_r)^n(1 + g)PVIF_{k,n}}{(k - g)} \tag{3.14}$$

and the symbols used are the same as those defined earlier.

APPLICATION
Stock Valuation
with Temporary
Above-Average
Dividend Growth

A stock with an expected rate of return of 15 percent paid a dividend of $2 last year. If the dividend grows by 10 percent a year for three years, 5 percent a year for the next two years, and then ceases to grow, what will be the value of the stock?

SOLUTION According to Equation 3.14,

$$P_0 = 2(1.10) \times PVIF_{15,1} + 2(1.10)^2 \times PVIF_{15,2} + 2(1.10)^3$$
$$\times PVIF_{15,3} + 2(1.10)^3 \times (1.05) \times PVIF_{15,4} + 2(1.10)^3$$
$$\times (1.05)^2 \times PVIF_{15,5} + \frac{2(1.10)^3 \times (1.05)^2 \times PVIF_{15,5}}{.15}$$
$$= 1.91 + 1.83 + 1.75 + 1.60 + 1.46 + 9.73$$
$$= \$18.28$$

Hence, the current price of the stock should be $18.28.

SUMMARY AND
CONCLUSIONS

Corporate securities promise more or less certain amounts of money in the future. This chapter shows how the techniques of present value analysis, introduced in Chapter 2, can be used to value these future cash flows. Competition between buyers and sellers ensures that the price at which a security trades will equal its value.

The cash inflows on a bond consist of the regular coupon payments of C per period plus the principal repayment F at maturity. With a required return or discount rate of r and a maturity of n years, the value of the bond will be

$$B = C \times PVIFA_{r,n} + F \times PVIF_{r,n}$$

Preferred stock pays a fixed dividend PD but has no set maturity date. Hence, it can be modeled as a perpetuity with a value

$$V_0 = PD/k_p$$

where k_p is the required return on preferred stock.

Common stock has neither a fixed maturity nor a fixed dividend. The only cash flows received by common stockholders are in the form of dividends (including a liquidating dividend), which are the residual corporate cash flows after all debt and preferred stock payments have been made and the firm has met all its financing needs. Therefore, the present value of a share of common stock is

$$P_0 = \sum_{t=1}^{\infty} \text{DIV}_t/(1 + k)^n$$

where DIV_t is the expected dividend per share in year t and k is the required return on equity capital.

In the special case where dividends are expected to grow forever at a compound annual rate of g, the present value of the infinite series of dividends is

$$P_0 = \text{DIV}_1/(k - g)$$

When dividends are a constant fraction b of earnings, this formula can also be used to establish the price–earnings ratio for the stock:

$$P_0/E_1 = b/(k - g)$$

where E_1 is the expected first-year earnings.

REFERENCES

Fama, Eugene F. "Efficient Capital Markets: A Review of Theory and Empirical Markets." *Journal of Finance*, May 1970, pp. 383–417.

Sharpe, William F. *Investments*. Englewood Cliffs, N.J.: Prentice-Hall, 1986.

QUESTIONS

1. According to a recent story in *Fortune* magazine (June 23, 1986, p. 27), the strategy for investing in the stock market is "Draw up a checklist for telling good managements from bad, and buy accordingly." Will picking stocks of well-managed companies be more rewarding than picking stocks of poorly managed companies? Comment.

2. Thirty-year, fixed-rate mortgages were common in the past for small homeowners. Today, variable-rate or short-term mortgages are more common. What can explain this change?

3. Before a recent change in government, the rate of return on short-term bonds averaged 18 percent, whereas the rate of inflation averaged 17 percent. Since the change in government, the rate of return on short-term bonds has averaged 12 percent and the rate of inflation has averaged 3 percent. The Head of State claims that his economic policies are to be applauded for lowering interest rates. Do you agree?

4. The Central Bank recently issued the following securities:

Day of Issue	Face	Terms
1 Oct 1988	$100	7 1/4s 2004
1 Oct 1989	$100	10 3/4s 2004

Both bonds trade freely in an organized market. In which bond would you prefer to invest $100,000?

5. Although the market-determined yield on 20-year corporate bonds is 11 percent, the treasurer of XYZ Corporation has been advised by the corporation's investment banker that it would be easy to sell a bond issue with a coupon at only 10 percent. The treasurer reasons that he will save the company interest expense by floating debt at only 10 percent. Do you agree? Why or why not?

6. XYZ Corporation currently has long-term bonds and preferred shares outstanding. The bonds have a face value of $1,000, 10 percent coupons, and are perpetuities. The preferred shares pay an annual dividend of $100 and have no early call provisions. Which security will sell for a higher price? Explain. Ignore taxes.

7. a. How is the value of a share of common equity determined?
   b. Given your answer to item a, why do stocks that pay no dividends sell at positive prices and often at high price/earnings ratios?

8. Comment on the following statement:

   Northern Telecom has a high P/E ratio while Gaz Métropolitain has a low P/E. Therefore, we should be buying more Northern Tel and dumping all our Gaz Métropolitain.

9. On October 19, 1987, the price of IBM stock dropped from $135 to $102. Because IBM's assets had not changed from one day to the next, this drop is prima facie evidence that the stock market is not efficient. Comment on this statement.

10. On January 2, a steel company's common equity sold for $50 a share. Over the course of the year, a $5 dividend was paid. On January 2, a pharmaceutical company's common equity sold for $100 a share, and a $1 dividend was paid over the course of the year. Which company has a higher rate of return for the year?

11. When is it valid to use the following stock valuation models?
    a. $P_0 = D_1/(k - g)$
    b. $P_0 = D/k$
    c. $P_0 = D_1/(1 + k)$

12. To determine the value of a stock, we discount the expected dividends to be received at a risk-adjusted rate.
    a. Write a general formula for stock valuation in terms of the present value of a series of dividends.
    b. Using the formula you wrote for (a), explain the two ways in which a change in anticipated future inflation can change a stock's price.

13. The executives of an oil company recently announced a large new investment in foreign oil fields. Although currently underdeveloped, the executives know the fields will be very profitable in ten to 15 years. Despite this, the oil company's stock price dropped after the announcement. Can you explain this puzzle with a simple stock valuation model?

14. On May 18, 1988, Hewlett-Packard announced gains of 30 percent in fiscal second-quarter profit, but its stock price fell about 8 percent. How do you account for this seemingly paradoxical stock price move?

15. Comment on the following statement by one stock analyst following the stock market crash on Black Monday:

    Investors are intolerant of disappointment of any kind. You have to do better than expected just to stay even in stock price in this market.

16. According to one analyst, the cause of the stock market crash in October 1987 is easy to explain:

    There is a simple answer why stock market values had to decline sooner or later. In mid-October interest rates were around 10 percent. This created a price-to-earnings ratio on bonds of ten-to-one. At the same time the price-to-earnings ratio in the stock market was twenty-to-one. In other words, it took twenty dollars to earn on the stock market what it took only ten to earn on the bond market—a clear sign of how overvalued most stocks were.

Comment on this statement in light of your understanding of how stock and bond prices are determined.

17. When a firm repurchases its own shares, it pays out cash and receives treasury stock that is of no productive value to the firm. In what way could shareholders possibly gain from such a transaction?

18. An investor is considering placing $100,000 in the stock of either Corporation A or Corporation B. Although each sells for $52 per share, A's common stock has a par value of $2, whereas B's common stock has a par value of zero. Given that the prices are equal, which share is the better investment?

19. Although stock in Fred's Bakeries, Ltd., currently sells for $50 a share, each shareholder now has preemptive rights to buy an additional share for $40. Construct an example to convince yourself that this does *not* represent an increase in real wealth for a shareholder.

20. A company issues $1 million of floating-rate perpetuities. The bonds are sold at face value, and the coupon rate is adjusted instantaneously to reflect interest rate changes. Demonstrate that the bond will always sell at face value.

21. As of mid-1988, the price/earnings ratio for the average Japanese share was 69 in contrast to a P/E ratio for the average American share of about 14. In trying to explain this apparent discrepancy, a recent article in *The Economist* (August 6, 1988, p. 59) argued that, "Japanese share prices do not reflect the value of future earnings growth but of the growth of future asset value. Thus, a price/earnings ratio, however adjusted, is a useless guide to share performance and a measure such as price/book value is more useful."

    a. Comment on this statement.

    b. What other factors might account for the high Japanese P/E ratios?

22. MacroCorp. has had a string of product successes and analysts are forecasting profitable growth in the future. By contrast, MicroCorp. has had a series of product failures and analysts are saying that the company's future is dismal. Which company should you invest in? Does it matter?

PROBLEMS

1. Suppose the market interest rate is 10 percent. You buy a Treasury bill that will pay you $1,000 in one year.

    a. What is the maximum amount you would pay for the bill?

    b. If you bought the bill for $892.86, what interest rate will you earn for the year?

2. A security pays $10,000 with certainty in one year. The rate of interest is 8 percent per year.

    a. How much should you pay for the security?

    b. How much should you pay for the security if it pays off in two years instead of one?

    c. How much must a security pay at the end of two years to make it equal in value to the security paying $10,000 in one year?

3. You have purchased a two-year, $1,000 face value bond with a 10 percent coupon payment.

    a. If the required yield to maturity on the security is 10 percent, what will be its current price?

    b. If the current price is $1,000, at what price must you be able to sell the bond in one year to earn 10 percent on the investment if you buy the bond today?

    c. If the interest rate is 5 percent, for what price will the bond sell?

    d. Given a current price of $1,092.97, at what price must you be able to sell the bond in one year in order to earn 5 percent on your investment?

    e. Suppose you purchase the bond for $1,000 to yield 10 percent a year. One year later, the market interest rate has changed to 5 percent. What will be the price of the security then?

    f. Repeat (e), except assume the market interest rate has risen to 20 percent.

    g. With returns at 10 percent, what is the future value of the cash flows from the bond? That is, how much money will you have from the investment of your coupon income at 10 percent for two years plus your final principal repayment at maturity?

4. The Treasury is planning to sell a new, $1,000 face value, ten-year note with a 10 percent coupon.

    a. If the rate on similar securities is 10 percent, for how much will the note sell (assume semiannual coupon payments)?

    b. If rates on such securities rise to 12 percent, what will be the note's price?

    c. If rates remain at 12 percent, what will be the note's price one year from today?

    d. With rates remaining at 12 percent, what will the note's price be one year from maturity?

5. Refer to the Treasury note in problem 4.

    a. If the note is priced at $750, what is the note's rate of return?

    b. If the note is priced at $1,250, what is its rate of return?

6. Three bonds have a "10 percent" coupon rate. One pays 10 percent annually, one pays 10 percent semiannually (5 percent every six months), and one pays 10 percent monthly (10/12 percent each month). Which bond has the highest effective annual yield? What is the yield?

7. The price of the Ford bond at a 12 percent yield was $834.42.

    a. What will be the price of the bond if interest rates fall to 6 percent?

    b. What will be the price of the bond if interest rates rise to 18 percent?

8. An investor buys a two-year, 8 percent coupon bond, $1,000 par value.

    a. If the yield to maturity is 8 percent, what will be the price of the bond?

    b. For how much must the investor sell the bond in one year (after interest is received) to obtain an 8 percent rate of return on her investment?

    c. If the interest rate today is 10 percent, what will be the price of the bond?

    d. If the investor bought the bond for the price in (c), for how much must she sell the bond in one year to obtain a 10 percent rate of return on her investment?

9. The principal value of each of the following bonds is $1,000. The current yield on Treasury securities (of all maturities) is 12 percent.

> U.S. Treasury bond, 10 percent coupon, 10-year maturity
> U.S. Treasury note, 5 percent coupon, 10-year maturity
> U.S. Treasury bond, 10 percent coupon, 20-year maturity
> U.S. Treasury zero-coupon bond, 10-year maturity
> U.S. Treasury zero-coupon bond, 20-year maturity

Note: A zero-coupon bond pays no interest until maturity. Instead, it sells at a discount to its face value sufficient to yield the required return.

    a. What are the current prices of the bonds?

    b. If inflation is expected to increase by 2 percent annually (interest rates rise to 14 percent), what will be the change in the value of each bond?

    c. Which bond suffers the greatest percentage price decline because of inflation? Why? Which suffers the least percentage price decline? Why?

10. Two zero-coupon bonds each have a face value of $10,000. One matures in two years, and the other matures in five years.

    a. If the market rate of interest is 8 percent, what will be the prices of the two bonds?

    b. If inflation suddenly causes the interest rate to rise to 20 percent, what will be the new prices for the two bonds?

    c. Which bond suffers a greater percentage decrease in its price when the interest rate rises? Why?

11. Two bonds have a face value of $1,000 and a maturity of two years. One pays a yearly coupon of $200, whereas the other pays a yearly coupon of $50. For these two bonds, repeat items 10(a), 10(b), and 10(c).

12. A $10,000 Treasury bill matures in three months and currently sells for $9,764.54. What is the annual yield on the bill?

13. You are considering investing in two corporate bonds of equal risk:

Coupon Rate (%)	Maturity	Face Value
5	1 year	$1,000
20	1 year	$1,000

a. If the market rate of interest is 11 percent, at what prices will the bonds sell?
b. Your income tax rate is 50 percent and your capital gains tax rate is 25 percent. Income taxes are paid on interest received, and capital gains taxes are paid at maturity on the difference between the face value and purchase price. Which bond would you prefer to invest in? What after-tax rate of return would each bond give you?

14. In early 1988, the Mexican government sought to swap about $15 billion of its outstanding bank debt for $10 billion in bonds. The principal amount of the Mexican bonds would be secured by 20-year, zero-coupon U.S. Treasury bonds having a face value of $10 billion. Because of doubts about Mexico's creditworthiness, Mexican bank debt was then valued by the market at about 50 cents on the dollar.
a. What is the value of the U.S. Treasury bonds securing Mexico's $10 billion of principal repayments? Assume that the market yield on the zero-coupon U.S. Treasury bonds is 8.25 percent.
b. What will the $10 billion in Mexican bonds be worth if Mexico's creditworthiness is unchanged by the swap?
c. What is the value of the $15 billion in bank loans to Mexico before the swap?
d. Based on your analysis, how eager were banks likely to be to swap their bank loans for Mexican bonds?
e. As noted previously, the Mexican promise to pay $1 in bank debt is worth about 50 cents. Suppose the bond interest payments are less risky than bank debt payments. How much must a Mexican promise to pay $1 in bond interest be worth for the bond swap to be worthwhile (e.g., 32 cents, 47 cents)?

15. On December 15, 1987, Southland Corporation issued bonds due December 15, 2002, in conjunction with its leveraged buyout. These bonds pay no interest until December 15, 1992, but pay an 18 percent annual coupon semiannually afterward (the first coupon will be paid on June 15, 1993). If these bonds are priced to yield 16 percent, compounded semiannually, what will be their price at issue?

16. What will be the price of the three Atlantic Richfield preferred issues (see Section 3.4) if the required rate of return on each stock is 9 percent?

✓17. An investor is considering the purchase of a preferred share, which will pay a dividend of $3 per year in perpetuity.
a. If the current market rate of interest is 8 percent, what is the maximum price the investor should pay for the share?
b. Suppose there is a call provision and the issuing company has the right to repurchase the issue at a price of $20 in five years. Does this change your estimate of the maximum price an investor should pay for the share? Explain. (*Hint*: Under what circumstances is the firm most likely to call the preferred stock?)

18. Commonwealth Edison $2.75 preferred is currently selling for $15. What is the required rate of return on the stock?

19. Calculate the price of the Aetna Life preferred share in the text if
a. expected inflation suddenly increased the required yield by 2 percent.
b. Aetna announces it will redeem the preferred stock for $54.95 in 20 years.

20. Apex Products has an issue of 6 percent cumulative preferred stock on which it has paid no dividends for the past three years. This year's net income after tax is $900,000. If there are 20,000 shares ($100 par value) of the preferred outstanding and 200,000 shares of common, what will be the largest common dividend that Apex can pay this year?

21. A railroad has outstanding 400,000 shares of $3.50 cumulative preferred with a $50

par value. A participation feature requires that one half of any dividend in excess of $.50 paid to common stockholders must also be paid to preferred. For example, if common receives a $1 dividend, preferred will receive an extra 25 cents participation dividend. Suppose there are 2 million common shares outstanding. What would the dividends per share for common and preferred equal, given the following levels of after-tax earnings?

   a. $1,200,000.

   b. $2,200,000.

   c. $4,000,000.

22. The DeVeers Gem Co. has suffered through a slump in the diamond industry and, as a consequence, has not paid dividends on its $50 million, 4 percent preferred cumulative stock issue in three years.

   a. By the end of the third year, how much does DeVeers owe the preferred stockholders?

   b. If DeVeers' common stock is currently selling for $35 a share, how many shares might each preferred holder accept in compensation for the dividend arrears? There are currently 1.2 million shares of common stock outstanding.

23. Suppose Atlantic Richfield $2.80 convertible preferred is selling for $123 a share and its $3.00 convertible preferred is selling for $349.

   a. At what stock price will it be worthwhile for the preferred holders to convert their preferred shares?

   b. On the same day, Atlantic Richfield common is selling for $51.75. Will preferred shareholders convert their shares? Why or why not?

24. If holders of Atlantic Richfield knew that the firm would go bankrupt in five years, what would be the market price of the preferred shares today? Assume the preferred dividends are paid as scheduled until bankruptcy, and the rate of return required is 11 percent.

25. To finance a new product, work-out jewelry, Harold's Sports Co. plans to issue a $1.35 cumulative preferred stock. If the work-out jewelry is forecast to provide a 15 percent rate of return, at what price must the preferred sell to avoid diluting earnings?

26. A new office services firm has issued its first shares of common stock. The shares have a par value of $.50 a share and an issue price of $37.50; 100,000 shares were issued.

   a. Show the balance sheet accounts for the stock after the offering.

   b. If a buyer eventually obtained 250 shares of the stock for $.25, what will be her liability in the event of bankruptcy?

27. A stock sells for $50 on January 1 and pays $2 in cash dividends over the course of the year.

   a. If the stock closes at $60 on December 31, what was the rate of return for the year?

   b. If the stock closed at $40, what was the rate of return for the year?

28. A stock selling for $12.50 is expected to pay $5 in dividends during the year and has an expected rate of return of 8 percent. What is the expected price at the end of a year?

29. A stock with an expected rate of return of 15 percent will pay a dividend of $2 this year.

   a. If this dividend is paid in perpetuity, what will be the value of the stock?

   b. If this dividend grows by 10 percent a year in perpetuity, what will be the value of the stock?

   c. If the dividend grows by 10 percent a year for five years, 5 percent a year thereafter for 20 years, and then ceases to grow, what will be the value of the stock?

30. Two stocks currently pay a $1 dividend and have a required rate of return of 15 percent. However, the first stock sells for $20, whereas the second stock sells for only $10. Can you use the dividend growth model to explain this difference?

31. What would happen to the value of IBM stock (see Section 3.7) if the company made an announcement that indicated its risk-adjusted required rate of return had increased by 2 percent, to 17 percent?

a. What would happen to the stock price if the jump in the required return were associated with an increase in expected inflation from 0 percent to 2 percent annually (assume IBM's dividend payment would keep pace with inflation)?

b. What would happen to the stock price in (a) if IBM's ability to adjust for inflation was only 50 percent of the inflation rate (i.e., IBM could only raise its dividend by 1 percent a year)? What would happen to IBM's stock price if no adjustment to inflation were possible (i.e., the dividend stays constant in nominal terms)?

32. The management of Unioil is interested in calculating the value of the company's stock under four possible scenarios. Under the first, the company will experience declining oil revenue as old wells are depleted and substitute wells are not found; the second forecasts a steady state for the company; under the third, the company will grow with the economy; and under the fourth, the company will strike an extremely profitable but short-lived well and then resume growing along with the rest of the economy. Currently, the company pays an annual dividend of $2.10 per share; current earnings are $3.85 per share annually. The required rate of return for a stock like Unioil is 11 percent and is expected to remain so under all four scenarios. Find the price, dividend yield, and P/E ratio under each of the four growth scenarios, given the following projected dividend growth rates associated with these growth scenarios.

Scenario	1	2	3	4
$g =$	−3.5%	0.0%	4.0%	15% for 5 years, then 4% thereafter

33. Stock A has a required rate of return of 20 percent, a current dividend of $20, dividend growth of 10 percent, and a current market price of $150. Stock B has a required rate of return of 13 percent, a current dividend of $8, dividend growth of 8 percent, and a current market price of $200. Should investors take any positions in the stocks?

34. Stock A has a current price of $20, a current dividend of $2, and a return on equity of 15 percent.

a. If 60 percent of earnings are paid out as dividends, what will be the growth rate of earnings?

b. If the book value of equity is currently $20, what will it be in two years?

c. What is the stock's required rate of return?

35. An all-equity-financed firm has as its only asset a silver mine that produces 10,000 ounces per year. Currently, reserves are known to be 30,000 ounces; the price per ounce is $10; and the discount rate is 10 percent.

a. Suppose the price of silver is expected to remain constant. What is the value of the company's stock?

b. Suppose the price of silver is expected to drop by 5 percent a year over the life of the mine. Now what is the value of the company's stock?

c. If there is no limit on reserves and output is expected to grow by 3 percent per year forever, what will be the value of the stock, assuming that the price of silver remains at $10 per ounce?

36. The Bilson Company has outstanding common stock, preferred stock, and bonds. The common sells for $100 a share and is expected to pay a dividend of $3.20 per share. This dividend is expected to grow by 7 percent a year. The preferred stock pays an annual dividend of $4.50 in perpetuity and has a current market price of $52.50. The bonds have a face value of $1,000, a maturity of 30 years, a coupon of $90 paid annually, and a current price of $1,450.

a. What is the required rate of return for each security?

b. Can you rank the securities by riskiness? Explain your reasoning.

c. Determine a new price for each security if required rates of return increase by 50 percent.

37. Hotshot Enterprises is enjoying a period of very rapid growth in sales, earnings, and dividends. Hotshot is expected to pay a dividend of $10 per share next year (year 1),

and dividends are expected to grow at a 20 percent rate during the following two years (years 2 and 3). However, such rapid growth cannot be sustained. Beginning with the dividend in year 4, Hotshot's dividends are expected to grow steadily at a 5 percent rate forever. The required return on Hotshot stock is 10 percent.

a. What is the current price of a share of Hotshot?

b. What is the expected price per share in year 1?

c. What is the total expected rate of return in year 1?

d. What are the expected prices and rates of return in years 2–4?

38. Here are some data on Consolidated Edison Company for the period 1969 to 1973.

	1969	1970	1971	1972	1973
EPS	$2.68	$2.30	$2.35	$2.06	$2.32
DPS	$1.80	$1.80	$1.80	$1.80	$1.80
ROE	8.6%	7.5%	7.5%	6.7%	7.6%
Stock price	$30	$25	$27	$26	$22
Book value	$31	$31	$31	$31	$31
Utility bond rate	8.9%	9.0%	8.4%	7.8%	8.5%
Inflation rate	5.4%	5.9%	4.3%	3.3%	6.2%

By early 1974, Con Ed's bond rate had risen to 10.5 percent, but the Public Services Commission did not permit it to raise its rates.

a. Why is Con Ed stock selling at below book value?

b. Estimate the likely growth rate of Con Ed's dividend as of early 1974.

c. Suppose that the required return on Con Ed's stock equals the bond rate plus 4 percent. Based on your answer to (b), estimate the price of Con Ed stock as of early 1974.

d. U.S. prices rose 11 percent in 1974. If this rate of inflation persisted, what would happen to Con Ed's dividend without rate relief?

39. Suppose that Paradise Corp. has assets that generate perpetual (cash) earnings per share of $5 annually. Since Paradise has no reinvestment opportunities, it will pay out all its earnings as dividends; the level of assets will be maintained over time.

a. If investors require a 12 percent rate of return, what is the price of this no-growth firm?

b. Now suppose that because of an unexpected increase in consumer demand the management estimates that Paradise can increase its sales by expanding its capacity. Management concludes that the firm can reinvest 40 percent of its earnings annually for the next 20 years (i.e., at $t = 1, \ldots, 20$). These reinvested earnings are expected to generate a permanent 20 percent return. After the growth period, there will be no new growth opportunities. If investors require a 12 percent rate of return, what will be the share price of Paradise Corp. with its new growth opportunities?

CHAPTER

4

Risk and Return

The earth is just too small and fragile a basket
for the human race to keep all its eggs in.

ROBERT A. HEINLEIN

Risk is the common denominator of virtually all financial decisions. Investors deciding which securities to purchase, marketing managers deciding whether to launch a new product, plant managers deciding on the installation of a new production line, and financial executives deciding how to finance the firm's present operations and future investments all face choices that involve uncertain future cash flows. Evaluating these risks and factoring them into decisions are thus essential aspects of financial decision making.

The objective in making these decisions is not to avoid risk—that is impossible—but to recognize its existence and to ensure that compensation is adequate for the risks being borne. Compensation is required because investors are generally risk averse; that is, all other things being equal, investors prefer less risk to more risk. Of course, all other things are usually not equal, and so managers and investors must constantly select among choices entailing different amounts of risk and promised returns. To ensure comparability among the various alternatives, it is necessary to convert the uncertain future cash flows associated with each of the alternatives into their present values. This requires discounting the future cash flows for both the time value of money and the degree of risk involved.

But to estimate the risk-adjusted discount rate—a task that we have ignored up to now—we must be able to correctly measure and price financial risk. It is for this reason that perhaps the most important development in finance in the past 30 years is the ability to quantify what we mean by risk. The ability to measure risk has led, in turn, to new theoretical and empirical work relating risk and return. The result has been a vast increase in our understanding of how risky assets and projects are valued in a competitive market.

This chapter covers four major aspects of risk and return. Its purpose is to define risk and establish the link between risk and the required rate of return associated with various risky assets. Section 1 examines the historical record to see how returns on securities of differing riskiness have varied over time. Appendix 4A provides some basic concepts from probability theory that are used in the remaining sections of this chapter. Section 2 discusses the nature of risk in a portfolio context and demonstrates how, for the same level of expected return, risk can be reduced through portfolio diversification. Section 3 explores the implications of modern portfolio theory for the pricing of risky assets in a competitive market. Sections 4 and 5 discuss the capital asset pricing model (CAPM) and the arbitrage pricing theory (APT). Both the CAPM and the APT provide techniques that enable us to estimate the risk-adjusted discount rate for choices involving uncertainty. Section 6 examines the effects of international diversification.

The subject matter of this chapter is inherently quantitative. It relies on a heavy dose of probability theory and algebra, and it is not easily digested. But it is important because it provides the theoretical foundation for the study of risk in all financial decisions. Despite the technical nature of this material, the emphasis here is on the basic insights into the trade-off between risk and return implied by modern capital market theory, rather than on the theoretical methodology itself.

4.1 HISTORICAL RETURNS IN THE CAPITAL MARKET

Much of our theory depends on the notion that over long periods of time individuals figure out what is going on in financial markets and respond rationally to this information. It is worthwhile, therefore, to examine the historical evidence regarding the rates of return realized by investors holding different types of securities.

Our intuition tells us that stocks are riskier than are corporate bonds, which in turn are riskier than are default-free government bonds. A long-term government bond, in turn, whose price fluctuates with interest rate movements, should be riskier than a Treasury bill, whose short maturity largely insulates it from price variations. Therefore, we would expect that over time stocks would yield the highest average returns, followed in descending order by corporate bonds, government bonds, and Treasury bills.

It is clear from Table 4-1 that the empirical evidence supports our expectations. The data indicate that over the 63-year period from 1926 to 1988, the riskiest investment, common stock, earned the highest rate of return—12.1 percent a year in nominal terms and 8.9 percent in real terms, indicating that

TABLE 4-1 Average Annual Security Returns: 1926–1988	Security	Nominal Rate of Return (%)	Real Rate of Return (%)	Risk Premium (relative to Treasury bills) (%)
	Stocks	12.1 (10.43)*	8.9 (8.5)	8.5
	Long-term corporate bonds	5.3	2.1	1.7
	Long-term U.S. government bonds	4.7	1.5	1.1
	Short-term U.S. Treasury bills	3.6	.4	0

SOURCES: Roger G. Ibbotson and Rex A. Sinquefield, *Stocks, Bonds, Bills, and Inflation: The Past and the Future* (Charlottesville, Va.: 1982), Financial Analysts Research Foundation (updates courtesy of SBBI Yearbook, Chicago: Ibbotson Associates, 1988); and Jack W. Wilson and Charles P. Jones, "A Comparison of Annual Common Stock Returns: 1871–1925 with 1926–1985," *Journal of Business* (April 1987): Table 3, p. 245, and Table 4, p. 248.

*Numbers in parentheses refer to data from 1871–1988. Comparable data were unavailable for the other securities.

inflation averaged about 3 percent over this period. Corporate bonds earned a lower return, in line with their lower risk, and long-term government bonds earned even less. The worst performance was turned in by the safest investment, Treasury bills, which yielded about 3.6 percent annually in nominal terms and .4 percent in real terms. Thus, investors in common stock received a risk premium that averaged 8.5 percent annually relative to the return on Treasury bills.

The data on inflation-adjusted stock returns are remarkably similar whether one uses the 63-year period from 1926 to 1988 or the 118-year period from 1871 to 1988. The real return on the stock market for the shorter period was 8.9 percent versus 8.5 percent for the extended period.

The rationale for computing average returns using over 60 years worth of data (118 years in the case of stocks) is that prices, and hence returns, fluctuate so much that return comparisons based on averages taken over shorter periods of time are pointless. This is especially true for stock prices, which are highly volatile. Figure 4-1 shows how variable an investment the stock market has been historically.

These returns vary from a gain of 53.9 percent in 1933, following the stock market crash of 1929–1932, to a loss of 43.3 percent in 1931. Even in the least volatile periods, the 1890s and 1960s, there were dramatic year-to-year price fluctuations.

Figures 4-2(a) and 4-2(b) show histograms, or frequency distributions, of annual nominal and real stock market returns. The variability of returns is apparent in the wide spread of the annual outcomes from investing in the stock market.

FIGURE 4-1

Year-by-Year Total Stock Market Return: 1871–1988

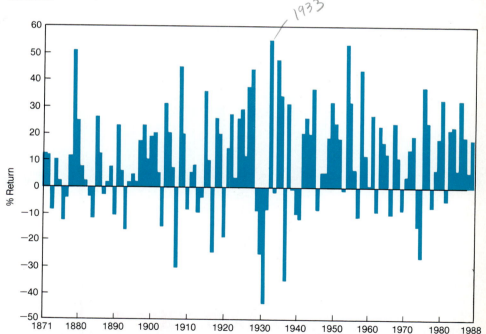

SOURCES: Jack W. Wilson and Charles P. Jones, "A Comparison of Annual Common Stock Returns: 1871–1925 with 1926–1985," *Journal of Business*, April 1987; Roger G. Ibbotson and Rex A. Sinquefield, *Stocks, Bonds, Bills, and Inflation* (SSBI). Updated in *SSBI 1987 Yearbook*. Ibbotson Associates.

FIGURE 4-2
(a) Histogram of
Nominal Annual
Rates of Return for
the U.S. Stock Mar-
ket: 1871–1988; (b)
Real Annual Rates
of Return for the
U.S. Stock Market

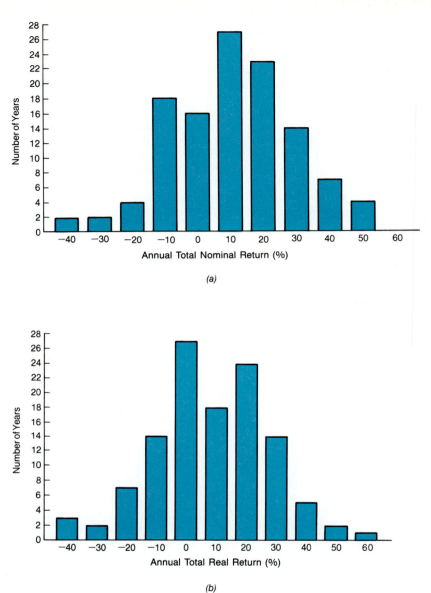

(a)

(b)

4.2
PORTFOLIO
RISK AND
RETURN

Appendix 4A shows how to estimate the risk and expected return for a single asset. To summarize, risk is usually thought of as the dispersion of possible outcomes around the expected return. Thus, the stock market is considered to be highly risky because of the wide range of year-to-year returns. The standard statistical measures of dispersion are the *variance* and *standard deviation*. They are defined as follows:

1. *Variance.* The variance, denoted by σ_R^2 and pronounced "sigma squared," is the sum of the squared deviations $[R_i - E(R)]$ between the actual returns, R_i, and the expected return, $E(R)$, weighted by the associated probabilities p_i:

$$\sigma_R^2 = \sum_{i=1}^{n} p_i[R_i - E(R)]^2$$

2. *Standard deviation.* The standard deviation of the return is simply the square root of the variance:

$$\sigma_R = (\sigma_R^2)^{1/2}$$

where σ (sigma) is the symbol for the standard deviation.

Most investors, however, do not put all their eggs in one basket. They typically own portfolios containing a variety of assets, including different stocks, bonds, real estate, and precious metals. What matters to well-diversified investors, therefore, is not the riskiness of individual securities held in isolation but the risk of their portfolios.[1] Thus, the relevant risk and return of a security to such an investor is the contribution of that security to the variability and return of the portfolio in which it is included. To fully explore the concept of contribution to portfolio risk requires a theory of portfolio risk and return. Before getting into all the technical details of portfolio theory, however, it is worthwhile to examine a concrete example of this somewhat abstract concept. The auto insurance business provides a good illustration.

An insurance company like State Farm holds a portfolio of auto insurance contracts. The net return on any one of these contracts, equal to the difference between the insurance premium and the claims paid out, is essentially unpredictable. It could be either positive, if no claim is filed, or significantly negative, if the insured gets into an expensive accident. Thus, any single insurance contract held by State Farm is highly risky.

But State Farm insures millions of cars and can predict with a great deal of certainty just how many accidents it will have to pay for. Therefore, the unpredictability of individual driving records contributes very little to the riskiness of State Farm's insurance portfolio. This means that most of the risk associated with the uncertainty of a specific individual's accident experience can be diversified away. Competition among insurance firms ensures that this individual risk is not priced in an automobile insurance contract; that is, insurance companies will charge a fee based on an individual's expected driving record; they will not charge an additional fee for bearing the risk associated with driver unpredictability. This is a basic principle of risk in finance: *Risk that can be eliminated through diversification does not command a risk premium.*

---

[1]Bondholders, managers, employees, customers, and other parties may well be concerned about the total risk of a company, and this will affect the company's future cash flows. But only the systematic component of risk should affect the discount rate. The effects of total risk on future cash flows are elaborated in Chapter 8.

Auto insurance portfolios do contain elements of risk that cannot be diversified away, however. Consider the effect of a shock such as the quadrupling of oil prices in 1973. The jump in oil prices induced people to drive significantly less. This meant fewer accidents per capita. In addition, the introduction of the 55-mile-per-hour speed limit further reduced the amount and severity of auto accidents. These factors systematically lowered claims costs, thereby raising the returns to State Farm on all its auto insurance contracts. On the other hand, because insurance premiums are set ahead of time, unexpectedly high inflation during the late 1970s led to unexpectedly high repair costs (because the cost of parts and labor rose in line with inflation) and therefore to unexpected losses on even the best-diversified insurance portfolio. From the standpoint of an insurance company, these risks are systematic; no matter how well diversified its portfolio of insurance contracts, returns on the portfolio are affected by oil price shocks and inflation. These risks systematically affect all assets to a greater or lesser extent and therefore will influence their required returns. This brings us to the second fundamental principle of risk in finance: *The market demands a return premium from an asset according to the asset's contribution to the risk of a fully diversified portfolio.*

APPLICATION
Lloyd's of London

The biggest loss in the 290-year history of Lloyd's of London—claims of up to $300 million—resulted from the insurance market's failure to distinguish adequately between diversifiable and nondiversifiable risk. The trouble began when Lloyd's devised an insurance contract protecting leasing companies against losing money on canceled computer leases. Such losses could arise from having to re-lease the computer at a lower rental. Lease terminations resulting from factors affecting specific businesses are clearly diversifiable. But Lloyd's failed to anticipate the risk of technological obsolescence that would systematically affect the value of all computers out on lease. This risk materialized in 1977 when IBM introduced a new, less expensive line of computers that outmoded the older 370s, for which most of the insurance was written. As customers canceled leases, the 370s had to be remarketed at distress prices and the leasing companies filed claims against Lloyd's.

Returning to the development of modern portfolio theory, we note that the motive for holding a diversified portfolio of risky securities is to reduce the variability of overall returns. *Diversification works because stock prices don't move perfectly in phase with one another.* At the same time that some stocks are moving up, others are moving down and still others are not moving at all. The result is that some of the fluctuations in individual stocks cancel out. In general, therefore, the variability of portfolio returns is less than the average variability of returns on its component assets. This is reflected in the following important rule: *The risk of a portfolio depends not only on the inherent riskiness of its component assets but also on how returns on those assets relate to one another.*

Figure 4-3 shows how diversification can almost halve the standard deviation of returns on a stock portfolio. According to recent data, the standard deviation of the average stock listed on the New York Stock Exchange (NYSE) is approximately 28 percent. This contrasts with a standard deviation of about 15

FIGURE 4-3
Market Risk and
Unique Risk

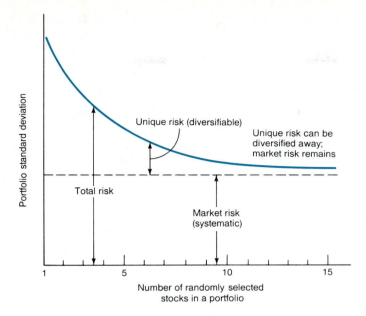

percent for the "market portfolio," the fully diversified portfolio consisting of all 2,081 stocks listed on the NYSE. Fortunately for the average investor, it is not necessary to hold all 2,081 NYSE-listed stocks to benefit substantially from diversification. Figure 4-3 reveals that most of the benefits of diversification can be achieved with as few as ten different stocks. As additional securities are added to the portfolio, its standard deviation decreases, but at a decreasing rate.

Systematic Versus Unsystematic Risk

Figure 4-3 also shows that the part of risk that is eliminated through diversification is risk that is unique to the stock or group of stocks in the portfolio. Market risk, which affects all stocks to a greater or lesser extent, cannot be diversified away. This division of risk summarizes the basic insight of modern portfolio theory:

$$\text{Total risk} = \text{Market risk} + \text{Unique risk}$$

Unique risk is known as **diversifiable** or **unsystematic risk**. It is an important component of risk because many of the uncertainties confronting the typical firm are unique to that firm and perhaps to some of its competitors. Diversifiable risks include such things as changing consumer tastes, labor strikes, new product developments, or marketing campaigns that affect a firm's competitive position, and fluctuations in raw materials prices. For example, major risks affecting Maxwell House, General Foods' coffee division, include unpredictable changes in its market share, fluctuations in the price of green coffee beans, and the uncertain number of people switching among coffee, tea, and soft drinks. Depending on what happens to the Brazilian coffee bean crop and therefore to the price of coffee beans and how many people shift from drinking coffee to, say, Coca-Cola or from Maxwell House to Nestle's Taster's Choice, Maxwell House could do better or worse than expected. Because these risk factors are limited to the small number of firms competing in the beverage industry, they can be diversified away.

No matter how well diversified you are, however, there is some risk you just can't avoid. This unavoidable component of risk is known as **market** or **systematic risk**. It exists because certain risk factors—such as variations in the GNP growth rate, changes in the level of real interest rates, or oil price shocks—systematically affect all firms in the economy to a greater or lesser extent. The existence of common risk factors explains why stocks tend to move together. It also means that no matter how many different stocks investors hold, they are still exposed to the vagaries of the market.

This was vividly demonstrated on October 19, 1987, when 1,973 of the 2,081 stocks traded on the New York Stock Exchange (95 percent) dropped in price. No matter how well diversified, a stock market investor would have suffered. However, even on Black Monday, Table 4-2 shows that although the NYSE stocks dropped an average of 19.2 percent, some stocks dropped far more, whereas others actually gained.

TABLE 4-2
Biggest Price Percentage Gainers . . . and Losers on October 19, 1987

NYSE	Close	Change	% Change		Close	Change	% Change
Newmont Gold	39½ +	3¾ +	10.5	US Home Corp	1⅝ −	2⅜ −	−59.4
Callahan Mining	32½ +	2¼ +	7.4	Amer Century	1 −	1¼ −	−55.6
Dallas Corp	12½ +	¾ +	6.4	Valley Indus	1½ −	1½ −	−50.0
Sunshine	5¾ +	¼ +	4.5	Unvl Matchbx	4 −	3¾ −	−48.4
Public Svc NH	3⅛ +	⅛ +	4.2	Malaysia Fund	5⅜ −	5 −	−48.2
Super Valu Str	20½ +	½ +	2.5	Telerate	10½ −	7⅝ −	−42.1
Benguet Corp	5½ +	⅛ +	2.3	Liggett Grp	7 −	4¾ −	−40.4
Northgate	6⅝ +	⅛ +	1.9	Brunswick	x14⅝ −	9¾ −	−40.0
Grwth Stk Outlk	9 +	⅛ +	1.4	Scudder Asia	6¼ −	4⅛ −	−39.8
ASA Ltd	65 +	⅛ +	.2	Holiday Corp	19⅜ −	11⅜ −	−37.0
OTC (Nasdaq NMS)							
Northview	18¼ +	4¼ +	30.4	Berkshire	170 −	720 −	−80.9
Durmed Pharm	5½ +	¾ +	15.8	Amer Integrity	2⅛ −	2⅜ −	−52.8
Silver State Mn	2 7/16 +	¼ +	11.4	Franklin Cmptr	5¾ −	4⅞ −	−45.9
Rpublc Auto Prt	6½ +	½ +	8.3	Higby's (J.) In	4¼ −	3 −	−41.4
Fed Sav Bk PR	14 +	1 +	7.7	Norsk Data A.S	20 −	14 −	−41.2
AMEX							
St. Joe Gold	16⅛ +	1 +	6.6	A. Tr Amoco.s	5 −	9¼ −	−64.9
Vintage Enterp	2⅛ +	⅛ +	6.2	A. Tr Exxon.s	17 −	14 −	−45.2
Inco Oppty Rlty	12¼ +	⅝ +	5.4	A. TrGM.s	6 −	4¾ −	−44.2
Cntrl Fd Cda	6½ +	¼ +	4.0	A. Tr Brstl.s	12¾ −	10 −	−44.0
American Cap	3⅞ +	⅛ +	3.3	GTI Corp	4⅛ −	3⅛ −	−43.1

SOURCE: *Wall Street Journal,* October 20, 1987, p. 73.

TABLE 4-3 Probability Distributions for Stocks A and B	State of the Economy	Probability	Return on Stock A (%)	Return on Stock B (%)
	Boom	.25	18	6
	Normal	.50	16	15
	Recession	.25	10	24

Stocks can be categorized as cyclical, countercyclical, or acyclical. A *cyclical* stock is one whose returns move in line with the state of the economy. It does well when the economy does well and poorly when the economy does poorly. Auto stocks are generally cyclical. A *countercyclical* stock, on the other hand, does well when the economy does poorly and poorly when the economy does well. An example here would be an auto replacement parts manufacturer because consumers tend to hold onto their cars longer during hard times, fixing them up as they break down rather than replacing them. A third group of stocks seems to be *acyclical*. Their returns may vary, but not with the business cycle. Acyclical stocks would include the shares of medical supply companies like Johnson & Johnson and Baxter Travenol. Demand for their products, sold to hospitals and doctors, is strong in good times and holds up in economic slumps. Most stocks are cyclical, moving in step with general economic conditions and, therefore, in line with one another. Hence, it is the countercyclical and acyclical stocks that supply the greatest degree of diversification.

To illustrate the benefits, and the limits, of diversification, consider the two stocks, A and B, whose returns are described in Table 4-3. Stock A is cyclical, and stock B is countercyclical. The means and standard deviations of these stocks are calculated in Table 4-4 and summarized in Table 4-5.

Suppose you had the choice of investing in one or both of these two stocks. It might seem logical to invest all your money in stock A because it has the same

TABLE 4-4 Calculation of Expected Returns and Standard Deviations for Stocks A and B	**Expected Return**
	Stock A $.25 \times 18\% + .50 \times 16\% + .25 \times 10\% = 15\%$
	Stock B $.25 \times 6\% + .50 \times 15\% + .25 \times 24\% = 15\%$
	Standard Deviation
	Stock A $\sigma_A^2 = .25(18 - 15)^2 + .50(16 - 15)^2 + .25(10 - 15)^2$
	$= .25(3)^2 + .50(1)^2 + .25(-5)^2$
	$= 9$
	$\sigma_A = (9)^{1/2}$
	$= 3\%$
	Stock B $\sigma_B^2 = .25(6 - 15)^2 + .50(15 - 15)^2 + .25(24 - 15)^2$
	$= .25(-9)^2 + .5(0) + .25(9)^2$
	$= 40.5$
	$\sigma_B = (40.5)^{1/2}$
	$= 6.4\%$

TABLE 4-5		Expected Return (%)	Standard Deviation (%)
Expected Returns and Standard Deviations for Stocks A and B	Stock A	15	3.0
	Stock B	15	6.4

15 percent expected return as stock B but a significantly lower standard deviation, 3 percent as opposed to B's 6.4 percent. Your intuition would be wrong if you think that.

By holding a portfolio containing both securities, you can achieve the same expected return, but with less risk than if you invested in only stock A. This is the magic of portfolio diversification. To see this, it is necessary to establish the formulas for calculating the expected return and standard deviation of a portfolio.

Portfolio Expected Return

Suppose you invested half your money in shares of A and the other half in shares of B. Your expected return on this portfolio is $.5 \times 15\% + .5 \times 15\% = 15$ percent. This illustrates the following general principle: *The expected return on a portfolio of securities is just the weighted average of the expected returns of the component securities, when the weights equal the fraction of the portfolio's value accounted for by each security.* In mathematical terms, this means that

$$E(R_p) = \sum_{i=1}^{n} w_i E(R_i)$$

and

$$w_i = V_i/I$$

where $E(R_p)$ is the expected return on the portfolio, $E(R_i)$ is the expected return on asset i, n is the number of assets in the portfolio, and w_i is the value of the investment in asset i, V_i, as a fraction of the total investment I in the portfolio.

Portfolio Standard Deviation

As mentioned, the contribution of an individual asset to a portfolio's risk is apt to be less than the asset's own standard deviation, owing to the diversification effect. We will now explore the exact nature of this diversification effect.

The weighted average of the individual standard deviations of a portfolio containing equal dollar amounts of stocks A and B is $.5 \times 3\% + .5 \times 6.4\% = 4.7$ percent. This is not, however, the standard deviation of overall portfolio returns. To aid in calculating the portfolio standard deviation, Table 4-6 contains the probability distribution of returns on a portfolio consisting of equal investments in both assets.

	State of the Economy	Probability	Return on Portfolio (%)	Deviation from Expected Return of 15% (%)
TABLE 4-6 Probability Distribution of the Portfolio	Boom	.25	12.0	−3.0
	Normal	.50	15.5	.5
	Recession	.25	17.0	2.0

The standard deviation of returns on this portfolio is

$$\sigma_p = [.25(-3)^2 + .50(.5)^2 + .25(2)^2]^{1/2}$$

$$= (3.375)^{1/2}$$

$$= 1.8 \text{ percent}$$

The portfolio standard deviation of 1.8 percent is 40 percent below the weighted average of the individual standard deviations, 4.7 percent, as calculated. Looking at Table 4-3, we see why this should be the case. Stocks A and B move out of phase with each other, thereby canceling out some of their individual variation. During a boom, when A is doing well, B is doing poorly, whereas in a recession, B's returns pick up at the same time A's returns are slumping. In technical terms, stocks A and B are said to be *negatively correlated* with each other. This means that on average, when returns on one stock are moving up, returns on the other stock are moving down. This brings up an important message: *To calculate the standard deviation of a portfolio of assets, it is necessary to take into account not only their individual standard deviations but also the comovement of returns on the assets.*

Portfolio Risk and Correlation

The extent to which security returns tend to move together can be measured by the *correlation coefficient*. The correlation coefficient between two securities i and j, r_{ij}, takes on values between -1 and $+1$. A positive correlation, such as exists between Ford and General Motors stock, indicates that the security returns tend to move in the same direction; securities that are negatively correlated tend to move in opposite directions. A zero correlation means that the security returns vary independently of each other. A related statistical measure of the tendency of two variables to move together that is often used in place of or in addition to the correlation coefficient is the *covariance*. The covariance between variables i and j, σ_{ij}, is $r_{ij}\sigma_i\sigma_j$.

The less positive or more negative the correlation or covariance among securities is, the greater the risk-reducing benefits of portfolio diversification will be; conversely, combining securities that are highly positively correlated into a portfolio provides little in the way of risk reduction. Thus, a portfolio containing Ford and GM stock provides less diversification than does one containing Ford and IBM stock. Perfect positive correlation ($r_{ij} = +1$) or negative correlation ($r_{ij} = -1$) is rare among securities. Most asset returns tend to move together, but not in lockstep. Thus, despite the generally positive correlation among asset returns, the risk-reducing benefits from diversification are enormous. Figure 4-3 shows that diversification can remove almost half the variation in the average stock.

The general formula for the standard deviation of a two-asset portfolio with correlation coefficient r_{12} and weights w_1 and w_2, where $w_1 + w_2 = 1$, is

$$\text{Portfolio standard deviation} = [w_1^2\sigma_1^2 + w_2^2\sigma_2^2 + 2w_1w_2r_{12}\sigma_1\sigma_2]^{1/2} \tag{4.1}$$

For example, suppose the standard deviations of the returns on Exxon and 3M stock are 31 percent and 44 percent, respectively, and the correlation between their returns is .14. According to Equation 4.1, a portfolio invested 60 percent in Exxon stock and 40 percent in 3M stock will have a standard deviation of

$$\sigma_p = [(.6 \times 31)^2 + (.4 \times 44)^2 + 2 \times .6 \times .4 \times .14 \times 31 \times 44]^{1/2}$$

$$= (747.38)^{1/2}$$

$$= 27.3 \text{ percent}$$

The portfolio standard deviation of 27.3 percent is less than the standard deviation of either Exxon or 3M. By contrast, the weighted average of the individual standard deviations is

$$.6 \times 31\% + .4 \times 44\% = 36.2\%$$

Thus, diversification reduces the portfolio's standard deviation, in absolute terms, by 8.9 percent (36.2% − 27.3%) or, in relative terms, by a fraction equal to 24.6 percent (8.9/36.2). In other words, the standard deviation of the portfolio is only about 75 percent of the average standard deviation of its component stocks. As we vary the weights attached to the stocks, the expected return and standard deviation of the portfolio will change in line with Equation 4.1.

APPLICATION
Estimating Portfolio Risk and Return

Two companies have the following risk characteristics:

	Expected Return (%)	Standard Deviation (%)
Brooklyn Cement Inc.	12	8
Bronx Power & Light	8	5

If the correlation between the two firms is .2, what will be the expected returns and standard deviations of the following portfolios?

Portfolio	Percentage Invested in	
	Cement	Power & Light
1	50	50
2	25	75
3	75	25

SOLUTION   For portfolio 1,

$$\text{expected return} = .5 \times 12\% + .5 \times 8\%$$

$$= 10\%$$

$$\text{standard deviation} = [(.5 \times 8)^2 + (.5 \times 5)^2 + 2 \times .5 \times .5 \times .2 \times 8 \times 5]^{1/2}$$

$$= 5.12\%$$

For portfolio 2,

$$\text{expected return} = .25 \times 12\% + .75 \times 8\%$$

$$= 9\%$$

$$\text{standard deviation} = [(.25 \times 8)^2 + (.75 \times 5)^2 + 2 \times .25 \times .75 \times .2 \times 8 \times 5]^{1/2}$$

$$= 4.59\%$$

For portfolio 3,

$$\text{expected return} = .75 \times 12\% + .25 \times 8\%$$

$$= 11\%$$

$$\text{standard deviation} = [(.75 \times 8)^2 + (.25 \times 5)^2 + 2 \times .75 \times .25 \times .2 \times 8 \times 5]^{1/2}$$

$$= 6.37\%$$

Figure 4-4 shows the expected returns and standard deviations for all possible portfolio combinations of Brooklyn Cement and Bronx Power.

FIGURE 4-4
Expected Returns
and Standard Devia-
tions for All Possible
Portfolio Combina-
tions of Brooklyn
Cement and Bronx
Power & Light

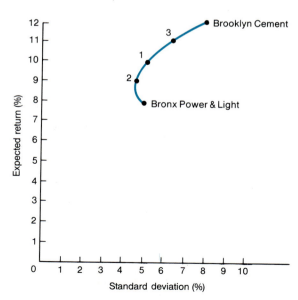

The covariance between the returns of two assets A and B can be calculated directly as

$$\sigma_{AB} = \sum_{i=1}^{n} p_i[R_{Ai} - E(R_A)][R_{Bi} - E(R_B)]$$

where p_i is the probability of outcome i occurring and R_{Ai} and R_{Bi} are the returns on assets A and B if outcome i occurs. $E(R_A)$ and $E(R_B)$ are the expected returns on assets A and B.

APPLICATION
Estimating Project Risk and Return

A firm faces two investment opportunities. A financial analyst has estimated the rate of return for each project for three levels of economic growth:

State of Economy	Probability of State	Project A Return (%)	Project B Return (%)
Recession	.2	−10	5
Normal	.6	15	10
Boom	.2	30	15

For each project, calculate the expected return and standard deviation. Then, calculate the covariance and correlation between the projects.

SOLUTION   For project A,

$$\text{expected return} = .2 \times -10\% + .6 \times 15\% + .2 \times 30\%$$

$$= 13\%$$

$$\text{standard deviation} = [.2(-10 - 13)^2 + .6(15 - 13)^2 + .2(30 - 13)^2]^{1/2}$$

$$= 12.88\%$$

For project B,

$$\text{expected return} = .2 \times 5\% + .6 \times 10\% + .2 \times 15\%$$

$$= 10\%$$

$$\text{standard deviation} = [.2(5 - 10)^2 + .6(10 - 10)^2 + .2(15 - 10)^2]^{1/2}$$

$$= 3.16\%$$

The covariance of returns between projects A and B is

$$\sigma_{AB} = .2(-10 - 13)(5 - 10) + .6(15 - 13)(10 - 10) + .2(30 - 13)(15 - 10)$$

$$= 40$$

The correlation between A and B is

$$r_{AB} = \sigma_{AB}/(\sigma_A \sigma_B)$$

$$= \frac{40}{12.88 \times 3.16}$$

$$= .983$$

A correlation this high means that the returns on these two projects vary very closely with each other. It also means there are minimal diversification benefits from undertaking both projects.

**4.3
MODERN
PORTFOLIO
THEORY AND
THE PRICING
OF CAPITAL
ASSETS**

It has long been recognized that diversification reduces risk, but that was the extent of knowledge about portfolios until 1952. In that year, Harry Markowitz, known as the "father of modern portfolio theory," published an article showing the exact relationship between stock return correlations and risk reduction.[2] But Markowitz was concerned with more than diversification per se; he was most interested in the basic principles of portfolio construction. These principles became the foundation for the study of the relationship between risk and return.

Markowitz recognized that a set of securities can be combined into an infinite number of portfolios by varying the weights assigned to the different securities. This is illustrated in Figure 4-5. Each cross represents the expected return and standard deviation associated with an individual security. By combining these securities into portfolios and varying the weights on the stocks, you can attain a much wider range of risk–return combinations. The shaded area shows all the possible combinations of expected return and standard deviation associated with the set of feasible portfolios.

FIGURE 4-5
Portfolio Creation
with Different Com-
binations of Stocks

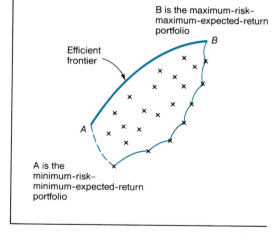

²Harry Markowitz, "Portfolio Selection," *Journal of Finance*, March 1952, pp. 77–91.

But investors, despite varying investment criteria, will be interested only in a subset of these feasible portfolios. This is the subset of efficient portfolios. An **efficient portfolio** is one that has the smallest possible standard deviation for its level of expected return *and* has the maximum expected return for a given level of risk. Only this subset is consistent with the two objectives common to all rational, risk-averse investors: *higher return* and *lower risk*. These portfolios, which lie along the solid dark line at the top of the feasible set, comprise the **efficient set**, more commonly termed the **efficient frontier**. The efficient set of portfolios can be computed using a mathematical programming technique known as *quadratic programming*.

Optimal Portfolio Selection

Even the efficient frontier contains an infinite number of possible portfolio combinations, ranging from the minimum-risk–minimum-return portfolio (portfolio A) to the maximum-risk–maximum-return portfolio (portfolio B). Each represents a different risk–return trade-off: The higher the expected return is, the more risk that must be assumed. No one portfolio is inherently better than any other. The optimal portfolio choice will vary from investor to investor and depend on the investor's degree of risk aversion. Those investors willing to take on added risk in the hope of earning a higher return will select a portfolio closer to B; those more risk averse will prefer a portfolio closer to A.

Optimal Portfolio Selection with a Risk-free Security. The opportunity to borrow or lend at a risk-free rate r_f has a powerful implication for optimal portfolio selection. If you invest part of your money in a riskless security like a Treasury bill and the remainder in an efficient portfolio—like C in Figure 4-6—you can obtain any combination of expected return and risk lying along the line connecting the points r_f and C. For example, if you invest half your funds in the Treasury bill and the other half in portfolio C, your risk–return combination will be point D, halfway between r_f and C. It is evident from Figure 4-6, however, that you can do better than point D. For example, point E has a higher expected return but no added risk, whereas point F has the same expected return as D but less risk. Points E and F both lie on the line connecting points r_f and M. This line contains all possible combinations of the risk-free security and portfolio M.[3] Investors will always prefer to hold combinations of the risk-free security and portfolio M because they offer a superior risk–return trade-off.

In fact, the points on line $r_f MG$, which is just tangent to the efficient frontier of risky portfolios, represent the best attainable combinations of risk and return. Thus, this line, which is known as the **capital market line** (CML), dominates all other lines. No matter which point on another line you select, you can earn a higher return with the same amount of risk or less risk for the same return by selecting combinations of the risk-free security and the tangency portfolio M. If you lend money at the risk-free rate r_f, you will wind up at a point on the line

---

[3] If w is the fraction of funds invested in the risk-free asset (with $1 - w$ being the fraction invested in portfolio M), then the expected return on the newly formed portfolio will be $wr_f + (1 - w)r_m$ and the standard deviation will be $(1 - w)\sigma_m$, where r_m and σ_m are the expected return and standard deviation of portfolio M. Thus both risk and expected return are linear in w. This means that the risk and expected return of all portfolios involving possible combinations of the risk-free asset and portfolio M lie on line $r_f MG$.

FIGURE 4-6

Selection of Optimal
Portfolio when
Riskless Investment
Is Available

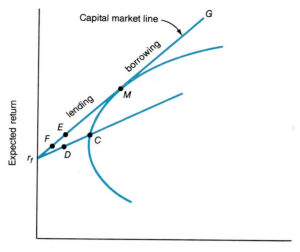

segment r_fM; if you borrow money to leverage your investment in portfolio M, you will be at a point on the line segment MG. Therefore, when riskless borrowing and lending is available, the set of efficient portfolios is represented by the CML; it is no longer the curved portion of the set of feasible risky portfolios connecting points A and B. Thus, *portfolio M is now the only efficient portfolio of risky assets.*

If all investors share the same probability beliefs, they all will hold only efficient portfolios that are linear combinations of the risk-free asset and portfolio M. For the market to be in equilibrium, M must be the **market portfolio**; that is, M must contain each asset in proportion to that asset's share of the total market value of all assets. This means that if IBM comprises 5 percent of the market value of all securities, then 5 percent of portfolio M must consist of IBM stock.

If all investors hold the market portfolio (or a reasonably well-diversified facsimile), which by definition contains no unsystematic risk, then only market risk will matter. This leads to one of the most important insights of modern finance theory: *Because the risk of a well-diversified portfolio depends only on the market risk of its component securities, the relevant risk of any security is its sensitivity to general market movements.*

The idea that only market or systematic risk matters underlies the pricing of risk. This can be seen by focusing attention on the capital market line. The CML has an intercept of r_f and a slope equal to $(r_m - r_f)/\sigma_m$, where r_m is the required return on the market portfolio and σ_m is the standard deviation of M. The term $r_m - r_f$ is known as the **market risk premium**. It depends on the average degree of investor risk aversion and the amount of market risk. Dividing the market risk premium through by σ_m yields the **market price of risk**:

$$\text{Market price of risk} = (r_m - r_f)/\sigma_m$$

The market price of risk is so called because it describes the risk premium expected by investors per unit of market risk, as measured by the standard deviation of the market return. For example, we saw earlier that historically, r_m = 12.1 percent, r_f = 3.6 percent, and σ_m = 15 percent, where the returns are in nominal terms. Thus, based on the historical data,

$$\text{Market price of risk} = (12.1 - 3.6)/15$$

$$= .57 \text{ percent}$$

This number means that historically, investors have received about .57 percent in added return for each additional unit of risk that they were willing to bear when holding an efficient portfolio.

Because any efficient portfolio P must lie on the CML, the relationship between risk and return for such a portfolio is linear:

$$\begin{array}{c} \text{Required return} \\ \text{on portfolio P} \end{array} = \begin{array}{c} \text{Risk-free} \\ \text{return} \end{array} + \begin{array}{c} \text{Market price} \\ \text{of risk} \end{array} \times \begin{array}{c} \text{Standard deviation} \\ \text{of portfolio P} \end{array}$$

$$r_p = r_f + \frac{(r_m - r_f)}{\sigma_m} \sigma_p \qquad\qquad \textbf{(4.2)}$$

Equation 4.2 says that the required return on an efficient portfolio P, r_p, equals the risk-free rate of interest plus a risk premium equal to the market price of risk multiplied by the standard deviation of the portfolio σ_p. An important implication of Equation 4.2 is that the risk premium on the efficient portfolio $r_p - r_f$ varies directly in proportion to its standard deviation. For example, doubling σ_p doubles the required risk premium.

It is always possible that investors will have access to different information, and so each will hold a different risky portfolio. This is highly unlikely, however, in an efficient market in which information is widely disseminated and available at nominal cost. In such a world, investors will wind up with similar beliefs and information. We have already seen that this will result in everybody's holding the market portfolio M. In that case, the relevant risk of a security is its contribution to the risk of the market portfolio. As noted earlier, this is the security's *systematic* or *market* risk.

Market Risk and Beta

The market risk of a security, in turn, depends on how sensitive it is to movements in the market portfolio. The sensitivity of an asset's return to market movements is called **beta** (β); beta measures the systematic risk of a security. Because the market portfolio's volatility relative to itself is 1, the market portfolio has a beta of 1.0. A stock with a beta of 1.5 will be one and a half times as volatile as the market is. When the market goes up 1 percent, the stock will go up, on average, 1.5 percent. Similarly, a stock with a beta of .5 will tend to move only about half as much as the market will. If the market goes up by 1 percent, the stock will generally rise only .5 percent. Conversely, a 1 percent drop in the market will cause the stock to drop by about .5 percent on average.

Technically, the beta of a risky asset i is the covariance of returns on that asset with returns on the market, σ_{im}, divided by the variance of the market return:

$$\text{Beta for asset } i = \frac{\text{Covariance between returns on asset } i \text{ and the return on the market portfolio}}{\text{Variance of the market portfolio}}$$

$$\beta_i = \sigma_{im}/\sigma_m^2$$

As defined earlier, $\sigma_{im} = r_{im}\sigma_i\sigma_m$. Making the substitution yields

$$\beta_i = r_{im}\sigma_i\sigma_m/\sigma_m^2 = r_{im}\sigma_i/\sigma_m \qquad \textbf{(4.3)}$$

As Equation 4.3 shows, another interpretation of beta is that it measures the fraction $r_{im}\sigma_i$ of the asset's standard deviation that contributes to the market

---

APPLICATION
Estimating Beta

Suppose the probability distribution of returns for the market and Davis, Inc. are as follows:

Market Conditions	Probability	Market Return (%)	Davis, Inc. Return (%)
Good	.2	22	55
Average	.4	17	25
Bad	.3	7	5
Worse	.1	−13	−25

What is the beta for Davis, Inc.?

SOLUTION Calculate the variance for the market, the covariance of the returns on the market and Davis, Inc., and then use Equation 4.3 to calculate beta.

Expected return for the market
$$= .2 \times 22\% + .4 \times 17\% + .3 \times 7\% + .1 \times -13\%$$
$$= 12\%$$

Variance of the market
$$= .2(22 - 12)^2 + .4(17 - 12)^2 + .3(7 - 12)^2 + .1(-13 - 12)^2$$
$$= 100$$

Expected return for Davis, Inc.
$$= .2 \times 55\% + .4 \times 25\% + .3 \times 5\% + .1 \times -25\%$$
$$= 20\%$$

Covariance of returns
$$= .2(22 - 12)(55 - 20) + .4(17 - 12)(25 - 20) + .3(7 - 12)(5 - 20) + .1(-13 - 12)(-25 - 20)$$
$$= 215$$

Beta of Davis, Inc.
$$= \frac{\text{Covariance between Davis and the market}}{\text{Variance of the market}}$$
$$= 215/100$$
$$= 2.15$$

portfolio's risk. Thus, if w_i is the weight of asset i in the market portfolio, $w_i\beta_i$ will be its relative contribution to the risk of the market portfolio. A stock with a beta exceeding 1.0 contributes a more than proportionate share of risk to the market portfolio. For example, Wang Labs has a beta of about 1.50. This means that it contributes 50 percent more risk than does the average stock in the market portfolio (because the average beta must be 1.0). By contrast, Consolidated Edison, with a beta of .70, contributes substantially less than its proportionate share to the market portfolio's riskiness. Because the total proportion of risk contributed by all stocks in the market portfolio must equal 1.0, we must have

$$\sum_{i=1}^{n} w_i\beta_i = 1.0$$

In general, *the beta of a portfolio equals the weighted average of the betas of the component securities*. This makes the market risk of any given portfolio easy to calculate.

Stocks with betas greater than 1.0 are often called *aggressive stocks* because they go up faster than the market in a "bull" (rising) market but fall faster in a "bear" (declining) market. *Defensive stocks*, which are stocks with betas less than 1.0, tend to fluctuate less than the market. Table 4-7 lists a number of commonly traded stocks ranked in terms of their betas.

The stocks with the highest standard deviations are not necessarily those with the highest betas; there is no necessary relationship between a stock's individual risk and its contribution to market risk.

Estimating Beta. Stock betas are usually estimated from historical data, even though they are based on expectations about *future* performance relative to the market. The technique used is called *regression analysis*, and it involves fitting a straight line through the points representing past combinations of returns on the market and the stock. This is shown in Figure 4-7. The line that fits the data best—in the sense of minimizing the sum of the squared deviations between the line and the data points—is known as the **characteristic line** for the stock. The

TABLE 4-7 Betas of Commonly Traded Stocks			
British Telecom	.60	Kellogg	1.00
Consolidated Edison	.70	McDonald's	1.00
Atlantic Richfield	.80	PepsiCo	1.00
Exxon	.80	Philip Morris	1.00
AT&T	.85	CBS	1.05
Coca-Cola	.90	3M	1.05
Procter & Gamble	.90	General Electric	1.10
Pacific Telesis	.90	Citicorp	1.20
Anheuser-Busch	.95	Ford Motor	1.20
Capital Cities/ABC	.95	Hewlett-Packard	1.20
General Motors	.95	Apple Computer	1.35
Merck	.95	Bethlehem Steel	1.50
IBM	1.00	Zenith Electronics	1.55

SOURCE: *Value Line Investment Survey*, November 4, 1988.

FIGURE 4-7
Estimating Beta from Stock Return Data: The Characteristic Line

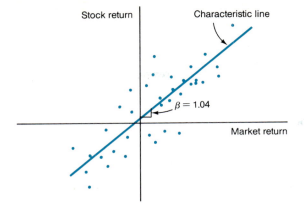

estimated beta equals the slope of the characteristic line and is the regression coefficient on market returns.

The validity of using historical data to estimate beta is contingent on past performance being a reasonable proxy for expected future performance. If the historical relationship is not expected to hold in the future, a different estimation procedure must be used. This could involve substituting expectations of the future for the historical data or weighting recent data more heavily than data further in the past.

Rather than calculating beta directly, you could use the services of investment advisory firms like Merrill Lynch or Value Line, which regularly provide updated estimates of the betas of actively traded stocks. Estimates vary from one service to another because of different time periods or estimation techniques used, but they should be similar.

A more serious problem in estimating beta is the inability to measure the true market portfolio consisting of all risky assets. Instead, it is necessary to use a market index that serves as a proxy for the actual market portfolio. Most market proxies, however, contain only a sample of domestic stocks; they generally exclude foreign stocks, bonds, real estate, human capital, precious metals, and other risky assets that people hold for investment and diversification purposes. The seriousness of this problem is still being debated.[4]

4.4
THE CAPITAL ASSET PRICING MODEL

The basic premise of all financial models is that investors are risk averse and therefore demand a premium for bearing risk. This means that higher-risk assets are priced to yield higher expected returns than do lower-risk assets. An implication is that the expected return on an asset can be decomposed into the risk-free return plus a risk premium:

[4]For different opinions on the seriousness of this problem, see Richard Roll, "A Critique of the Asset Pricing Theory's Tests. Part 1: On Past and Potential Testability of the Theory," *Journal of Financial Economics*, March 1977, pp. 129–176; and Robert Stambough, "On the Exclusion of Assets from Tests of the Two-Parameter Model," *Journal of Financial Economics*, November 1982, pp. 237–268.

$$\frac{\text{Expected return}}{\text{on a risky asset}} = \frac{\text{Risk-free}}{\text{return}} + \frac{\text{Risk}}{\text{premium}}$$

The risk-free rate compensates for the time value of money and is measured as the return on a riskless instrument like a Treasury bill.[5] The important issue now is what determines the risk premium for a given security or other asset. We have already seen that fully diversified investors holding the market portfolio care only about an asset's systematic risk as measured by its beta. But what is the expected risk premium for an individual security given its beta, that is, what is the relationship between a stock's beta and its required return? To begin with the simplest cases first, a stock that has a beta of 1.0, the same as the market portfolio, should yield a risk premium of $r_m - r_f$, whereas a riskless asset, with a beta of 0, should provide a return equal to r_f. Otherwise, it would be possible to earn arbitrage profits. But what about all the other assets with betas unequal to 0 or 1?

The answer to this question is contained in the **capital asset pricing model** (CAPM). Developed almost simultaneously in the early 1960s by three people—John Lintner, William Sharpe, and Jack Treynor—the CAPM provides the following key result: *The risk premium on any asset is proportional to its beta.*[6] This means that the expected risk premium on asset i with a beta of β_i must be

$$r_i - r_f = \beta_i (r_m - r_f) \tag{4.4}$$

where r_i is the required return on asset i. Rearranging the terms of Equation 4.4 yields the more familiar form of the CAPM:

$$r_i = r_f + \beta_i (r_m - r_f) \tag{4.5}$$

According to Equation 4.5, the required return on asset i equals the risk-free return plus a risk premium equal to the asset's beta multiplied by the market risk premium $r_m - r_f$. The linear relationship between an asset's expected return and its beta coefficient is known as the **security market line** (SML) and is depicted in Figure 4-8. The slope of this line is the market risk premium $r_m - r_f$.

The more risk averse investors are, the higher will be the required return for bearing risk. Less risk aversion leads to a smaller risk premium and a lower required return. The result is higher stock prices because the same cash flows will be capitalized at a lower discount rate, thereby increasing the present value of those cash flows. Conversely, an increase in risk aversion causes stock prices to decline.

---

[5]In reality, Treasury bills are free only of *default risk*. Because they are stated in nominal terms, investors in T-bills must still bear inflation risk. The CAPM can be modified to incorporate inflation risk.

[6]Jack Treynor's article on capital asset pricing was never published. The other referenced papers are William F. Sharpe, "Capital Asset Prices: A Theory of Market Equilibrium under Conditions of Risk," *Journal of Finance*, September 1964, pp. 425–442; and John Lintner, "The Valuation of Risk Assets and the Selection of Risky Investments in Stock Portfolios and Capital Budgets," *Review of Economics and Statistics*, February 1965, pp. 13–37.

FIGURE 4-8
Market Relationship Between Risk and Return

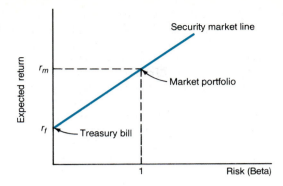

APPLICATION
Using the CAPM

The market has an expected rate of return of 15 percent, the riskless rate of interest is 5 percent, and a common stock has a beta of 2. Using the CAPM, what is the expected rate of return of the stock?

SOLUTION   Apply the CAPM as follows:

$$\text{Expected return on the stock} = r_f + \beta(r_m - r_f)$$

$$= 5\% + 2(15\% - 5\%)$$

$$= 25 \text{ percent}$$

Assumptions Underlying the CAPM

Modern financial theory rests on two key assumptions:

1. Securities markets are highly competitive and populated by highly sophisticated, well-informed buyers and sellers.
2. Securities markets are dominated by rational, risk-averse investors, who seek to maximize the risk-adjusted returns from their investments.

The first assumption implies that markets are efficient; that is, relevant information is readily and universally available and quickly reflected in security prices. The consequences of the second assumption are that investors prefer more wealth to less and demand a premium in the form of higher expected returns for bearing risk.

The formal development of the CAPM requires additional specialized assumptions:

1. Financial markets are frictionless. This means there are no taxes, transaction costs, or restrictions on borrowing, lending, and short selling (selling stock that one doesn't own in the hope of buying it back later at a lower price). Otherwise, expected returns will be affected by an individ-

ual's tax position, cost of trading, or access to information, and there may not be a definite relationship between risk and expected return in the market.

2. Either security returns follow specific probability distributions, or there are restrictions on what investors' preferences can be.[7] If these conditions fail to hold, investors may be interested in other measures of risk besides standard deviation (like the skewness of returns—the degree to which returns are not symmetrical around the expected return) and the relationship between these measures of risk and expected return will generally not be linear.

3. Investors share common beliefs as to the probability distributions of returns. If individuals disagree on the expected returns and risks associated with different assets, it becomes more difficult to imagine a common pricing mechanism that all can agree on.

Although these assumptions are clearly unrealistic, some simplification of reality is always necessary in order to develop useful models. Much research has gone into examining the implications of relaxing these restrictive assumptions. The result has been more complex models, but ones that are generally consistent with the simple version of the CAPM contained here. The basic insight of the CAPM—that only the systematic component of total risk is priced—still holds. Ultimately, of course, what matters is not how fancy or "realistic" a model is but how well it fits the facts.

Empirical Tests of the CAPM

There have been numerous tests of the CAPM, the best known being the studies by Fischer Black, Michael Jensen, and Myron Scholes and by Eugene Fama and James MacBeth.[8] Most of these studies, including the aforementioned, examined returns on portfolios rather than individual securities to avoid some measurement problems. With few exceptions, these studies have reached similar conclusions:

1. Security returns appear to be linearly related to beta as predicted by the CAPM. Inclusion of a factor representing unsystematic risk appears not to explain past returns any better.

2. There is a positive relationship between beta and past returns; that is, higher betas tend to lead to higher returns.

3. The empirical SML appears to be less steeply sloped than the theoretical SML is. This means that low-beta stocks earn a somewhat higher return than the CAPM predicts, whereas high-beta stocks earn less than predicted. This could be due to measurement problems.

4. The intercept term is somewhat greater than its theoretically predicted value of r_f.

---

[7]Specifically, either investors have quadratic utility functions in wealth or portfolio returns are normally distributed. The latter assumption is less questionable than the former assumption.

[8]See Fischer Black, Michael C. Jensen, and Myron Scholes, "The Capital Asset Pricing Model: Some Empirical Tests," in Michael C. Jensen, ed., *Studies in the Theory of Capital Markets* (New York: Praeger, 1972); and Eugene F. Fama and James D. MacBeth, "Risk, Return and Equilibrium: Empirical Tests," *Journal of Political Economy*, May 1973, pp. 607–636.

TABLE 4-8		March 1966	December 1970	December 1980	September 1988
Stock Market Capitalizations As Percent of World Total (20 main markets)	Japan	3%	5%	15%	42%
	United States	71	66	53	31
	Europe	19	20	20	21
	Rest of World	7	9	12	6

SOURCE: *Morgan Stanley Capital International.*

The net result of these tests is that although they don't provide unequivocal support of the CAPM, they are consistent with its major implications. Beta, the measure of systematic risk, is linearly and positively related to past returns. Other asset-pricing models have not proved clearly superior to the CAPM, which appears to be a remarkable example of a theoretical construct, based on limiting assumptions, that explains a great deal of real-world behavior.

Unfortunately, these tests are less supportive of the CAPM than they appear to be. According to Richard Roll, all empirical tests of the CAPM suffer from two basic flaws.[9] First, he claims that all the results of tests like those of Black, Jensen, and Scholes, and Fama and MacBeth are tautological; that is, the linear relationship between beta and expected stock returns follows directly from the assumption that the market portfolio is on the efficient set of portfolios. Hence, the only real prediction of the CAPM is that the market portfolio is efficient (in the sense that the portfolio is on the efficient frontier).

This brings us to the second basic problem with testing the CAPM. Roll argues that it is not even conceptually possible to test whether the market portfolio is efficient. Because the market portfolio consists of all economic assets in the world, not just stocks listed on the New York or American stock exchanges, any proxy for the market contains only a subset of these assets. (This is the same problem alluded to earlier in the discussion about estimating beta.)

Moreover, the distortion associated with using an index of stocks listed on the New York Stock Exchange as a proxy for the true market portfolio has gotten more severe over time. Over two-thirds of the world's stock market capitalization is in non-U.S. companies and this fraction has been increasing over time (see Table 4-8).

To reject the CAPM, you must find that the *true* market portfolio is inefficient, that is, not on the efficient set. But even if the true market portfolio is efficient, it is unlikely that a subset of the market will be on the efficient set. Thus you can't reject the CAPM because of a finding that a proxy for the market is inefficient. An analogy would be to reject the CAPM because you find that a portfolio restricted to auto and steel stocks is not on the efficient set relative to the stock market as a whole. It is important to realize that Roll's critique does not invalidate the CAPM; it calls into question the results of previous tests of the CAPM. The *arbitrage pricing theory*, introduced in the next section, does not suffer from being unable to identify the correct market portfolio, although it does have its own empirical problems.

[9]Roll, "A Critique of the Asset Pricing Theory's Tests."

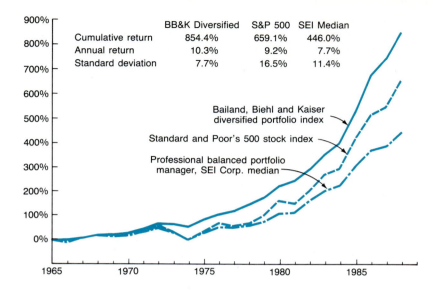

	BB&K Diversified	S&P 500	SEI Median
Cumulative return	854.4%	659.1%	446.0%
Annual return	10.3%	9.2%	7.7%
Standard deviation	7.7%	16.5%	11.4%

Bailand, Biehl and Kaiser
diversified portfolio index

Standard and Poor's 500 stock index

Professional balanced portfolio
manager, SEI Corp. median

Common sense tells us that expanding the universe of assets available for investment should lead to higher returns for the same level of risk or less risk for the same level of expected return. This is evident in Figure 4-9, which shows that between 1965 and 1988, a diversified investment index has outpaced the U.S. stock market and the typical professional portfolio manager. The index consists of five equally weighted parts: U.S. stocks, foreign stocks, U.S. corporate and government bonds, real estate, and Treasury bills. This index grew at a 10.3 percent rate during the 23-year period, compared with 9.2 percent for the S&P 500 stock index and 7.9 percent for the median U.S. money manager invested in both stocks and bonds.

Most of the extra gains came from foreign stocks and real estate, which raced ahead of U.S. stocks for much of the 1970s and 1980s. Note too that the more fully diversified portfolio was less volatile, even as it delivered higher returns. Just as movements in different stocks partially offset one another in an all-equity portfolio, so also movements in different types of assets cancel out each other somewhat. International diversification in particular can lead to a significant reduction in risk. The advantages of international diversification are elaborated in Section 6.

Applying the CAPM

Suppose you want to find the required return on a stock like Hewlett-Packard. The CAPM tells you that you need three numbers to do this: r_f, β_{HP}, and $r_m - r_f$. In November 1988 the return on 30-day Treasury bills, the standard proxy for a risk-free rate, was 6.0 percent. Based on the historical record, shown in Table 4-1, a reasonable estimate of the market risk premium is about 8.5 percent. From Table 4-7 the beta of HP is given as 1.20. Thus, the CAPM-based estimate of the required return on HP stock is

$$r_{HP} = .06 + 1.20 \times .085 = 16.20 \text{ percent}$$

TABLE 4-9
Required Returns of Commonly Traded Stocks

	Beta*	Expected Return (%) $r_f + \beta(r_m - r_f)$		Beta	Expected Return (%) $r_f + \beta(r_f - r_m)$
British Telecom	.60	11.10	Kellogg	1.00	14.50
Consolidated Edison	.70	11.95	McDonald's	1.00	14.50
Atlantic Richfield	.80	12.80	PepsiCo	1.00	14.50
Exxon	.80	12.80	Philip Morris	1.00	14.50
AT&T	.85	13.23	CBS	1.05	14.93
Coca-Cola	.90	13.65	3M	1.05	14.93
Procter & Gamble	.90	13.65	General Electric	1.10	15.35
Pacific Telesis	.90	13.65	Citicorp	1.20	16.20
Anheuser-Busch	.95	14.08	Ford Motor	1.20	16.20
Capital Cities/ABC	.95	14.08	Hewlett-Packard	1.20	16.20
General Motors	.95	14.08	Apple Computer	1.35	17.48
Merck	.95	14.08	Bethlehem Steel	1.50	18.75
IBM	1.00	14.50	Zenith Electronics	1.55	19.18

*Estimates of beta are taken from *Value Line*, November 4, 1988.

Similar estimates of the required returns as of November 1988 for the other stocks listed in Table 4-7 are contained in Table 4-9.

The Basic Message of the CAPM

The basic message of the CAPM is that if you want to earn a higher return, you must be prepared to bear greater risk. There is no "free lunch" in an efficient market. Moreover, the CAPM says that if you are holding a less than fully diversified portfolio, you are bearing risk (diversifiable risk) for which you are not being compensated. To see this, suppose the market rewarded total risk, as opposed to systematic risk alone. This means that the rate at which future dividends are discounted would bear a risk premium based on total risk. Because total risk exceeds the systematic component of risk, a total risk-based discount rate would be greater than one based only on systematic risk. In order for stocks to provide this higher expected return, stock prices must be lower than if systematic risk alone mattered. Therefore, if total risk matters, stocks will be underpriced relative to the case in which the risk premium is based only on the systematic component of risk. By discounting the same cash flows but at a lower rate, the CAPM-derived value must exceed the value based on a total risk-derived discount rate.

If this were the case, you could easily earn a fortune. Here's how: Put together a well-diversified portfolio of stocks. This portfolio will have a required return below the average of the required returns of the component securities. (Remember that the contribution of any given security to the total risk of a portfolio is just the security's systematic risk weighted by its share of the portfolio's value.) You could then sell shares in the portfolio to the public at a price higher than the prices of the component securities. This is because the same cash flows would be priced to yield a return below the average discount rate of the component securities.

This is a money machine: Buy individual securities, repackage them in well-diversified portfolios, and then resell them to the public at a price that exceeds the cost of forming the portfolios. In the process of taking advantage of this money machine, arbitrageurs will force up the prices of the individual securities today, thereby lowering their future expected returns. Arbitrage will continue until all securities prices are based on their systematic risk alone. This illustrates one of the basic rules of finance: *Money machines quickly self-destruct*.

To the extent that information is not free and transaction costs exist, this money machine may not function as described. In fact, however, mutual funds and other security packages sell at their net asset values (aside from a small convenience cost). The bottom line, therefore, seems to be that arbitrage takes place despite various market imperfections. The arbitrageurs include financial institutions—pension funds, insurance companies, and mutual funds—as well as individuals.

4.5 THE ARBITRAGE PRICING THEORY

In the early 1970s, Stephen Ross developed the **arbitrage pricing theory**, or APT, a generalized version of the CAPM.[10] According to the APT, the expected return on security or asset i is

$$\begin{array}{c}\text{Expected}\\\text{return on}\\\text{asset } i\end{array} = \begin{array}{c}\text{Riskless}\\\text{return}\end{array} + \begin{array}{c}\text{Sensitivity}\\\text{of asset } i\\\text{to factor}\end{array} \times \begin{array}{c}\text{Factor risk}\\\text{premium}\end{array}$$

$$E(r_i) = r_f + \beta_i \lambda \qquad (4.6)$$

where r_f is the risk-free interest rate, β_i is security i's systematic risk, and λ is the market price of risk.[11] A security's systematic risk is due to a random risk factor, like changes in gross national product (GNP), shared by all securities to a greater or lesser extent. Arbitrage across the common factor ensures that only systematic risk is priced. If this sounds similar to the logic underlying the CAPM, it should. The main difference between the CAPM and the APT is that the CAPM specifies that the common risk factor is the random return on the market portfolio, whereas the APT does not prespecify the common risk factor(s).

One advantage of the APT is that it can be expanded to encompass several risk factors. The CAPM is limited to one common risk factor. The general multifactor APT can be expressed as

$$E(r_i) = r_f + \beta_{i1}\lambda_1 + \beta_{i2}\lambda_2 + \cdots + \beta_{in}\lambda_n \qquad (4.7)$$

where β_{ij} is security i's systematic risk associated with the jth risk factor, λ_j is the market price of risk for the jth risk factor, and n is the number of common

---

[10]Stephen A. Ross, "The Arbitrage Theory of Capital Asset Pricing," *Journal of Economic Theory*, December 1976, pp. 341–360.

[11]When a risk-free asset doesn't exist, an alternative approach is to substitute the return on a zero-beta portfolio, one whose weights are set so that the portfolio has a beta of zero.

factors. Empirical research based on Equation 4.7 seems to indicate that there are no more than three to five common factors affecting stock returns. The four factors mentioned most often include unexpected changes in industrial output, in inflation, in the difference between the yield on a long-term and a short-term Treasury bond, and in bond risk premiums.[12]

These variables make intuitive sense as risk factors because unanticipated changes in them systematically affect the values of all assets. Thus investors who hold securities that are more exposed to these factors will find that their securities' market values fluctuate more over time. Investors will purchase these riskier securities, therefore, only if they expect to be compensated by a higher total return in the long run.

APPLICATION
Using the APT

Suppose that a firm has the following factor sensitivities: .7 to the factor relating to industrial production, .3 to the factor relating to unanticipated inflation, .9 to the factor relating to the term structure of interest rates, and .4 to bond risk premiums. Further, suppose that the risk premiums for the factor sensitivities are 10 percent for industrial production, 6 percent for inflation, 4 percent for the term structure, and 3 percent for the bond risk premium. These risk premiums mean, for example, that an asset with a factor sensitivity of 1.0 to inflation risk will have an expected return that is 6 percent greater than the expected return of an otherwise identical asset that has a factor sensitivity of 0 to inflation. The risk-free interest rate is 7.5 percent. What is the expected return on this stock according to the APT?

SOLUTION Applying the APT yields

$$E(r) = E(r_f) + \beta_1\lambda_1 + \beta_2\lambda_2 + \beta_3\lambda_3 + \beta_4\lambda_4$$
$$= 7.5\% + .7 \times 10\% + .3 \times 6\% + .9 \times 4\% + .4 \times 3\%$$
$$= 21.1 \text{ percent}$$

In some instances, the APT sends out messages about the riskiness of various stocks that are at odds with what the CAPM says. The CAPM, for example, depicts utilities as low-risk defensive stocks whereas the APT shows them to be very sensitive to inflation risk and, therefore, extremely risky in an environment characterized by high and variable inflation.[13]

There is a great deal of research activity going on in the area of arbitrage pricing. Unfortunately, one outcome of this research is to call into question the testability of the APT. Although the issues raised are highly technical, one problem is that as the sample of securities used to extract common factors increases, the number of estimated factors increases as well. Hence, if you find that the

---

[12]See, for example, Nai-Fu Chen, Richard Roll, and Stephen A. Ross, "Economic Forces and the Stock Market," *Journal of Business*, July 1986, pp. 383–403.

[13]See, for example, Richard Roll and Stephen A. Ross, "Regulation, the Capital Asset Pricing Model, and the Arbitrage Pricing Theory," *Public Utilities Fortnightly*, May 26, 1983, pp. 22–28; and Dorothy H. Bower, Richard S. Bower, and Dennis E. Logue, "A Primer on Arbitrage Pricing Theory," *Midland Corporate Finance Journal*, Fall 1984, pp. 31–40.

price of a factor varies from one portfolio to another—ordinarily, a prima facie case for rejecting the APT—the possibility always remains that your sample of securities is too small and the APT was wrongly rejected. This is analogous to the problem confronting tests of the CAPM. Another problem is the inability to identify clearly the economic forces that underlie the factors affecting security returns, particularly when these forces affect security returns in complex ways.[14] Each factor may be a construct representing the movements of several economic variables. For example, one factor may represent the interaction of inflation and changes in the difference between long-term and short-term interest rates on asset values. The jury is still out on the APT as it is on the CAPM.

4.6 THE BENEFITS OF INTERNATIONAL DIVERSIFICATION

The expanded universe of securities available internationally suggests the possibility of achieving a better risk-return trade-off than by investing solely in U.S. securities. This follows from the basic rule of portfolio diversification: The broader the diversification, the more stable the returns and the more diffuse the risks.

Prudent investors know that diversifying across industries leads to a lower level of risk for a given level of expected return. Ultimately, though, the advantages of such diversification are limited because all companies in a country are more or less subject to the same cyclical economic fluctuations. By diversifying across nations whose economic cycles are not perfectly in phase, investors should be able to reduce still further the variability of their returns. In other words, risk that is systematic in the context of the U.S. economy may be unsystematic in the context of the global economy. For example, an oil price shock that hurts the U.S. economy helps the economies of oil-exporting nations, and vice versa. Thus, just as movements in different stocks partially offset one another in an all-U.S. portfolio, so also movements in U.S. and non-U.S. stock portfolios cancel out each other somewhat.

The value of international equity diversification appears to be significant. Donald Lessard and Bruno Solnik, among others, have both presented evidence that national factors have a strong impact on security returns relative to that of any common world factor.[15] They also found that returns from the different national equity markets have relatively low correlations with one another.

Table 4-10 contains some data on correlations between the U.S. and non-U.S. markets. The betas for the foreign markets relative to the U.S. market are calculated in the same way that individual asset betas are calculated:

$$\text{Foreign market beta} = \frac{\dfrac{\text{Correlation with}}{\text{U.S. market}} \times \dfrac{\text{Standard deviation}}{\text{of foreign market}}}{\text{Standard deviation of U.S. market}}$$

For example, the Canadian market beta is .60 × 21.9/18.2 = .72.

---

[14]Jay Shanken, "The Arbitrage Pricing Theory: Is It Testable?" *Journal of Finance*, December 1982, pp. 1129–1140.

[15]Donald R. Lessard, "World, National, and Industry Factors in Equity Returns," *Journal of Finance*, May 1974, pp. 379–391; and Bruno H. Solnik, "Why Not Diversify Internationally?" *Financial Analysts Journal*, August 1974, pp. 48–54.

	Correlation with	Standard Deviation	Market Risk (beta)
TABLE 4-10 How Foreign Markets Correlate with the U.S. Market (1974–1983) **Country**	**U.S. Market**	**of Returns (%)**	**from U.S. Perspective**
United States	1.00	18.2	1.00
Canada	.60	21.9	.72
United Kingdom	.33	34.4	.62
France	.25	28.8	.40
West Germany	.31	19.4	.33
Switzerland	.46	23.5	.59
Italy	.19	31.5	.33
Netherlands	.60	22.6	.75
Belgium	.36	22.0	.44
Austria	.21	15.0	.17
Spain	.06	20.9	.07
Sweden	.30	21.7	.36
Norway	.25	35.5	.49
Japan	.38	20.5	.43
Hong Kong	.34	45.5	.85
Singapore	.39	41.1	.88
Australia	.43	29.3	.69
EAFE Index*	.47	17.2	.44
World Index†	.91	17.1	.86

SOURCE: Based on data appearing in *Capital International Perspective.*

*The Morgan Stanley Capital International Europe, Australia, Far East (EAFE) Index is the non-American world index and consists of stock markets from those parts of the world.
†The Morgan Stanley Capital International World Index has a combined market value of $2.1 trillion, covers 19 countries including the United States, and includes about 1,600 of the largest companies worldwide.

Measured for the ten-year period 1974–1983, foreign markets correlated with the U.S. market from a high of .60 for Canada and the Netherlands to a low of .06 for Spain. The relatively high correlations for Canada and the Netherlands reveal that these markets tracked the U.S. market's ups and downs. Spain's low correlation, on the other hand, indicates that the Spanish and U.S. markets have tended to move largely independently of each other.

Notice also that the investment risks associated with these different markets can be quite different—with the Hong Kong market showing the highest level, the Austrian market the lowest. Indeed, all but the Austrian market had a higher level of risk, as measured by the standard deviation of returns, than the U.S. market. Yet the internationally diversified Morgan Stanley Capital International World Index had the next lowest level of risk—lower even than the U.S. market. The reason, of course, is that much of the risk associated with markets in individual countries is unsystematic and so can be eliminated by diversification, as indicated by the relatively low betas of these markets.

These results imply that international diversification may significantly reduce the risk of portfolio returns. As indicated in Figure 4-10, the risk reduction benefits from international diversification are significantly greater than those that can be achieved solely by adding more domestic stocks to a portfolio.

Moreover, between 1971 and 1986, the compound annual return for the Morgan Stanley Capital International World Index was 13.0 percent compared

FIGURE 4-10

Effect of International Diversification on Risk

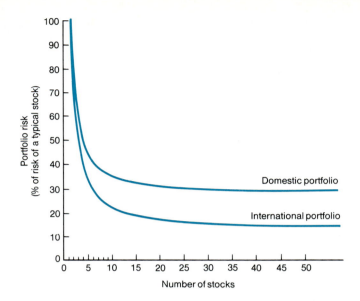

with 10.0 percent for the U.S. market. The obvious conclusion is that international diversification pushes out the efficient frontier, allowing investors simultaneously to reduce their risk and increase their expected return. This is illustrated by Figure 4-11.

One way to estimate the benefits of international diversification is to consider the expected return and standard deviation of return for a portfolio consisting of a fraction a invested in U.S. stocks and the remaining fraction, $1 - a$, invested in foreign stocks. Let r_{us} and r_{rw} be the expected returns on the U.S. and rest-of-world stock portfolios. Similarly, let σ_{us} and σ_{rw} be the standard deviations of the U.S. and rest-of-world portfolios. The expected return r_p can be calculated as

$$r_p = ar_{us} + (1 - a)r_{rw}$$

and the portfolio standard deviation, σ_p, is (see Equation 4.1)

$$\sigma_p = [a^2\sigma_{us}^2 + (1 - a)^2\,\sigma_{rw}^2 + 2a(1 - a)\sigma_{us}\sigma_{rw}r_{us,rw}]^{1/2} \qquad (4.8)$$

where $r_{us,rw}$ is the correlation between the returns on the U.S. and foreign stock portfolios.

To see the benefits of international diversification, assume that the portfolio is equally invested in U.S. and foreign stocks, where the EAFE Index represents the foreign stock portfolio. Using data from Table 4-10, this implies that $\sigma_{us} = 18.2$ percent, $\sigma_{rw} = 17.1$ percent, and $r_{us,rw} = .47$. According to Equation 4.8, this implies that the standard deviation of the internationally diversified portfolio is

$$\sigma_p = [.5^2(18.1)^2 + .5^2(17.1)^2 + .5^2 \times 2 \times 18.2 \times 17.1 \times .47]^{1/2}$$

$$= .5(912.57)^{1/2}$$

$$= 15.1 \text{ percent}$$

FIGURE 4-11
Effect of International Diversification on an Efficient Frontier

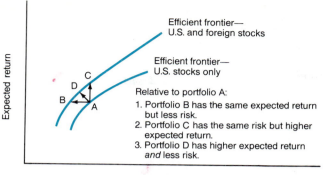

Efficient frontier—
U.S. and foreign stocks

Efficient frontier—
U.S. stocks only

Relative to portfolio A:
1. Portfolio B has the same expected return but less risk.
2. Portfolio C has the same risk but higher expected return.
3. Portfolio D has higher expected return *and* less risk.

Here the risk of the internationally diversified portfolio is considerably below the risk of the U.S. portfolio. Moreover, as indicated earlier, the expected return is much higher as well.

Although there are barriers to international diversification by investors, many of them are being eroded. Money invested abroad by both large institutions and individuals is growing dramatically.

There are several ways in which U.S. investors can diversify into foreign securities. A small number of foreign firms—fewer than 100—have listed their securities on the New York Stock Exchange (NYSE) or the American Stock Exchange. It is believed that a major barrier in the past to foreign listing has been the NYSE requirements for substantial disclosure and audited financial statements. However, the gap between acceptable NYSE accounting and disclosure standards and those acceptable to large foreign companies has narrowed substantially in recent years. Moreover, Japanese and European multinational firms that raise funds in international capital markets have been forced to conform to stricter standards. This may encourage other foreign firms to list their securities and gain access to the U.S. capital market.

Investors can always buy foreign securities in their home markets. One problem with buying stocks listed on foreign exchanges is that it can be expensive, primarily because of steep brokerage commissions. Owners of foreign stocks also face the complications of foreign tax laws and the nuisance of converting dividend payments into dollars.

In the absence of investing in an internationally diversified mutual fund, of which a growing number are available, there is a simpler way of investing overseas: buy American Depository Receipts of non-U.S. companies. ADRs, as they are commonly called, are receipts for foreign shares held in trust by a bank—usually a foreign branch of an American bank—and they are increasing rapidly. For a small fee, five New York banks will handle all the paperwork and remit dividends converted into U.S. dollars.

SUMMARY AND CONCLUSIONS

The primary objectives of this chapter are to (1) define risk, (2) show how it can be measured, and (3) explain how it affects expected asset returns. We began by examining one of the fundamental premises of modern financial theory: that on average, financial markets are dominated by people who are risk averse. The corollary is that to induce investors to bear the risk that is naturally present in all financial decisions, they must be compensated with a higher expected rate of return. The historical data support the view that risk hath its reward. Over the past 63 years, the riskiest investment, common stocks, has yielded an average annual return of 12.1 percent, approximately 8.5 percent more than the 3.6 percent annual return on the safest investment, short-term Treasury bills.

We then used the intuitive notion that risk is related to the unpredictability of future returns to show that a quantitative measure of this uncertainty is provided by the standard deviation of the probability distribution of returns. We saw that the riskiness of an individual stock can be divided into two components—diversifiable or unsystematic risk, which is eliminated in a well-diversified portfolio, and systematic or market risk, which remains even in the best-diversified portfolio. Because investors hold diversified portfolios of stocks, thereby eliminating unsystematic risk, they are primarily concerned with the market risk of the individual stocks they hold. Only this latter risk, measured by the beta coefficient, contributes to the riskiness of their portfolios.

Beta measures the tendency of a stock to move up or down with the market. The market portfolio has a beta of 1.0, as does a stock of average riskiness. A stock with a beta greater than 1.0 tends to be more volatile than the overall stock market, whereas a stock with a beta less than 1.0 is more stable than the market.

The insight that systematic risk is the relevant risk in financial markets provides the basis for the capital asset pricing model (CAPM). According to the CAPM, the expected or required return on asset i, r_i, is equal to the risk-free interest rate, r_f, plus a risk premium. This risk premium equals the difference between the expected return on the market, r_m, and the risk-free rate multiplied by the stock's beta coefficient. Formally,

$$r_i = r_f + \beta_i(r_f - r_m)$$

This formula is also known as the security market line (SML).

An alternative approach to measuring risk and return is provided by the arbitrage pricing theory (APT). According to the APT, security returns are affected by a number of common factors, instead of the CAPM's single-factor approach. Arbitrage across the common factors results in a market price of risk for each common factor and a required return for each security based on the security's sensitivity to these factors.

REFERENCES   Bower, Dorothy H., Bower, Richard S., and Logue, Dennis E. "A Primer on Arbitrage Pricing Theory." *Midland Corporate Finance Journal*, Fall 1984, pp. 31–40.

Fama, Eugene F., and MacBeth, James D. "Risk, Return and Equilibrium: Empirical Tests." *Journal of Political Economy*, May 1973, pp. 607–636.

Jensen, Michael C., ed., *Studies in the Theory of Capital Markets*. New York: Praeger, 1972.

Lintner, John. "The Valuation of Risk Assets and the Selection of Risky Investments in Stock Portfolios and Capital Budgets." *Review of Economics and Statistics*, February 1965, pp. 13–37.

Markowitz, Harry. "Portfolio Selection." *Journal of Finance*, March 1952, pp. 77–91.

Roll, Richard. "A Critique of the Asset Pricing Theory's Tests. Part 1: On Past and Potential Testability of the Theory." *Journal of Financial Economics*, March 1977, pp. 129–176.

Ross, Stephen A. "The Arbitrage Theory of Capital Asset Pricing." *Journal of Economic Theory*, December 1976, pp. 341–360.

Sharpe, William F. "Capital Asset Prices: A Theory of Market Equilibrium Under Conditions of Risk." *Journal of Finance*, September 1964, pp. 425–442.

QUESTIONS

1. List four common shares likely to have a high standard deviation of return and four stocks likely to have a low standard deviation of return. Then list two pairs of stocks likely to be highly correlated and two pairs likely to be relatively uncorrelated.

2. Comment on the following statement: "Risky stocks offer the investor a good shot at very high profits, and so these stocks should sell at a premium."

3. True or false?
   a. Because investors like to hold diversified portfolios, a conglomerate's shares are more prized than are shares of a company with only one business.
   b. The CAPM implies that an asset with a negative beta has an expected rate of return lower than the risk-free interest rate.
   c. A stock with a beta of .5 has a required return one half as high as the market.
   d. Diversification will have no value if the returns of all risky assets are perfectly correlated.
   e. If an asset lies above the security market line, it is overvalued.
   f. If an asset lies inside the mean-variance frontier, it is overvalued.
   g. An undiversified portfolio with a beta of 2 is as risky as the market portfolio.

4. What factors could increase the diversifiable risk of a stock? What factors could increase the nondiversifiable risk of a stock?

5. Which situation would offer the best chance to reduce risk by forming a portfolio from two stocks?
   a. Perfect correlation between the stocks.
   b. No correlation between the stocks.
   c. Perfect negative correlation between the stocks.

6. The capital asset pricing model asserts that the expected return on an asset depends on
   a. the nondiversifiable risk of the asset.
   b. the expected return on the market.
   c. the risk-free interest rate.
   d. all of the above.
   e. none of the above.

7. The return on T-bills is 6 percent and the expected return on the market is 14 percent. If a stock has a beta of 1.1, then what will be the expected return on the stock?
   a. 13.2 percent.
   b. 21.4 percent.
   c. 16.3 percent.
   d. 23.7 percent.
   e. none of the above.

8. Investors can achieve diversification benefits from all the following methods except
   a. buying corporate bonds with different ratings and different maturities.
   b. buying securities with a low correlation among returns.
   c. randomly selecting ten stocks.
   d. buying stocks with a high (but not perfect) correlation among returns.
   e. buying only long-term government bonds.

9. Comment on the following statements:

   a. If we assume stocks follow a normal distribution, we err because the normal distribution has a positive probability of an infinitely negative value. We know, however, that the rate of return on a limited liability asset like stock cannot be less than −100 percent.

   b. If I buy several hundred "penny" mining shares, I don't care about risk. The stocks can go up very high in price or, at worst, I can lose just a few dollars.

   c. Although our company has a very low beta, we feel it is misleading to our shareholders because our company is subject to very wide fluctuations in sales and profits.

10. If the market portfolio actually yields a rate of return different from the expected return predicted by the CAPM, does this mean the CAPM is a bad model?

11. What is the definition of covariance? What is the definition of correlation? What is an intuitive explanation of the difference between the two?

12. Given what you know about the benefits of diversification, what advice would you have for an assembly-line worker in an auto plant who puts most of his savings into shares of auto companies?

13. Gold pays no dividends, is costly to store, and has often undergone long periods of price decreases. Why would investors ever want to hold this asset?

14. Many insurance companies sell auto insurance at competitive rates, yet none will offer earthquake insurance at any price. Can you explain this puzzle?

15. Sketch the efficient set of risky assets in a diagram with expected return on the vertical axis and standard deviation on the horizontal axis. Show how an investor's opportunity set will change if she can borrow and lend at the same interest rate. Now, show how the investor's opportunity set will change if the rate of interest at which she can borrow exceeds the rate of interest at which she may lend.

16. Common shares of Empire State Petroleum have a beta of .75, but a very high unsystematic risk that the beta does not reflect. If the expected return on the market is 25 percent, and the riskless rate is 5 percent, the expected return on Empire State will be

   a. 20 percent.
   b. 18.75 percent.
   c. indeterminate but clearly more than 20 percent because of the extra risk.
   d. indeterminate unless we know the interest rate and the market premium for unsystematic risk.

17. We may write the expected return on a stock as $E(r) = a + \beta E(r_m)$ where $E(r_m)$ is the expected rate of return on the market portfolio. For this formula to be consistent with the CAPM, it must be the case that

   a. $a = r_f$, the rate of return on the riskless asset.
   b. $a = (1 - \beta)r_f$.
   c. $a = 0$.
   d. $a = (1 - r_f)$.

18. As seen in Table 4-10, Hong Kong stocks are about 2.5 times more volatile than U.S. stocks. Does that mean that risk-averse American investors should avoid Hong Kong equities? Explain.

19. What characteristics of foreign securities lead to diversification benefits for American investors?

20. Comment on the following statement: On October 19, 1987, the U.S. stock market crashed. As the globe turned the following day, the devastation spread from New York to Tokyo, Hong Kong, Sydney, and Singapore, and on to Frankfurt, Paris, and London, then back to New York. The domino-style spread of the crash from one market to the next accelerated as international investors attempted to outrun the wave of panic selling from Tokyo to London and back to New York. It is difficult to imagine that some investors thought they had been able to diversify their investment risks by spreading their money across different stock markets around the world, when in fact their downside risks were actually multiplying as one market followed another into decline.

PROBLEMS

1. Mary Smith has invested two thirds of her money in GM stock and the remainder in Chrysler. On past evidence, the standard deviation is 22 percent for GM and 44 percent for Chrysler. Suppose the correlation between GM and Chrysler is −1.0. What is the standard deviation of Mary Smith's portfolio?

2. Two stocks are available for investment, AA Auto Parts and ZZ Appliances. Their probability distributions of returns are given below:

Probability	.10	.15	.10	.20	.15	.20	.10
AA	−15%	−10%	0%	5%	10%	12%	15%
ZZ	−25%	−10%	−5%	0%	15%	25%	35%

  a. What is the expected return of AA? Of ZZ?
  b. Calculate the variance and standard deviation of return of both stocks.
  c. If the distributions were continuous and normal, what probability statements could be made regarding the return of the two securities?

3. Two over-the-counter stocks, Dunked Donuts and Crai Computer, have the following characteristics:

	Expected Return	Standard Deviation of Return
Dunked	.15	.10
Crai	.25	.125

  a. Calculate the expected return and standard deviation of return of a portfolio containing 50 percent investments in both Dunked and Crai if the correlation coefficient between the two stocks is .10.
  b. Calculate the expected return and standard deviation of return of a portfolio containing 50 percent of each stock if the correlation coefficient is .75.
  c. Calculate the expected return and the standard deviation of return of a portfolio containing 50 percent of each stock if the correlation coefficient is −.50.

4. The probability distribution of two securities, Stamford and Clarkmont, over five possible states of the world are as shown. The initial purchase price for Stamford is $10, for Clarkmont, $5.

Market Conditions	Probability	Price of S	Price of C
Bull market	.10	$20	$7.50
Mild expansion	.25	15	6.50
Steady state	.20	12	5.50
Mild recession	.35	10	4.50
Bear market	.10	8	3.50

  a. What is the expected return and standard deviation of return of Stamford? Of Clarkmont?
  b. Calculate the covariance between the pair.
  c. What is the correlation coefficient of the pair?
  d. Would combining Stamford and Clarkmont in a portfolio serve to decrease an investor's risk?

5. An investor is considering forming a portfolio from two stocks, Atlantic Telesis and Valley Bell. They have a correlation coefficient of .50.

	Atlantic Telesis (%)	Valley Bell (%)
Expected return	10	12.5
Standard deviation	5	6.0

a. What is the expected return and standard deviation of return of a portfolio with 50 percent invested in AT, 50 percent invested in VB?

b. What is the expected return, standard deviation of return of a portfolio with 25 percent invested in AT, 75 percent in VB?

c. What is the expected return, standard deviation of return of a portfolio with 75 percent invested in AT, 25 percent in VB?

d. Trace the efficient frontier composed of the two securities, Valley Bell and Atlantic Telesis.

6. Two assets have expected return and standard deviation of return as shown below:

Asset	Expected Return (%)	Standard Deviation (%)
A	15	25
B	25	25

The two assets have a correlation coefficient of .20.

a. If the securities are included in a portfolio with equal weights, what will be the expected return and standard deviation of return of the portfolio?

b. A third security C is available for inclusion. Its expected return is 20 percent and the standard deviation of return is 20 percent; its correlation coefficient with both A and B is .20. What will be the expected return of a portfolio with C added, if each security is weighted equally in the portfolio?

c. The general formula for the standard deviation of return for a portfolio of n securities is

$$\text{Standard deviation of portfolio} = \left(\sum_{i=1}^{n} \sum_{j=1}^{n} w_i w_j \sigma_{ij} \right)^{1/2}$$

What will be the risk (standard deviation) of a portfolio with C added, if each security is weighted equally in the portfolio?

d. How many extra variance terms are added to the standard deviation formula with a fourth security? If each security is weighted equally, what weight will be given to each variance term? What does this indicate about the importance of a security's own variance as n increases?

7. Two securities, Campbell Co. and Stuart Co., are available for inclusion in a portfolio. The expected return of Campbell is 10 percent, and its standard deviation is 7.5 percent; the expected return of Stuart is 7.5 percent, standard deviation is 4 percent.

a. Graph a 100 percent investment in each of the two securities within the expected return–standard deviation space as in Figure 4-4.

b. Assume the two securities are perfectly correlated. Graph the possible expected return–standard deviation combinations if the two securities are combined in a portfolio with proportions of .25:.75. With proportions of .50:.50. With proportions of .75:.25.

c. What is the minimum portfolio risk (standard deviation) possible with the two securities? What proportion is invested in Campbell?

d. If the two securities are not correlated at all (correlation coefficient of 0), the portfolio risk will be minimized if the proportion of funds invested in Campbell is 22 percent. What is the expected return and standard deviation of return with this proportion?

e. Using the weights in (b), draw the efficient frontier.

f. If the two securities are perfectly negatively correlated (correlation coefficient is -1.0), the portfolio risk is minimized if the proportion of funds invested in Campbell is 35 percent. What is the expected return and standard deviation of return attainable with this proportion?

g. Using the weights in (b), draw the efficient frontier.

8. The market portfolio's rate of return has a variance of 400, and the covariance of the market with a steel company's stock is 800.
    a. What is the steel company's beta?
    b. If a great number of stocks with the some beta as the steel company were combined into a diversified portfolio, what would be the standard deviation of the rate of return of that portfolio?
    c. What is the average beta for all stocks?
    d. If the market portfolio yields 7 percent less than expected, how much less than expected should the steel company's stock yield?

9. Suppose the beta for an oil company has been estimated to be 1.5. The expected return on the market is 20 percent and the riskless rate of return is 10 percent.
    a. If the expected rate of return on the oil company's stock is 22 percent, what should an investor do?
    b. What if the stock's expected rate of return is 28 percent?

10. The standard deviation of the rate of return of the market portfolio is .15.
    a. What is the standard deviation of a well-diversified portfolio with a beta of .75?
    b. What is the standard deviation of a well-diversified portfolio with a beta of 0?
    c. What is the beta of a well-diversified portfolio with a standard deviation of .25?

11. An oil company has an expected return of .25 and a beta of 1.5, whereas a bank has an expected return of .175 and a beta of .75. What is the expected return on the market and the riskless rate of interest?

12. Risk-free securities are currently expected to yield 7.5 percent, and the market risk premium is expected to be 4 percent.
    a. What is the market return?
    b. If a security has a beta of 1.5, what will be its expected return?
    c. If the return on the security in (b) was expected to be 10 percent, what would we expect to happen to the security?
    d. If a security has a beta of 2, and an expected dividend yield of 5 percent, what capital gains (in percent) can one expect if one holds the stock?

13. Over the past ten years, the year-end price of GoldMine Co. has been as shown. The closing level of the S&P 500 is also included:

Year	1	2	3	4	5	6	7	8	9	10
GoldMine	$25.00	$24.50	$25.00	$27.50	$30.00	$35.00	$45.00	$41.00	$44.00	$44.00
S&P 500	94.28	97.80	107.78	135.76	122.30	141.24	164.93	173.86	210.25	230.75

    a. From the historical data, what is the standard deviation of return of GoldMine Co.?
    b. What is the expected return of GoldMine Co.?
    c. Estimate the beta of GoldMine Co.
    d. If the risk-free rate of return is 7.5 percent and the market risk premium is 4 percent, what will be the expected return of GoldMine Co. stock?
    e. Is GoldMine a good investment to hold in a portfolio?

14. The risk-free rate of return is 7.5 percent and the market risk premium is 4 percent.
    a. The beta of ITT stock has been estimated at 1.00. Given its current price of $10, what is its expected price one year from now (assume all return to the stock is in the form of capital gains)?
    b. If Martin Metals stock has a beta of −.2, and its price is expected to be 45 next year, how much would you be willing to pay for the stock today?

15. The beta of Golf and Eastern Corp. is 1.35. The risk-free rate is 10 percent and the market risk premium is 8 percent.
    a. Calculate the expected return of G&E.
    b. Assume G&E has a constant growth of dividends of 10 percent. If dividends are expected to be $1.05 next year, what is the current price of the stock?

c. If inflation rose by 5 percent, what would happen to the risk-free rate, the market return, and the expected return of G&E?

d. If inflation increases as in (c), what will happen to the stock price of G&E?

16. The risk-free rate is 7.5 percent and the market return is 10.5 percent.

a. With a beta of 2.00, what is the expected return of the stock of Amp Electronics?

b. If Amp Electronics has been growing at 5 percent and dividends are expected to be $2.10, what is the price of the stock?

c. If the corporation's management institutes changes that decrease AE's risk, the stock's beta will decline to .65. Assuming the same growth in dividends as before, what will happen to the price of its stock?

17. Agricorp just paid its annual dividend of $1.75. At the same time, the president of the company announced that the goal of management was to double the dividend in each of the next five years and then to have the annual dividend double every ten years thereafter. The risk-free interest rate is 8 percent and the expected return on the market is 17 percent. The market applies a 14 percent discount rate to Agricorp's stock.

a. What is Agricorp's stock worth, assuming the market believes the president will be able to fulfill her dividend intentions?

b. What is the stock's beta?

18. Westbrook Partners, Inc., a venture capital firm, is considering an investment in a new product. The partners have estimated the expected net after-tax cash flows from investing in the project and the expected level of the Dow-Jones Industrial Average for each of six possible scenarios, as follows:

Scenario	1	2	3	4	5	6
Cash flow ($ millions)	2.5	2.7	3.0	3.2	3.3	3.4
Dow-Jones	1510	1660	1700	1750	1825	1880

a. If Westbrook values the new product line as an investment asset similar to a stock, what would the product line's beta be?

b. If the market risk premium is expected to be 7 percent and the risk-free rate is expected to be 9 percent, what rate of return should the firm require from the product line?

c. If markets for assets like new product lines are efficient, how much should Westbrook be willing to pay for the product line? Assume the six scenarios are equally likely and the project lasts for one year only.

19. Three factors have been found to influence the return of Unoil stock: an index summarizing energy costs (I1), changes in the level of the stock market (I2), and changes in the dollar in relation to a weighted average of exchange rates (I3). The betas associated with each risk factor are .7, .3, and 1.1, respectively. The risk premium for I1 is 3 percent, for I2 is 5 percent, and for I3 is 7.5 percent. The risk-free rate is 5.5 percent.

a. What is the expected return for Unoil according to the APT?

b. What is the expected return according to the CAPM?

c. Would the inclusion of the two extra factors explain the usual empirical result in tests of the CAPM that the zero-beta security has a rate of return greater than the risk-free rate and that the market risk premium estimated empirically is usually less than the actual market risk premium?

20. A portfolio manager is considering the benefits of increasing his diversification by investing overseas. He can purchase shares in an individual country fund with the following characteristics:

	United States (%)	United Kingdom (%)	Spain (%)
Expected return	15	12	5
Standard deviation of return	10	9	4
Correlation with the United States	1.0	.33	.06

a. What is the expected return and standard deviation of return of a portfolio with 25 percent invested in the United Kingdom, 75 percent in the United States? With 50 percent invested in the United States, 50 percent in the United Kingdom? With 25 percent invested in the United States and 75 percent in the United Kingdom?

b. What is the expected return and standard deviation of return of a portfolio with 25 percent invested in Spain, 75 percent in the United States? With 50 percent invested in the United States and 50 percent invested in Spain? With 25 percent invested in the United States, 75 percent invested in Spain?

c. Plot these two sets of risk–return combinations, (a) and (b), as in Figure 4-4. Which leads to a better set of risk–return choices, Spain or the United Kingdom?

Measuring Risk and Return
for a Single Asset

Because the future itself is always uncertain, the cash flows associated with possible projects and activities are also uncertain. As the future unfolds, actual cash flows are revealed, and to the extent that they diverge from those that were expected, security values adjust to reflect the new information. Thus, for example, few people forecast the decline in oil prices in the early 1980s, and so when it happened, oil stocks tumbled.

It is this uncertainty, the inability to forecast the future accurately and reliably, that we intuitively understand as risk. Intuition takes us only so far, however. What we need is a more precise definition of risk that will enable us to compare alternative ventures in terms of both risk and return. This is possible using probability theory.

Probability Distributions

The *probability* of an event is defined as the likelihood that the event will occur. For example, the chances of drilling successfully for oil in west Texas may be one out of ten. This is equivalent to saying that the probability of finding oil is .10 or 10 percent. In general, the probability of a particular outcome must lie between zero and one. Impossible events have a zero probability; if an event is certain (a sure thing), its probability is one. Most event probabilities, like the odds of heads on the flip of a coin, fall somewhere in between.

A complete description of all possible outcomes, along with their associated probabilities, is known as a *probability distribution*. The probabilities represented by a probability distribution must sum to 1; otherwise, some possible event has been omitted. This means that if the probability of finding oil is .10, the probability of drilling a dry hole must be .90; it can't be .89 or .91.

From the data supplied by these probability distributions, we can compute two statistical parameters that are crucial to financial analysis: (1) the *expected return*, which describes the average of all possible outcomes, and (2) the *standard deviation*, which is a measure of the dispersion or variability around the expected outcome.

Expected Rate of Return.   Because the actual return on an investment is unknown at the time the investment is made, investors usually focus on the "likely return." The most common measure of "likely return" is the *expected return*, which is a weighted average of all possible returns multiplied by the associated probabilities. More precisely,

$$E(R) = \sum_{i=1}^{n} p_i R_i$$

where $E(R)$ is the expected return, R_i is the return for the ith possible outcome, p_i is the probability of earning that return, and n is the number of different possible returns.

APPLICATION **Valuing a Lottery**	A magazine subscription agent offers a free lottery to encourage magazine sales. Prizes and the probabilities of winning the different prizes are as follows:

	Amount	Chance of Winning
First prize	$1,000,000	1 in 10,000,000
Second prize	$100,000	1 in 2,000,000
Third prize	$50,000	1 in 1,500,000

If a stamp to mail in the lottery entry costs 22 cents, should you enter the lottery?

SOLUTION   Find the expected return from entering the lottery. This expected return is just the difference between the expected payoff of the lottery and the cost of entering the lottery.

$$\text{Expected payoff of lottery} = \$1,000,000 \times 1/10,000,000 + \$100,000$$
$$\times 1/2,000,000 + \$50,000 \times 1/1,500,000$$
$$= \$.183$$

Because the cost of a stamp is $.22, the expected return from entering the lottery is $.183 − $.22 = −$.037. Therefore, you should not enter the lottery.

In all likelihood, the expected return will not materialize. Were this not so, there would be no risk. In fact, in many cases, as in the lottery illustration, the expected return cannot occur because it is not one of the possible outcomes! Financial risk, therefore, can be thought of as the possibility that the return on a security or project will deviate from what was expected. The dispersion of possible outcomes around the expected return is usually measured by either the variance or the standard deviation.

Variance.   The variance, denoted by σ_R^2 (sigma squared), is the sum of the squared deviations $[R_i - E(R_i)]$ between the actual returns and the expected return, weighted by the associated probabilities p_i:

$$\sigma_R^2 = \sum_{i=1}^{n} p_i [R_i - E(R)]^2$$

Standard Deviation. Because the variance is expressed as squared returns, a concept difficult for most people to grasp, the standard deviation of the return, which is the square root of the variance, is often used as an equivalent measure of risk. That is,

$$\sigma_R = (\sigma_R{}^2)^{1/2}$$

where σ (sigma) is the symbol for the standard deviation.

APPLICATION
Du Pont

Suppose an investor believed that the possible one-year returns (dividends plus price appreciation) on Du Pont stock could be described by the following probability distribution:

Probability Distribution of One-Year Returns on Du Pont Stock

Probability of outcome	.10	.15	.15	.20	.15	.15	.10
Return (%)	−6	−2	4	8	12	18	27

What are the variance and standard deviation of this distribution?

SOLUTION First calculate the expected return. Then weight the squared deviations from the expected return by their probabilities of occurring to find the variance. Finally take the square root of the variance to find the standard deviation.

The expected return is

$$E(R) = -6 \times .10 - 2 \times .15 + 4 \times .15 + 8 \times .20 + 12 \times .15$$
$$+ 18 \times .15 + .27 \times .10$$
$$= 8.5 \text{ percent}$$

This yields a variance of

$$\sigma_R{}^2 = .10(-6 - 8.5)^2 + .15(-2 - 8.5)^2 + .15(4 - 8.5)^2 + .2(8 - 8.5)^2$$
$$+ .15(12 - 8.5)^2 + .15(18 - 8.5)^2 + .10(27 - 8.5)^2$$
$$= 21.03 + 16.54 + 3.04 + .05 + 1.84 + 13.54 + 34.23$$
$$= 90.25 \text{ (difference due to rounding errors)}$$

and a standard deviation of

$$\sigma_R = (90.25)^{1/2}$$
$$= 9.5 \text{ percent}$$

Observe that the standard deviation is expressed in percentage terms, the same units of measurement as the expected return.

FIGURE 4A-1

Two Probability Distributions with Identical Expected Returns but Different Standard Deviations

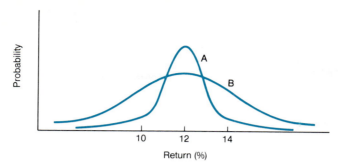

A probability distribution with a low variance or standard deviation is said to be "tight" because possible returns are more tightly bunched around the expected return. The tighter the distribution is, the closer the actual return is likely to be to the expected return and, therefore, the lower the risk of the investment will be. Distribution A in Figure 4A-1 is tighter than distribution B.

Properties of the Standard Deviation.   The standard deviation as a measure of risk has four important features:

1. *In the absence of any variation, the standard deviation is zero.* This is a desirable property because it says that for a riskless investment, our measure of risk is zero.
2. *The deviations from the mean are squared.* This means that values further from the mean are given a proportionately heavier weight. The rationale is that large deviations represent substantially more risk than do smaller deviations.
3. *The squared deviations are multiplied by the probability of that deviation's occurring.* The result is that deviations with a greater chance of occurring have a larger effect on the standard deviation.
4. *The standard deviation is expressed in the same units as is the expected return.* This enables a direct comparison between the two statistics. The units could be dollars, percentage per annum, or any other measurement quantity.

Continuous Probability Distributions

The probability distribution for Du Pont stock is called a *discrete* distribution; that is, probabilities are assigned to only a finite number of specific values. Most probability distributions used in finance are treated as *continuous* (even if they are actually discrete); that is, they assign probabilities to intervals between two points of a continuous curve. Individual points have a zero probability. Consequently, with continuous distributions, like the ones depicted in Figure 4A-1, it is more appropriate to talk about the probability of earning a return of at least, say, 15 percent than to talk about the probability that the actual return will be 15 percent. Continuous probability distributions are also good at answering questions such as "What is the probability that the return will lie somewhere between 10 and 20 percent?"

The Normal Distribution.   The most important probability distribution used in finance is the normal distribution, the familiar bell-shaped curve. Many phenomena, from weather patterns to IQ measurements, are normally distributed. Over short intervals of time, stock returns are approximately normal as well. This is fortunate for investors because a normal probability distribution can be completely characterized by just two numbers, its expected return and its standard deviation. Thus an investor need only be concerned with these two measures of risk and return.

Four features of the normal distribution deserve mention:

1. *It is perfectly symmetric around the expected return*. This means, for example, that there is a 50 percent probability that the actual return will exceed the expected return and a 50 percent probability that the actual return will be less than the expected return.
2. *The probability that the return will be within plus or minus one standard deviation from the expected return is 68.3 percent*. In other words, about two out of three times, returns will be within one standard deviation of the expected return. Because the normal distribution is symmetric, this means that the probability of a return's being more than one standard deviation above the expected return is 15.9 percent (31.8/2). For example, if the expected return is 15 percent and the standard deviation is 6 percent, then there is a 68.3 percent probability that the actual return will be between 9 percent and 21 percent (15 percent plus or minus 6 percent).
3. *About 95 percent of the time (95.4 percent to be more precise), the return will be within two standard deviations of the expected return*. Therefore, the odds of the actual return's exceeding the expected return by more than two standard deviations is 2.3 percent (4.6/2). In the example in item 2, there is a 95.4 percent probability that the actual return will be between 3 percent and 27 percent (15 percent plus or minus 2 × 6 percent).
4. *Almost 100 percent of the time (actually 99.7 percent), the return will lie within three standard deviations of the expected return*. Thus, with a 15 percent expected return and a 6 percent standard deviation, there is a 99.7 percent probability that the actual return will lie between −3 percent and 33 percent.

These characteristics of the normal distribution are displayed in Figure 4A-2. Other probability ranges for the normal distribution can be found in Appendix Table 5 at the back of the book.

FIGURE 4A-2
Normal Distribution

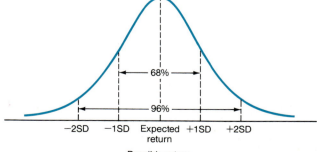

CHAPTER

5

Options and Corporate Finance

If chance will have me king, why, chance may
crown me.

SHAKESPEARE, *Macbeth*

In April 1973, trade in stock options began on the floor of the Chicago Board Options Exchange (CBOE). The succeeding years have witnessed enormous growth in the variety of options available to investors. Options on stocks, stock indexes, commodities, foreign currencies, and government securities are listed on over a dozen exchanges worldwide. There has been a corresponding explosion in investor interest. The number of contracts traded increases yearly, and volume on the CBOE often exceeds that of the New York Stock Exchange.

The reason for discussing options in a corporate finance text, however, is not because they are an interesting or actively traded form of financial contract. Rather, it is because many investment and financing choices contain options in disguise. For example, an investment in a new technology or a new distribution network may allow the company to expand into new products or markets at a later date. In each case, the company is investing money today for the option of making further investments in the future. If the future projects appear to be profitable, the company will invest in them; otherwise it will let its option expire. Similarly, we will see that all financial securities contain options embedded in them.

The two main purposes of this chapter are to show you how the concepts and techniques developed in the option valuation literature can be applied to many problems in corporate finance and to orient you to this method of looking at value. It covers the basic concepts of options and option pricing and introduces a number of problems in corporate finance in which an option-pricing approach is useful. This will set the stage for a more detailed study of options and corporate finance in subsequent chapters. Waiting until later to introduce this material would preclude the use of option-pricing concepts and models before then.

5.1
THE BASICS
OF STOCK
OPTIONS

Options come in many forms, but all share the following characteristic: The holder has the right—but not the obligation—to buy (call) or sell (put) an asset at a set price and date. The seller of the put or call option must fulfill the contract if the buyer so desires it. The option not to buy or sell has value, and so the buyer must pay the seller of the option a *premium* for this privilege. An option that would be profitable to exercise at the asset's current price is said to be **in the money**. Conversely, an **out-of-the-money** option is one that would not be profitable to exercise at the current asset price. The price at which the option is exercised is the **exercise** or **strike** price. If the option can be exercised only at the expiration date, it is called a **European option.** An option that can be exercised at any date prior to expiration is an **American option.**

Call Options

The relationship among the expiration price, the strike price, and the profitability of a European option contract is shown in Figure 5-1. Figure 5-1(a) illustrates the profits available on a **call option** with an exercise price of $25 and a call premium of $3. At a price of $25 or lower, the option will not be exercised, resulting in a loss of the $3 option premium. At a price above $28, the option is sufficiently deep in the money to cover the option premium and yield a net profit. For example, if the expiration price is $32, the option will be worth $7 ($32 − $25), and the profit net of the $3 premium will be $4.

Between $25 and $28, the option will be exercised, but the gain is insufficient to cover the cost of the premium. For example, if the expiration price is

FIGURE 5-1
Profit from Options

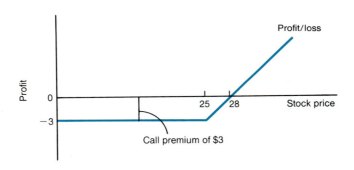

(a) Buy a call option

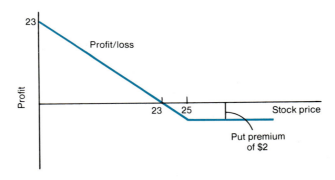

(b) Buy a put option

$27, the option will yield $2 ($27 − $25), but the overall impact is a $1 loss net of the $3 premium.

In general, the value, C, of a call option at expiration with stock price S at that time and exercise price X is

$$C = \max\{0, S - X\}$$

where max refers to the maximum value of $S - X$ and 0. In other words, the call option is worth the difference between the current stock price and the exercise price or zero, whichever is greater. If the stock price happens to equal the exercise price, the option is said to be **at the money**, and the investor will be indifferent between exercising it for a zero gain or allowing it to expire. The profit to the call option buyer is $C - a$, where a is the call premium. Because the call option contract is a zero-sum game, the profit from selling a call is the negative of the profit from buying the call.

Put Options

Figure 5-1(b) illustrates the profit from buying a **put option** with an exercise price of $25 and a premium of $2. As the asset's price rises toward $23, the profit falls. In particular, each $1 rise in the price of the asset causes the profit on the put option to drop by $1. For example, if the price of the asset goes from $15 to $16, the value of the option will drop from $10 to $9, and the profit on the option net of the $2 premium will fall from $8 to $7. At $23, the net profit on the put option is zero and becomes a loss of the $2 put premium at $25 and up. In general, the value of a put option, P, at expiration with exercise price X and stock price S on that date is

$$P = \max\{0, X - S\}$$

If the put premium is b, then the buyer's profit on the put option will equal $P - b$. The seller of the put option will realize profits that are the negative of the buyer's profits.

5.2 OPTION PRICING

The pricing of options is one of the most complex tasks in corporate finance. Until fairly recently, option prices could be determined for only very simple options. But in 1973 Fischer Black and Myron Scholes derived a formula to value European options.[1] The **Black–Scholes option pricing model** depends on the ability of investors to replicate exactly the payoffs from a call option by holding an investment in the underlying asset that is financed in part with borrowed money. In equilibrium, the value of the option must equal the cost of creating the option equivalent. If it does not, a risk-free arbitrage opportunity will exist.

The reason for introducing this material now is to give you some understanding of the factors that affect the value of an option and the way in which these factors affect option values. This understanding will be useful later in

---

[1]Fischer Black and Myron Scholes, "The Pricing of Options and Corporate Liabilities," *Journal of Political Economy*, May–June 1973, pp. 637–659.

recognizing how certain factors affect investment and financing decisions that have optionlike characteristics.

Using Arbitrage to Value an Option

To see how the Black–Scholes arbitrage technique for valuing options works, consider the following simple example: Suppose that the current price of Meridian Inc. is $100 per share, which is also the exercise price of a one-year call option. To keep matters simple, we will assume that at the end of one year Meridian's price will either rise to $110 or fall to $90. Given a one-year interest rate of 5 percent, we can show that the option must be worth $7.143.

If the stock's price at the expiration of the call turns out to be $110, the call option will be in the money, and its value will be $10. On the other hand, if the stock price in one year is $90, the call will expire worthless. The possible payoffs to the option are

	Stock price = $90	$110
Value of call option	0	10

The payoffs from this option can be exactly duplicated by buying one share of Meridian's stock, financed in part with $85.714 of borrowed money.[2] This portfolio has a current net value of $14.286, equal to the $100 price of the stock less the $85.714 of borrowed money. The payoffs in one year from this portfolio are as follows:

	Stock price = $90	$110
Value of one share	90	110
Repayment of loan plus interest @ 5%	90	90
Total payoff	$0	$20

Because the payoffs from this portfolio exactly duplicate the payoffs from owning *two* call options, their values must be identical. Therefore, given a current value of the portfolio equal to $14.286, the call option must be worth half that amount, or $7.143. If the market price of the call option should differ from this number, riskless arbitrage profits could be earned. But such a situation could not last for long. In the process of capitalizing on this profitable opportunity, arbitrageurs would drive back the price of the call option to its equilibrium value of $7.143.

---

[2]To construct a levered position in the underlying stock that gives exactly the same payoffs as the call option, it is necessary to borrow an amount equal to $(S_L - C_L)/(1 + r)$, where S_L is the possible low value for the end-of-period stock price, C_L is the end-of-period option contract value per share of stock when the stock finishes at S_L, and r is the borrowing rate. Substituting in the numbers given in the text yields a borrowing amount equal to

$$(90 - 0)/1.05 = \$85.714$$

The Black–Scholes Model

The assumption that only two possible stock price movements could occur during the year is fanciful. But if we change the word *year* to the word *period* and then shrink the period to an interval approaching zero, the assumption that the stock price will move either slightly up or slightly down during the next microsecond becomes quite realistic. Of course, the degree of leverage (the amount of money borrowed) would have to be updated continually as the price of the stock and the time until expiration changed.

Although the task of valuing this levered investment may sound daunting, Black and Scholes derived the formula that does the trick. The resulting value of a European call option prior to its expiration date is

BLACK–SCHOLES CALL OPTION PRICING FORMULA

$$C(t) = SN\{d_1\} - Xe^{-rt}N\{d_2\}$$

where

$C(t)$ = current value of the call option with an amount of time t remaining before expiration

t = time until expiration of the option

S = current price of the stock or other asset

X = exercise price of the option

e = 2.71828 (base of the natural system of logarithms)

r = (continuously compounded) risk-free rate of interest

$N(d)$ = value of the cumulative normal density function at d[3]

$$d_1 = \frac{\ln(S/X) + (r + .5\sigma^2)t}{\sigma\sqrt{t}}$$

$$d_2 = \frac{\ln(S/X) + (r - .5\sigma^2)t}{\sigma\sqrt{t}} = d_1 - \sigma\sqrt{t}$$

ln = natural logarithm

σ = standard deviation per period of the rate of return on the stock (continuously compounded)

This formula has several important implications for valuing options. Specifically, the option increases in value as

1. *The asset's price becomes more volatile.* An increase in the standard deviation increases the chance of an extremely high or low stock price at the time the option expires. The higher chance of a very high stock price benefits the call owner, whereas the higher chance of a very low

---

[3]$N(d)$ is the probability that a normally distributed random variable (see Chapter 4, Appendix 4A for a discussion of the normal distribution) will take on a value less than or equal to d.

stock price is irrelevant: The option will be worthless for any stock price less than the striking price, whether the stock price is "low" or "very low." Because the effect of increased volatility is beneficial, the value of the option is higher.

2. *The time to expiration increases.* A longer time to maturity increases the probability of a large change in the price of the asset over the life of the option. As noted, the possibility of large changes benefits the holder of a call option.

3. *The risk-free rate goes up.* The option value should increase as the effective cost of exercising decreases. As the rate of interest rises, the present value of the exercise payment, Xe^{-rt}, declines, thereby increasing the value of the option.

4. *The ratio of the stock price to the exercise price increases.* An increase in the ratio S/X results from an increase in S or a decrease in X. Because the option is worth a maximum of zero or S minus X, an increase in S or a decrease in X increases the chance of a large positive value of $S - X$, increasing the expected value of the payoff on the option.

The risk aversion of investors does not affect the value of the option explicitly.[4] This is because the risk associated with selling a call option can be perfectly hedged by holding the underlying asset in an amount that varies in line with the asset's price.[5] "Perfectly hedged" means that any profit resulting from an increase in the price of the asset being held would be exactly offset by a loss on the option position, and vice versa. Because the hedged position is riskless, the rate of return on the position must equal the riskless rate. Similarly, although the asset's expected return affects the price of the asset, it does not affect the value of the option.

The relation between the value of the option prior to expiration, the value of the underlying asset, and the 45° parity line, $S - X$, is shown in Figure 5-2. The distance between the value of the option C and the parity line is known as the **premium over parity**. The heavy solid line is the **intrinsic value** of the option. It equals the amount by which the option is in the money. In other words, it represents the immediate exercise value of the option. An out-of-the-money option has no intrinsic value. Figure 5-2 shows that the intrinsic value of the option is zero for asset values less than X. Any excess of the option value over its intrinsic value is called the **time value** of the contract.

Before expiration, an out-of-the-money option has only time value, and an in-the-money option has both time and intrinsic value. At expiration, an option can have only intrinsic value. The time value of an option reflects the probability that its intrinsic value will increase before expiration; this probability depends, among other things, on the volatility of the underlying asset. As shown in Figure 5-2, the time value of an option declines as the expiration date draws nearer; an option with a shorter life has less chance of going deeper in the money before it expires. Once the expiration date arrives, the option's time value is zero, and the option's only value is its intrinsic value.

---

[4]Although risk does not explicitly enter the valuation formula of the option, risk aversion is present among traders in the market who, in the aggregate, determine the return-generating process.

[5]The required ratio of stock shares to option-controlled shares is called the *hedge ratio*. In the previous example, this ratio was 1:2.

FIGURE 5-2

The Value of a Call Option Prior to Maturity

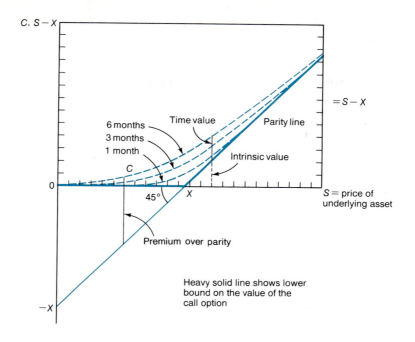

Figure 5-2 also shows that as S approaches zero, C approaches zero and as S becomes infinitely large, the value of the option approaches $S - X$. In other words, the time value of an option goes to zero (leaving the asset with only its intrinsic value) as the option goes deep in or out of the money and as the option approaches its expiration. In addition, the time value is greatest when the option is at the money.

These results arise as follows: A stock price of zero means that there is no chance the asset will be worth anything in the future.[6] If so, the option will expire unexercised and worthless, giving it a present value of zero. Alternatively, as the asset's price rises, the chance that it will fall below X in the future declines, increasing the probability that the option will be exercised eventually at a profit of $S - X$. If S becomes large enough, exercise is virtually ensured and the value of the option will just equal $S - X$.[7] Under both price extremes—$S = 0$ and $S = \infty$—the time value equals zero because there is no chance that future events will alter the decision of whether to exercise the option. Otherwise, the option price will always exceed its value, $S - X$, if exercised today.

The fact that an option has a positive time value prior to expiration results in an important decision rule: An option on a non-dividend–paying stock should never be exercised before expiration. Exercise yields the holder $S - X$ dollars, but at any time before expiration the option is worth a premium above $S - X$. A holder who wishes to cash out early should always prefer to sell the option to someone else and receive $S - X$ plus the time value.

[6]If there were any possibility that the asset would be worth *something* in the future, no matter how little, its present value would be positive.

[7]Actually, the value of the option is $S - Xe^{-rt}$, where Xe^{-rt} is the present value of the future exercise price with t units of time remaining until expiration.

We can see that the Black–Scholes formula offers simple and interesting implications. There is a complementary formula for the value of a European put option that yields similar implications.

5.3 THE BLACK–SCHOLES MODEL AND ACTUAL STOCK OPTION CONTRACTS

In deriving their option-pricing formula, Black and Scholes made several assumptions to simplify the mathematics of the derivation. Some of these assumptions conflict with the features of actual option contracts and option markets.

First, Black and Scholes assumed that the underlying stock pays no dividend and the option is of the European type, which can be exercised only at the instant before it expires. The previous section showed that the possibility of early exercise is not a problem as long as the underlying stock does not pay dividends. However, virtually all listed stock options are written on stocks that pay dividends and are *American* options, which can be exercised at any time during their life, not just at the end. Robert Merton has derived an option-pricing formula for the case when the stock continuously pays a dividend at a fixed percentage of the stock price.[8] Other authors have published models that account for periodic dividends and possible early exercise of an American option. However, the realistic features of these models are not without cost: They are considerably more difficult to use than is the Black–Scholes formula.

Though more complex, these models address issues that are important to actual participants in option markets. Consider the owner of an in-the-money option on a stock that is about to pay a large dividend. By exercising the option, the owner loses the value of the option *premium*, the value in excess of the cash flow that would be received from exercising immediately:

$$\text{Call option premium} = \text{Call option price} - \max\{0, S - X\}$$

But by not exercising the call and taking delivery of the stock, the owner will forfeit the large dividend forthcoming on the stock. Once that dividend is paid, the owner has an option on an asset that has dropped in value by approximately the amount of the dividend. Thus, the value of an in-the-money option will drop by about the amount of the dividend. The option holder will exercise if the benefit (the big dividend) exceeds the cost (the option premium that will be lost). However, these important considerations are not factored into the Black–Scholes formula.

For example, suppose the call option price is $3.50, the exercise price is $45, and the current stock price is $47. Then the call option premium is $1.50. If the stock is about to pay a dividend of $2.50, the option holder will prefer to exercise the option now and realize the $2 value of the option currently, even though the $1.50 option premium is lost. Otherwise, by retaining the option, the holder will lose the $2.50 dividend. Following payment of the $2.50 dividend, the price of the stock will drop by approximately that amount. Because the holder now has a call option that can be exercised at $45 on an asset that is worth approximately $44.50, the value of the option will drop considerably.

Other assumptions of the Black–Scholes model may not match real-world option markets. If interest rates are random, the assumption of a constant in-

[8]Robert C. Merton, "Theory of Rational Option Pricing," *Bell Journal of Economics and Management Science*, Spring 1973, pp. 141–183.

terest rate may lead to inaccurate option price estimates from the Black–Scholes model. If the variance of the stock's return is constantly changing with the firm's fortunes and information quality or if the stock's return is not normally distributed, the model may, once again, provide poor results. Finally, if transactions costs impede the ability of investors to set up duplicating portfolios of stocks and bonds, the model may not match actual market option prices.

Similar complications will arise when we seek to analyze corporate finance problems using basic option valuation concepts. Despite these problems, the usefulness of the simple Black–Scholes approach to option pricing for corporate finance will be immediately apparent if we take a quick look at a few problems.

5.4 OPTION VALUATION AND INVESTMENT DECISIONS

The corporation must value the set of available investment projects in order to decide which are worth undertaking. As we will see in the next chapter, the recommended approach is to estimate the cash flows that a project is expected to generate and to discount them at a risk-adjusted cost of capital. However, many investments have very uncertain payoffs that are best valued with an options approach.

Consider a firm that must decide whether to make a $50,000 down payment on an undeveloped piece of land. The down payment will permit the firm to purchase the property outright by paying an additional $500,000 at any time during the next six months. If the additional payment is not made, the $50,000 will be forfeited. The down payment agreement is a call option, with the $50,000 down payment equivalent to the option price; the extra money needed to complete the deal ($500,000) is the striking price; and the uncertain value of the land after it is developed is the "stock" price. The decision to "exercise the option," that is, to pay the additional $500,000 to own the land, depends on whether the value of the land exceeds $500,000 at the time the agreement is about to expire. Before entering into this agreement and spending the $50,000 option price, the company must determine whether $50,000 is a fair price for the option. Clearly, the Black–Scholes formula could be used for this purpose. Figure 5-3 shows how the value of this option varies with the price of the land in six months.

Other explicit and implicit contracts to which a firm is a party can be thought of (and valued as) options. A lease with an option to cancel can be viewed as a put option. If the value of leasing the property drops below the value of the lease payments, the lease will be canceled and the property will be "returned" to its owner, just as a stock will be sold to a put writer if its value drops sufficiently low. For example, a federal crop price support program is equivalent

FIGURE 5-3

Value of a Call Option on Land at Expiration

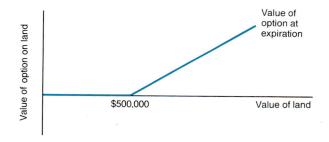

to issuing put options to farmers. A farmer would prefer to sell his crop at a higher price in the market but can always sell to the government at the guaranteed price if the market price plummets. The purchase of an insurance policy on property can also be thought of as a put: If the property is not damaged and remains valuable, the insurance contract will not be used; if a fire or earthquake damages the property, it will be forfeited in return for the contracted insurance payoff. It is analogous to exercising a put option when the price of the stock drops below the exercise price.

Any investment that requires an additional infusion of funds for its completion and offers an uncertain payoff can be viewed as an option. Consider the value of a patent on an untested cure for cancer. The price of obtaining the patent is the option price; the cost of developing, producing, and marketing the drug is the striking price; and the market value of profits on sales of the drug is equivalent to the stock price. The extra funds required to start production will be invested only if this cost is less than the payoff in the form of subsequent profits from the sale of the drug.

The opportunities that a firm may have to increase the profitability of its existing product lines and benefit from expanding into new products or markets may be thought of as **growth options**. Similarly, a firm's ability to capitalize on its managerial talent, its experience in a particular product line, its brand name, or its other resources may provide valuable but uncertain future prospects. Growth options are of great importance to new firms. New ventures often have few, if any, tangible assets; their assets consist primarily of the knowledge and skills of an entrepreneur. Yet such firms have value because of the profitable possibilities their intangible assets provide. As we will see in Chapter 7, these growth options may constitute a large fraction of firm value. For example, Genentech, a gene-splicing company, had a stock market value of over $3 billion in late 1986, even though its earnings for the year were only $11 million, giving it a P/E ratio of over 270 to 1. Clearly, the market was valuing Genentech's future ability to capitalize on its research in areas like anticancer therapy and blood clot dissolvers for heart attack victims.

Any firm that faces a continuing series of operating decisions may be thought of as having investment options. Consider a gold mine. Its owners may increase or decrease the mine's gold output depending on the current price of gold and expectations of future gold prices. The mine can be shut down and then reopened when production and market conditions are more favorable, or it can be abandoned permanently. Each decision is an option from the viewpoint of the mine's owners. The value of these options, in turn, affects the value of the mine.

APPLICATION
Valuing a Gold Mine

A gold mine is currently shut down but could be reopened at a cost of $1 million. The current value of the mine can be thought of as a call option on the value of the gold in the mine: The striking price equals the cost of reopening, and the stock price equals the value of the gold that could subsequently be produced. The mine will be reopened only if the value of the gold to be mined exceeds the cost of reopening, just as a call option will be exercised only if the stock price exceeds the exercise price. In Chapter 7, we will learn how to value such a mine. For now, it serves to illustrate the usefulness of option valuation concepts for capital budgeting and valuation purposes.

Consideration of competitive conditions is what separates growth options from stock options. Growth options are valuable because they allow the firm to delay investments to learn more about the value of the underlying growth opportunities. But because these options are (1) often shared with other competitors and (2) cannot generally be traded, competition provides an incentive to exercise the option early and invest in the opportunity before competitors do. This is equivalent to the early exercise of an option on a dividend-paying stock.

5.5 OPTION VALUATION AND CORPORATE FINANCING DECISIONS

In addition to deciding which investment projects to undertake, a financial manager must approach the capital markets with new issues of securities to obtain the funds needed to complete the firm's investment program. The range of possible securities to issue and the possible channels through which to sell them must be ranked according to their costs and benefits to the firm. A crucial insight by Black and Scholes was their recognition that all corporate securities can be viewed as special types of options and valued accordingly. Thus, option valuation concepts can help the manager determine an appropriate financing package. Much of the material in this section is a precursor to subjects that will be covered in more detail in Parts III and IV of the text.

Raising Equity Capital with a Rights Offering

A firm that has decided to issue new equity has several ways of getting the securities into the hands of investors. The firm's objective is to sell the entire new issue at the highest price possible. A *direct* or *private placement* is possible if the firm can find a large investor willing to purchase the entire issue. Alternatively, the new issue can be sold by issuing *rights* to existing stockholders of the firm. Rights grant to the holder the option to buy a prespecified number of new shares at a set price over a short period of time and are similar to call options. The subscription price (i.e., the exercise price) is usually set below the stock's current price. This means that the rights are in the money and increases the likelihood that they will be exercised.

However, the stock price may drop below the subscription price and make it uneconomic for shareholders to exercise their rights. One way to guard against this possibility and ensure that the firm's equity sale goes as planned is to execute a **standby agreement** with an investment banker. Under such an arrangement, the firm will try to sell the securities at the highest price the market will bear, but the investment banker agrees to take any unsold securities at a predetermined price. In return, the investment banker receives an initial payment regardless of whether there are unsold shares.

Clearly, the standby agreement is identical to a put option: The fee paid to the investment banker is the cost of the put; the fixed price the banker will pay for any unsold securities is the exercise price; and the uncertain price that the securities can fetch in the open market is equivalent to the stock price. Before signing a standby agreement, the issuing firm should use a put-pricing model to determine whether the investment banker's fee is a reasonable price for this put option.

APPLICATION
Hanson Trust
Issues Rights
Suppose Hanson Trust issues rights to its shareholders to purchase 5 million shares at a subscription price of $43. In return for a fee of $1 million, Goldman Sachs, a large investment bank, agrees to purchase at a price of $43 apiece any unsold shares. As long as the share price remains above $43, shareholders will exercise their rights and purchase the shares. But if the share price falls below $43, Hanson will exercise its put option and sell the shares directly to Goldman Sachs. If the price drops below $42.80, Goldman Sachs will lose money on the standby agreement. (Why?[9])

The Leverage Decision

In their paper on option valuation, Black and Scholes also pointed out that the equity of a *leveraged* corporation, one that uses debt financing to increase the returns on equity, may be thought of as a call option on the value of the firm's assets. Consider a firm that has borrowed $2 million that must be repaid next year. Because the corporation is a **limited liability** entity (i.e., the stockholders' liability is limited to the money they have already invested in the company), the owners can choose to make the payment and stay in business or default on the payment. In the latter case, the owners must turn over the firm and its assets to its creditors.

The owners' decision rule here is simple: They will pay the $2 million if the value of the firm's assets exceeds $2 million because they will get to keep the difference. Conversely, if the cost of keeping the firm going (the $2 million debt repayment) exceeds the value of the firm, the owners will default on the loan payment. The decision to pay or default is identical to the decision faced by the owner of a call option: He will exercise it if the stock price exceeds the exercise price and gain the difference, or he will allow the call to expire worthless if the stock price is less than the exercise price.

The Black–Scholes formula can be applied directly to the valuation of the levered firm's equity. The value of the firm's assets and the standard deviation of the return of the firm's assets replace in the formula the stock price and the standard deviation of the stock's return. The strike price and time to expiration are replaced by the face value and maturity of the firm's debt. The resulting formula yields the value of the equity. Furthermore, the implications of the model are also applicable:

1. The value of equity increases as the standard deviation of the firm's assets increases.
2. The value of the equity increases as the ratio of assets to debt in the firm increases.
3. The value of equity increases with the time to maturity of the debt.
4. The value of equity increases with the rate of interest.

The concept of equity as a call option will be discussed more at a later point in the chapter and later on in the book. We will see that because of the

---

[9]Each one cent drop in the price below $43 costs Goldman Sachs $50,000. With a fee of $1 million, Goldman Sachs will lose money if the price drops by more than $.20 per share.

optionlike nature of levered equity, managers and stockholders of a levered firm may have an incentive to select investment and financing strategies that will differ from those they would choose in an all-equity–financed firm.

Valuing Complex Securities

Firms frequently issue securities with complicated contractual features. As we will see in Parts III and IV, many corporate securities, including bonds and preferred stock that are convertible into a fixed number of common shares at the owner's option, bonds that are secured with some of the firm's assets as collateral, and warrants (call options on stock issued by the firm), have complex, optionlike features. Before issuing these securities, the financial manager can apply option-pricing techniques to determine their fair price.

5.6 OPTION VALUATION AND CONFLICTS AMONG CORPORATE STAKE-HOLDERS	The interests of stockholders, bondholders, and corporate managers do not always coincide. When conflicts arise, considerable explicit and implicit costs may be incurred by all the firm's stakeholders. Solutions consist of identifying the problem and creating more precise contracts between the parties involved. Concepts and models from the option valuation literature can help us understand these problems and design solutions.

Conflicts Between Stockholders and Bondholders

Return to the idea that the equity of a leveraged firm can be thought of as a call option on the value of the firm's assets. Specifically, recall the first implication of the Black–Scholes model:

> 1. The value of the call option rises as the standard deviation of the return from the underlying stock increases.

The intuition is that increased volatility benefits the option holder: He enjoys the increased chance of very high outcomes and does not care about the increased chance of very low outcomes because the option will be out of the money and worthless at any stock price below the strike price.

This optionlike characteristic of equity suggests an obvious conflict between stockholders and bondholders: Stockholders may be able to increase the value of their equity by switching the firm's assets into investment projects or lines of business with a higher standard deviation of return. The stockholders benefit from the increased chance of very high returns. The increased chance of *very* low returns does not concern them because *any* low return will bankrupt the firm.

Consider the case of the firm introduced in the previous section that owed $2 million to bondholders. Suppose the current probability distribution of future asset values is given by *A* in Figure 5-4(a). The value of the equity at the debt's maturity behaves like a call option and is shown by the 45° line originating at $2 million.

FIGURE 5-4

Valuing Equity as a Call Option on the Firm's Assets

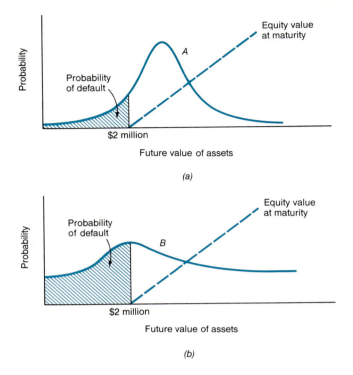

(a)

(b)

If the shareholders were to switch the firm's assets into riskier projects so as to produce a new probability distribution *B*, shown in Figure 5-4(b), they would be better off. The reason they are better off now is that the chance of a high payoff is greater in the case of distribution *B*, whereas the higher chance of a low payoff does not concern them; whether the firm's assets end up being worth $1.9 million or $1, the value of their equity is still zero. By contrast, they care greatly about whether the assets will wind up being worth $2.1 million or $5 million.

Stockholders will be restrained from taking on high-risk projects only if the firm owns valuable intangible assets whose value will be jeopardized by financial difficulties. Thus, stockholders of firms with few intangible assets have an incentive to gamble. Knowing this, investors will be unwilling to purchase bonds of such firms unless they offer a very high expected return. A possible solution to this problem is to design a bond contract that constrains the stockholders from moving the firm into a very risky business to the detriment of bondholders. By carefully designing the bond contract to prohibit the stockholders from switching the firm's assets into a riskier business, the potential conflicts between bondholders and stockholders and the potential costs of these conflicts (the lower price investors will pay for a new issue of corporate bonds and the costs imposed on other stakeholders) can be reduced. The option-pricing notion that levered equity can be thought of as a call option permits us to reach this conclusion and search for a solution.

Conflicts Between Owners and Managers

Consider a firm with many equity owners. The owners will wish the firm to engage in investment projects that maximize the value of their shares, even if those projects are highly risky. By contrast, the managers will tend to look to low-risk projects that minimize the possibility of bankruptcy: If the firm goes bankrupt, the managers will face considerable costs in finding a new position and may suffer a permanent loss of reputation. This puts the managers and owners in direct conflict.

One possible solution is to alter the managers' compensation contract in such a way that the interests of the managers and owners are aligned. Consider the impact of an employee stock option plan: Managers are given packages of out-of-the-money warrants in addition to their fixed salary and bonuses. The value of the options will increase if the managers direct the firm away from low-risk projects. Therefore, managers are encouraged to invest in those projects that the owners also find desirable. At the same time, the owners must be careful not to grant too many warrants to the managers; otherwise, the managers may be tempted to undertake risky investments to the point that the value of stockholder equity is reduced.

5.7 COMBINING STOCKS AND OPTIONS WITH BORROWING OR LENDING

Sections 5.1 and 5.2 outlined the payoffs from basic option positions. A European call pays the difference between the stock price and exercise price if the stock price exceeds the exercise price at expiration. A European put pays the difference between the exercise price and the stock price if the stock price is less than the exercise price at expiration. This section analyzes the payoffs from more complex combinations of puts, calls, stock, and money borrowed or lent. Doing so highlights some simple-option pricing principles and illustrates a variety of payoff patterns that can be achieved with options. The following notation will be used:

$$C = \text{current value of a European call option}$$

$$c = \text{current value of an American call option}$$

$$P = \text{current value of a European put option}$$

$$p = \text{current value of an American put option}$$

$$S = \text{current price of the underlying stock}$$

$$X = \text{exercise price of an option}$$

$$t = \text{time at which an option expires}$$

$$r = \text{continuously compounded riskless interest rate}$$

Bounds on the Values of European Puts and Calls

Without reference to the Black–Scholes model or any other specific theory, European option prices must obey several restrictions. Consider options on a stock that will pay no dividends over the life of the options. Because options can, at worst, expire unexercised and worthless, they cannot be worth less than zero:

$$C \geq 0 \tag{5.1}$$

$$P \geq 0 \tag{5.2}$$

Upper bounds on European option values are equally simple. Consider a call option. At best, it will be exercised and give its owner the underlying stock. Otherwise, it will not be exercised and expires worthless. Thus, the call cannot be worth more than the underlying stock:

$$C \leq S \tag{5.3}$$

Now consider the European put. At best, it will be exercised and give the owner a payment of X. Otherwise, it expires worthless. Therefore, the put cannot be worth more than a certain payment of X:

$$P \leq X \tag{5.4}$$

Combining puts or calls with the underlying stock and riskless borrowing or lending yields the following bounds:

$$C \geq S - Xe^{-rt} \tag{5.5}$$

$$P \geq Xe^{-rt} - S \tag{5.6}$$

The validity of these boundaries can be proved by comparing payoffs from options to payoffs from portfolios of stock and riskless borrowing or lending. Consider the call boundary, Equation 5.5. Compare the payoffs from a portfolio consisting of one share and Xe^{-rt} dollars borrowed to the payoffs from the call option. The borrowing is repaid with accumulated interest for a total cash out-flow of X dollars at time t. If the stock price at expiration, $S(t)$, exceeds the strike price, the option is worth $S(t) - X$. At the same time, the portfolio is worth the value of a stock minus the repayment of the borrowed dollars, $S(t) - X$. Therefore, the payoffs from the portfolio and the call are identical when the stock price exceeds the exercise price.

If the stock price at expiration is less than the strike price, the option is worthless but the portfolio is worth $S(t) - X$. However, in this case $S(t) - X$ is less than zero, so the payoff from the call (zero) exceeds the payoff from the portfolio. The current price of the call, C, must exceed the current price of the portfolio, $S - Xe^{-rt}$ because the payoff from the call is at least as great as, and sometimes greater than, the payoff from the portfolio:

$$C \geq S - Xe^{-rt} \tag{5.7}$$

Combining Equation 5.7 with condition 5.1 yields the European lower bound for calls:

$$C \geq \max\{0, S - Xe^{-rt}\} \tag{5.8}$$

The boundary for European puts, Equation 5.6, can be proved in a similar manner. A put pays $X - S(t)$ if the stock price is less than the exercise price or zero. A portfolio of Xe^{-rt} dollars lent and a share of stock sold short pays $X - S(t)$ regardless of whether $S(t)$ is less than or greater than X. The payoffs are equal if the stock price is less than the strike price while the payoff from the put is greater if the stock price is greater than the strike price. Since the put always pays at least as much as the portfolio and sometimes more, its current price must exceed the current price of the portfolio:

$$P \geq Xe^{-rt} - S \tag{5.9}$$

Combining this condition with Equation 5.2 yields the European lower bound for puts:

$$P \geq \max\{0, Xe^{-rt} - S\} \tag{5.10}$$

Put–Call Parity

By combining puts, calls, bonds, and shares of the underlying stock we can produce an equality for European option prices:

$$S + P = C + Xe^{-rt} \tag{5.11}$$

This condition is known as **European put–call parity** and can be proved by looking at the payoffs from two portfolios. The first portfolio consists of one share of stock and one put option. The potential payoffs can be shown as follows:

Payoffs on Portfolio of One Share of Stock and One Put Option at Expiration for Different Stock Prices

	$S(t) > X$	$S(t) < X$
Stock	$S(t)$	$S(t)$
European put option	0	$X - S(t)$
Stock plus put option	$S(t)$	X

These payoffs are shown in Figure 5-5(a). The dashed line in the sum of the stock and put payoffs for each closing price of the stock. For example, if $S(t) = X$, the value of the stock plus put is just X.

The second portfolio consists of one call and a riskless pure discount bond that pays X at time t. "Pure discount" means that no interest is paid till maturity. Then, the present value of the bond is Xe^{-rt}. The potential payoffs, which are shown in Figure 5-5(b), can be calculated as follows:

Payoffs on Portfolio of One Call Option and a Riskless Bond at Expiration for Different Stock Prices

	$S(t) > X$	$S(t) < X$
European call option	$S(t) - X$	0
Riskless bond	X	X
Call option plus bond	$S(t)$	X

FIGURE 5-5
Demonstration of
European Put–Call
Parity

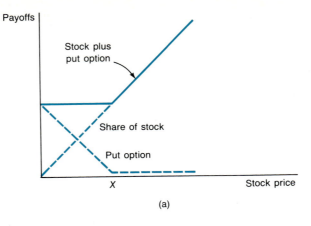

(a)

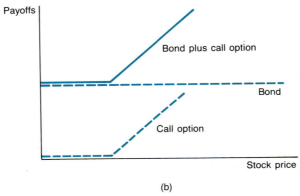

(b)

As can be seen in the tables and Figures 5-5(a) and 5-5(b), the payoffs from the two portfolios are identical. Given identical possible payoffs, the current values of the two portfolios must be identical and the European put–call parity equality is valid.

The preceding analysis shows how European put and call prices are restricted by stock and exercise prices and how prices for the two types of options are directly related though put–call parity. Option prices must obey these restrictions regardless of any particular option-pricing model.

**SUMMARY AND
CONCLUSIONS**

The key features of stock options can be summarized as follows: Put and call options are contracts between individuals. In return for an initial payment, one party to the contract has certain rights to buy or sell securities with the other party. The owner of the contract must determine whether to exercise those rights or to allow them to expire unused. It is important to remember that the option price is a sunk cost that the investor will regain only if the option is exercised at a profit. This makes the purchase price of an option a risky investment. But despite their risk, stock options are actively traded worldwide.

Although the frantic trading in stock options that occurs daily may appear to have little to do with the investment and financing decisions faced by financial managers, this is not the case. The growth in investors' interest in options has spawned a new branch of financial economics that has provided many concepts, models, and insights applicable to numerous issues in corporate finance. Option valuation can help managers both understand and solve fundamental problems in corporate finance.

These problems include the valuation of investments whose returns are contingent on how investors respond to unknown future states of nature, the effects of debt financing on both the risks and returns of equity capital, the valuation of complex securities and mechanisms for issuing those securities, and conflicts between stockholders and bondholders and between stockholders and managers.

REFERENCES

Black, Fischer, and Scholes, Myron. "The Pricing of Options and Corporate Liabilities." *Journal of Political Economy*, May–June 1973, pp. 637–659.

Cox, John C., and Rubinstein, Mark. *Option Markets*. Englewood Cliffs, N.J.: Prentice-Hall, 1985.

Kester, W. Carl. "An Options Approach to Corporate Finance," in Edward I. Altman, ed., *Handbook of Corporate Finance*, 2nd ed. New York: Wiley, 1986.

QUESTIONS

1. Insurance can be considered a put option from the policyholder's point of view. What is the exercise price and maturity of your car insurance? Do you think it is valued fairly?

2. As part of its month-long grand opening celebration, Rocky Burgers gives its customers a coupon entitling the holder to purchase two Rockyburgers for the price of one. Is this an option? How would you value it?

3. Imagine that the price of copper rises to the point that the copper value of a penny is worth more than $.01. As a result, pennies disappear from circulation. Your firm uses copper in its production process, and you can melt pennies down and retrieve their copper content at zero cost. At present, you have a six-month supply of copper reserves and you have also managed to collect 1 million pennies. Should you melt the pennies down and add the copper to your stockpile? Why or why not?

4. A new accounting firm has agreed to rent its office furniture and equipment for a year with an option to purchase all of it at the end of the lease for $500,000 extra. What is the strike price of the option? What is the price of the option?

5. According to the option-pricing model, shareholders *prefer* a riskier firm, other things being equal. Support this.

6. As interest rates rise, stock prices should fall, because the price of equity is the discounted value of future expected cash flows. Would this statement be true under the option-pricing model?

7. From an equityholder's point of view, what is the optimal amount of debt for a firm?

8. Under the option-pricing model, what are the key determinants of a convertible bond's value?

9. Equity is considered an option on the firm's value after the bondholders are paid off. Are bondholders "paid off" in most firms? What does this say about the value of equity?

10. A multidivisional corporation is planning a "spinoff" of a subsidiary to its shareholders. This would result in two firms, one of which, the old division, would be wholly

owned by the shareholders (100 percent equity). Will the bondholders approve of this spinoff? Will the shareholders?
11. Will a gold mine ever be shut permanently? Why or why not?
12. Should the coupon interest rate on convertible debt be greater or less than the coupon rate on a regular issue of debt from the same company if both are issued simultaneously at par? Why?
13. The U.S. government, through the Federal Savings and Loan Insurance Corporation (FSLIC), guarantees the safety of depositors' money. In return, savings and loans pay the FSLIC a fixed deposit insurance premium per dollar of deposits regardless of how risky the S&L's loan portfolio is.
    a. In what sense can FSLIC insurance be considered an option?
    b. How is the risk-taking behavior of S&Ls likely to be affected by the current FSLIC insurance system? How is the market value of its equity likely to affect an S&L's risk-taking behavior?
    c. How are depositors likely to respond to an S&L's risk-taking behavior under the current system?
    d. The market value of the assets of many Texas S&Ls is less than the face value of their liabilities. Why does the common stock of these S&Ls still sell at a positive price?

PROBLEMS

1. You have purchased a call option on AC stock for $5. The call option has an exercise price of $15.
   a. Calculate the profit on the option if the final price of AC stock is expected to be $35, $30, $25, $10, and $5.
   b. Graph the profit on the option as in Figure 5-1(a).
2. A put option on Unoil stock is selling for $2.35. The put exercise price is $10.
   a. Calculate the profit on the put option if the final price of Unoil is expected to be $20, $15, $10, $5, $2.50.
   b. Graph the profit on the option as in Figure 5-1(b).
3. A call option on the stock of Q Mart has an exercise price of $50 and expires in one year.
   a. If Q Mart rises to $55 from its current value of $50, how much will the option be worth at expiration?
   b. If Q Mart falls to $45 from $50, how much will the option be worth at expiration?
   c. You can duplicate the payoff on this option by taking a long position in one share of the stock and borrowing the amount ($45.00 − 0)/1.10 = $40.91 at 10 percent interest toward the purchase price. What is the payoff from this position?
   d. How much should the option be worth?
4. Call options are currently traded on Control Data Corp. stock. The exercise price of one of the call options is $30. The current price of Control Data is $27\frac{1}{2}$; the option maturity is in two months. The risk-free rate is 5 percent, and the stock's standard deviation of return is 10 percent.
   a. Calculate the price of the CD option.
   b. Assume the stock is more volatile and has a standard deviation of 15 percent. Calculate the price of the CD option.
   c. If the maturity of the option declines to one month from two, calculate the price of the CD option (assume a standard deviation of 10 percent).
5. GE options are traded on the Chicago Board Options Exchange. The current risk-free rate is 6.5 percent, and the standard deviation of GE's rate of return is 12 percent. The current price of GE is $46\frac{1}{4}$.
   a. Calculate the price of GE 45 calls if the expiration of the option is in eight months.
   b. Calculate the price of GE 45 calls if the expiration is in two months.
   c. Calculate the value of the option in (b) if it is expiring now.
   d. Will an option ever be exercised before maturity? Why or why not?